GW00602722

FROM RAGS TO GAGS

FROM RAGS TO GAGS

THE MEMOIRS OF A COMEDY WRITER

VINCE POWELL

Forewords by Cilla Black OBE
& Barry Cryer OBE

APEX PUBLISHING LTD

Hardback first published in 2008 by

Apex Publishing Ltd

PO Box 7086, Clacton on Sea, Essex, CO15 5WN, England

www.apexpublishing.co.uk

British Library Cataloguing-in-Publication Data
A catalogue record for this book
is available from the British Library

ISBN HARDBACK: 1-906358-07-9   978-1-906358-07-5

Typeset in 11pt Baskerville Win95BT

Production Manager: Chris Cowlin

Cover Design: Anthony Powell and Siobhan Smith

Printed and bound in Great Britain by
Biddles Ltd., King's Lynn, Norfolk

For my children:

Dominic, Genevieve & Anthony

FOREWORD

Vince Powell is arguably one of Britain's top television comedy writers who has been respondible for creating and writing many popular and successful TV situation comedy series during the past 40 years.

His autobiography traces his rise from the back street of Manchester and his early struggles which led him to a glittering career during which he wrote a host of TV hits, most of which were rarely out of the top ten national TV ratings.

His list of credits reads like a history of television comedy, and his memoirs evoke many happy memories of that wonderful era, now reffered to as the 'Golden Years of Comedy'.

I first met Vince when he became my Programme Associate for over a decade, working on 'Surprise Surprise', 'Blind Date' and many of my one-hour TV Specials, during which time we became good friends in spite of him being a Manchester United supporter!

If, like me, you would like to recapture those nostalgic memories of the time when comedy reigned supreme, you will enjoy Vince's book, with its stories and anecdotes of the many famoud celebrities who he has written for and worked with and his step by step rise to fame.

luv Cilla xx

Cilla Black OBE

FOREWORD

At last! The lid is off! Vince Powell was there and tells it how it happened. The Montgomery of comedy writing took on the Rommel of the ratings with shows that sparked controversy. A long career much of it with his partner, Harry Driver, a roller coaster of ribaldry, a ferris wheel of fun. If you ever wondered what went on behind the scenes of TV comedy, it's all here. Plus! Give us a clue, the long-running mime show that made a deafening impact with silence. Get this book early to avoid disappointment.

If you really want to know what a comedy writer's life is really like, it's all here, warts and all. And now and again, you'll remark "Oh, what a lovely wart". The detail is amazing and the self awareness is always there. Sit back, pour yourself a large glen close and enjoy!

Barry Cryer OBE

Acknowledgements

Thanks to all the talented actors and writers who have contributed to my success. Without your help this book could never been written.

To my dear friend Jack Ripley who spent hours researching the facts and even longer hours correcting my grammar and spelling mistakes.

And finally to my dear wife Geraldine who, for my sake, left her native home and family in Australia to share my life in England and encourage me through the many trials and tribulations familiar to all comedy writers.

Prologue

THE GOOD LIFE
"Oh the good life
Full of fun, seems to be the ideal
Yes the good life
Makes you hide all the sadness you feel"

The velvet voice of Tony Bennett at full volume echoed across the Esterel Massif from the car stereo as I drove my gold Rolls Bentley along the Moyenne Corniche, one of the three famous coastal routes of the French Riviera, a magnificent roadway which connects St Raphael to Menton. Sitting beside me taking in the wonderful scenery was my closest friend Anthony Parker, a Thames Television producer who had been responsible for producing and directing many of the successful television programmes which I had written. The sun shone down from a clear blue sky and sparkled and shimmered on the aquamarine waters of the Mediterranean Sea, glimpses of which we caught sight of with each bend of the road. We were on our way to the beautiful and picturesque former fishing village of St-Jean-Cap-Ferrat situated between Nice and Monaco.

Tony Bennett's words were so very apt that day and mirrored my mood exactly because awaiting me in St-Jean was a beautiful villa complete with four bedrooms each with an en-suite bathroom, a huge living room with French windows which opened on to a terrace leading to the garden and a swimming pool. Adjacent to the villa was a cottage in which lived Justa - a Spanish live-in femme de menage - housekeeper to you - and her gardener husband, Manuel. For the next twelve months, Villa Solanam was to be home to my wife Judi, myself and our two year old son Dominic. No, I had not won the football pools, robbed a bank or been left a fortune in the will of an elderly relative. Believe it or not,

1

my forthcoming sabbatical year was by courtesy of the Inland Revenue.

My writing partner, Harry Driver, with whom I had written for the past twenty years, had sadly finally succumbed to the polio virus which he had contracted in the great polio epidemic of 1957, and which had left him a quadriplegic, condemned to spend the rest of his life in a wheelchair and only able to move his head. At the time he passed away, we were both under an exclusive two year contract to Thames Television, as Comedy Advisers and Script Editors, plus a guarantee of writing thirteen situation comedies each year, which gave us an income of £25,000 a year each. After Harry died, I undertook to take on our joint contractual obligations which meant that my income virtually doubled. Very nice, you might think, and it would have been - but for the fact that, with the top rate of Income Tax being an exorbitant 80 pence in the pound, I would be paying most of my earnings to the Inland Revenue. My accountant advised me that the only solution was to go and live abroad for an entire tax year - April to April. This meant that, because I was self employed, I could fulfil my contractual obligations to Thames without being liable to pay any English tax on my earnings, while at the same time, if I went to live in France, I would be able to live there for a year before becoming liable to pay French tax. What a wonderful state of affairs!

Naturally, I didn't need telling twice. As soon as I could, I booked a flight to Nice, found a friendly estate agent and spent a wonderful three days being shown round several villas on the Cote d'Azur available to rent. I had been a devout Francophile ever since my first glimpse of the French Riviera many years ago when, serving in the Royal Navy on HMS Mauritius, we sailed into Villefranche-sur-Mer, and I fell in love with the South of France. (But more about that later in this book) When I left the Navy and could eventually afford to spend a holiday abroad, the first place I made for was Villefranche. And now, here I was, being given the glorious opportunity of living there for a year!

It didn't take me long to find a suitable villa, sign the necessary documents, and return home to arrange with a local estate agent for my house in Weybridge, Surrey to be put on his list of desirable properties to let. As it happened, before the agent had time to advertise the fact, a deal was done. The agent and I met in a local pub to discuss the letting contract over a drink, and our conversation was overhead by an American couple at a nearby table. They spoke to us; we took them to see my house and agreed a twelve month rental there and then. What luck!

My wife and I decided that I would travel ahead to Villa Solanam in my Rolls Bentley via Calais and the Auto Couchette, to set up the villa, before flying back to load up my wife's Mini and return on the Auto Couchette. My wife would then fly out to join me with our two year old son, Dominic.

For those of you who are not familiar with the term Auto Couchette, it's by far the best way to travel to the South of France with one's car without all the hassle of driving across France. You drive to Dover, put the car on the ferry to Calais, and then drive to the Gare Maritime where your car is loaded on to a rail transporter. You are shown to your cabin in the sleeping car where, you are served a light supper accompanied by a bottle of wine.

After your cabin attendant has made your bed, you settle down to a good night's sleep, to be woken up the following morning at Marseilles with breakfast. You can enjoy your Petit Dejeauner of croissants, crisp bread rolls with butter and piping hot coffee as the train travels along, what is for me, the most beautiful coastline in the world.

I had earlier suggested to my friend Tony Parker that he might like to accompany me on my initial journey and he jumped at the chance.

The great day arrived. I kissed my wife and son goodbye, climbed into the Rolls Bentley and set off on what was to be the most incredible year of my life. The Bentley was packed to capacity with all sort of things which my wife felt we may need during our year in France. The boot was practically bulging, and the rear seats were packed almost to the roof with suitcases, cardboard boxes and plastic carrier bags. There was just enough room for Tony Parker to squeeze in when I picked him up at his house in Putney.

We drove to Dover where we loaded the car on to one of

the cross-channel ferries and just over ninety minutes and two large scotches later, we drove off again having arrived in Calais. We headed toward Customs and joined the queue of cars. Tony became alarmed when he noticed that they were doing spot checks on some of the cars, indicating the drivers to pull to one side, while a Customers Officer searched the car. Tony turned to me.

What if they search us?"

"Relax Tony," I replied, "they won't search us."

"But what if they do? God knows what your wife's packed in the boot. They might think we're smugglers."

"Tony. They don't search quality cars like Rolls Royces or Bentleys. Just stop worrying."

By now we had reached the head of the queue. I smiled winningly at the Customs Official and handed him our passports and the official documents which confirmed that I and my family had been granted a 'Permit de Sejour' - permission to reside in France for a year. He barely glanced at the documents and handed them back. I thanked him, shot a triumphal 'told you so' look at Tony and prepared to move off, when to my dismay and Tony's horror, the official directed me to pull over to one side and park behind a dusty and shabby looking van which was being gone over by another Customs Official.

Tony shot me a 'told you so' look. His face had turned a decided shade of grey. He ran his fingers agitatedly through his beard and lit a cigarette. I tried to appear calm and waited. The Customs Official waved the van off and turned to me. He opened the driver's door and indicated for me to get out. "S'il vous plait m'sieu"

I climbed out and handed him the passports and 'Permit de Sejour'. He examined them meticulously, taking what seemed like an age before handing them back. I breathed a sigh of relief. He peered into the rear of the car at the various items.

"What is all this" he asked?"

I tried to explain in my best schoolboy French that they were all essential items which we needed if we were going to spend a year living in France. He looked into one cardboard carton which was full of cans of Heinz baked beans, took a

4

can out then gave me a questioning look. I told him that Heinz baked beans were not readily obtainable in France. Therefore we were taking our own supply. He shrugged, muttered something derogatory about 'Les Anglais' and indicated that he wanted to look in the boot. I unlocked it and raised the lid. There, on top of a huge mound of clothes were over a dozen ladies dresses all on hangers and in polythene bags fresh from the dry cleaners. The Customs Official looked at them, raised his eyebrows and shrugged as only the French can shrug. I quickly explained that the dresses all belonged to my wife. The official stared at me then walked slowly and deliberately round to the front of the Bentley and stared in at the bearded Tony. Tony smiled nervously and shrugged. The official shrugged back and returned to me, convinced that Tony and I were both a couple of gays. He closed the lid of the boot and waved us on. I got back in the car switched on the ignition and started to move off. I had hardly gone a few yards, when I heard a police whistle. The Customs Officer was running after the car blowing a whistle and waving his arms. My heart sank. What now? I stopped the car and wound down the window. The Customs Official came up to the open window and held out the can of beans which he was still holding. He smiled, handed me the can and winked suggestively at Tony and I. "Bon appetit Messieurs et bon voyage!"

I drove off, found the Gare Maritime where we loaded the Bentley on to the overnight Auto Couchette to Frejus, opened one of the duty free bottles of Bells whisky we had purchased on the ferry, and between us, drank the lot before collapsing into our respective bunks.

The following morning we awoke as the train pulled into Marseilles, where we were served breakfast before continuing our journey. I stared out of the window at the passing scenery as we sped along the coast through such exotic sounding places as Le Lavandou, St-Tropez, St-Maxime and St-Raphael before arriving at Frejus where we unloaded the car and set off for Cap Ferrat.So here we were, Tony Parker and I, gliding smoothly and happily along the Corniche in the warm sunshine toward Cap Ferrat accompanied by Tony Bennett now halfway through telling us he'd left his heart in

San Francisco, heading for my personal paradise, with me looking forward to a fantastic year ahead. It was my intention to spend the year writing a book - a crime novel - something I'd always wanted to do but never seemed to find the time. I even had a plot - and a title - "Countdown to Murder". It would win an Oscar and I would go on to write a succession of best sellers. That was the plan. However, as Mr Burns once remarked - Robert not George - 'the best laid schemes o' mice an men, Gang aft a-gley' as you will find out. But I'm getting ahead of myself.

Back on the Moyenne Corniche we approached Nice and joined the lower road, the Basse Corniche which swept along the Promenade des Anglais, built in 1822 by the British residents of Nice, hence its name, a truly elegant dual carriageway divided by a central reservation filled with rows of palm trees interspersed with exotic and colourful blooms. On one side the sparkling Mediterranean and, on the other, luxury hotels such as the Negresco, the Meridian and the Westminster.

I drove round the harbour and along the coast road leading to Villefranche-Sur-Mer. My excitement grew as I drew near to a particular bend in the road from which the whole panoramic view of the bay of Villefranche and the bay of Beaulieu can be seen, separated by the promontory of Cap Ferrat, the most expensive piece of real estate in Europe. A playground for the rich with exclusive villas and luxury yachts jostling for a space in the marina.

We turned right off the lower Corniche on to the Avenue Denis Semeria past the Musee Ephrussi de Rothschild completed in 1912. The guide books will tell you its well worth a visit and they're absolutely right. It's terrific and puts most of our British stately homes to shame. Further on, as we turned on to the Boulevard General de Gaullle, we passed the road leading to the Zoo. Now this is definitely worth a visit. Built by King Leopold II of Belgium in the 19th century, it houses an interesting collection of animals and even more important - a bar, in which one can enjoy a sandwich, a cold beer or a glass of wine.

Eventually, we turned right into the Boulevard du Plan des Abeilles and pulled into the drive of Villa Solanam. To my surprise, Justa and her husband Manuel were standing at the open front door. Justa was holding a bunch of flowers and Manuel was holding a tray on which was a bottle of champagne in an ice bucket and four glasses. Tony and I got out of the car, and Justa, not at all fazed by being confronted by the bearded Tony when she expected to see my wife, handed him the flowers, while Manual opened the champagne and poured us each a glass. After a conversation of broken English, broken French and broken Spanish, we managed to convince Justa and Manuel that Tony and I were just good friends and that my wife would be arriving the following week.

We finished the champagne and started to unload the car. Justa informed us that she would be preparing lunch for us on the terrace and it would be ready in about an hour. Being British, Tony and I were anxious to obtain the English newspapers. It was Sunday and we were both eager to discover the latest news from home - not that we were deep into political issues - no this was much more serious than that. For Tony it was to discover if Chelsea had avoided being relegated from Division I to Division 2 and for me, had Manchester United been promoted from Division 2 back to Division 1. United had played Oldham Athletic at Old Trafford the day before and a win for them would virtually clinch promotion.

It was decided that Tony would finish unloading the car while I would walk down to the newsagents in nearby St Jean, where I had been assured that I could obtain the English papers. However, when I arrived at the newsagents, I discovered that the English papers hadn't arrived. Apparently the plane bringing them from England was late in arriving. The good news was that the papers had been unloaded and were on their way. I decided to wait. As I stood outside the shop I noticed several other people standing around, obviously also waiting for the papers to arrive. I glanced at them curiously. My eye was taken by a dapper, slim gentleman who looked remarkably like David Niven. He caught my eye, smiled and nodded. 'My God?' I thought. 'It **is** David Niven!' I gazed round at the other people waiting. That man looking in the window of the patisserie - surely it couldn't be - it was - Rex Harrison. And the man chatting to a gendarme was unmistakably Gregory Peck. I couldn't believe my eyes. I found out later that Jack Hawkins and Kenneth More both had apartments on the Cap. All these famous actors lived in this small exclusive area of the Cote d'Azur and for the next twelve months would be my neighbours.

I decided to go and speak to David Niven, but before I could do so, a white van came round the corner and screeched to a halt. The papers had arrived and the moment had gone. Within minutes everyone had collected their newspapers and had dispersed. I bought The Times and the Sunday Express and started to walk back to Villa Solanam. On the way, still bemused by the thought of rubbing shoulders with so many of my celluloid heroes, I paused for a moment to take in the breathtaking view across the bay to Beaulieu and Eze. It was a beautiful day. There wasn't a cloud in the sky and the blue sea was as smooth as a mill pond.

My mind went back over 40 years to the incredible set of circumstances which had led me from the slums of Manchester to my present situation.

Chapter One:
GROWING PAINS

I was born in Manchester and for the first ten years of my life lived at 229 Bradford Road, Miles Platting a working class suburb of Manchester. It was directly opposite the gasworks and two huge gasometers. It was like a Lowry painting. For years I assumed that the smell from the gasworks was fresh air. The only blades of grass, or trees or flowers I ever saw as a child, was when my parents took me to the cemetery to visit my grandfather's grave.

The house itself was a small, two up, two down terraced property situated in a row of identical houses, the front doors of which led directly on to the pavement. Trams rattled noisily up and down the road which was illuminated by gas lighting. One of my earliest memories was peering out of my bedroom window watching a lamplighter turning off the street gas lights. Another memory was the 'knocker up'. This was a man who, for a few coppers, would tap on your bedroom window with a long pole at whatever time you wished to be woken up - a kind of human alarm clock. Though why anyone would need to be woken, with the noisy trams clattering up and down outside every few minutes, was a mystery to me.

The house had a backyard which contained an outside lavatory with bare whitewashed walls from one of which protruded a nail on which was hung a piece of string threaded through several squares of newspaper carefully torn from the pages of the Manchester Evening News. Not for us the luxury of soft, 3 ply toilet tissues. However, it did have one advantage - there was always something to read whilst sitting there.

From the yard, a back door led to what was called the back entry, a long narrow passage which separated our row of terraced houses from those at the back. This back entry was used by all and sundry for a variety of functions including, a playground for all the kids in the neighbourhood, a lovers' lane and a place where numerous cats and dogs came to relieve themselves, not to mention the odd husband on his way home from the local pub.

The house had no electricity and was lit by gas lighting. There was a hallway which also served as a cloakroom with a collection of overcoats, raincoats and jackets hanging from a row of coat-hooks. A door led from the hall to a front parlour, sometimes referred to as the best room. This was rarely used except on the occasional Sunday, when it was our turn to entertain relatives to Sunday tea. Sunday tea was always the same. The best china tea service came out and the ladies prepared the meal which was either tinned salmon and salad or slices of tongue and ham and brown bread and butter. This was followed by tinned sliced peaches and carnation cream. Meanwhile, the men would be in the pub on the corner drinking pints and discussing world affairs and the relative merits of United and City until they were summoned back by one of us kids shouting through the pub door 'Teas ready'. Parlours were also used, whenever a member of the family died, to display the body in an open coffin so that relatives could visit and pay their last respects.

At the end of the hall a door led to the living room which was dominated by a large black enamel structure consisting of a grate for the coal fire with an oven on one side, and a hob on the other. Hanging down over the fire from the chimney was a hook on which we used to hang a large kettle to boil water for making tea. My father also used to hang strips of bacon and an occasional sausage on the hook - a kind of primitive barbecue. I promise you, I've never had bacon or sausages since that tasted so delicious. Off the living room was the scullery, as kitchens were called in those days. From the hall a flight of steep and narrow stairs led up to a landing off which was the main bedroom, barely large enough to contain a double bed, a wardrobe and a dressing table. There was also a second bedroom with a single bed and a chest of drawers.

There was no bathroom. Every Friday night, a galvanised iron bath was brought into the kitchen from the back yard, and filled with several kettlefuls of boiling water. My mother bathed first, then it was my turn and finally my Dad's, all of us using the same water with an occasional topping up to keep it warm.

Warmth was an essential commodity in those days, especially during the winter months. We had no central heating and although the living room was fairly warm providing one kept near enough to the fire, leaving it to go up to bed was an ordeal. My bedroom was like an igloo. Invariably there was a coating of ice on the inside of the window. Not having the luxury of a hot water bottle, I used to sleep wearing a pullover on top of my pyjamas. Once in bed, I used to pull the bedclothes above my head and breathe in and out rapidly to create a cocoon of warm air. I also used to sleep with my socks on to avoid the risk of frostbite in the mornings when my feet came into contact with the icy linoleum which covered the floor.

Looking back on those days now, life was positively Dickensian. Television was still several years away although we owned a wireless set run off a battery which had to be re-charged at regular intervals. As a treat my mother used to send me to the corner shop and tell me to ask for a stale cream cake. I didn't know what the word stale meant - to me it was just another kind of cake. It wasn't until later that I found out that they were yesterday's cream cakes in which the cream had turned sour. I wasn't aware that we were poor and lived in a slum. I was happy. My mother and father gave me lots of love and affection. I didn't know that we ate bread and dripping because we couldn't afford butter. I loved bread and dripping. I didn't know that we bought broken biscuits from the Co-op because they were cheap. To me they tasted every bit as good a normal biscuits. I was an only child but I never felt lonely. We lived in a close Catholic community with a sense of belonging. Our neighbours were kind and friendly - everybody helped each other. It was good to be alive.

But I was soon to discover that life has a habit of delivering a shock when you least expect it. It was September 1933. I was just five years old. My mother was thirty-three and had been unwell with stomach pains for most of the previous day and night.

That morning, my father bundled me off early to his sisters, my Auntie Ethel who lived nearby, before taking my mother to the doctors. Auntie Ethel and Uncle Tom had three children, the youngest of whom, James, was my age. We had both just started to attend the infants class at the local Catholic school Corpus Christi and we were good friends. Auntie Ethel took me and James to school where we spent a few hours playing with building bricks and drinking the obligatory half bottle of milk before being picked up in the afternoon by Auntie Ethel. I waited at my auntie's for my Dad to call for me, but he didn't arrive. A message came from a neighbour. My mother had been taken to Ancoats Hospital and my Dad had gone with her and didn't know what time he would be home. It was decided that I would stay the night at my aunties and sleep with my cousin James. To a five year old boy this was an adventure. I wasn't really concerned about my mother. Looking back now, this must have seemed rather callous on my part, but at the time I was far too excited about staying the night at my aunties to worry about anything else.

The following day, Auntie Ethel took us to school again and in the afternoon, when it was time for us to leave, James and I made our way to the school gate where I was surprised to find my Dad waiting with Auntie Ethel. After dropping James back home, the three of us went to the hospital to visit my mother. Ancoats Hospital was a bleak and forbidding building and smelt of disinfectant. I held on tightly to my Dad's hand as we walked down a gloomy corridor and into a large ward in which were at least twenty women patients all in beds. I looked for my mother but couldn't see her. Then my Dad led me to the far end of the ward to a bed surrounded by curtains. We went behind the curtains and there was my mother, propped up on several pillows, her eyes closed and looking very pale. At the sound of my Dad's voice she opened her eyes. When she saw me, she smiled. My Dad lifted me up so that I could kiss her and she put an arm around me and held me close. We stayed with her for a while until a nurse came to give her some medication. We came out from behind the curtain and my Dad told me that I was to go back to auntie Ethel's and he would stay with my mother.

Auntie Ethel took my hand we walked back down the ward through the rows of beds. I kept turning round to try and see my mother, but all I could see were the curtains round the bed. Suddenly I heard my Dad call my name and I turned to see that my Dad had drawn the curtains back so that my mother and I could see each other. I waved to her and she waved weakly back.

That was the last time I ever saw my mother alive. 'Peritonitis' it said on the death certificate - as a result of food poisoning. Nowadays, with modern drugs and antibiotics such as penicillin and sulphonamides this condition, if properly and promptly treated, is rarely fatal. But then, in the early thirties it was a killer.

My memories of the next few days are rather vague. I had not yet come to terms with the concept and finality of death. I can remember my Dad saying to me, 'Mam's gone away Vincent. She's gone to be with the Angels in Heaven.' I had a mental picture of my mother walking in a beautiful garden surrounded by winged angels. It was only years later that I came to understand what anguish my Dad must have gone through.

My mother's body was brought home from the undertakers, and true to Catholic tradition was put in the front parlour in an open coffin. An unending number of grieving relatives came to say a prayer for her soul. I can recall my Dad lifting me up to see my Mother so that I could kiss her for the last time. There were lots of flowers, particularly lilies and to this day the smell of lilies reminds me of that day.

Of the funeral I remember very little. I recall that the house was full of relatives, many of whom gave me a penny. And after the actual burial we all went to a pub where, in an upstairs room we sat down to ham sandwiches, pork pies and trifle.

For the next two or three years my life settled into a regular pattern. My Dad would get me up, dress me, give me my breakfast then take me to Auntie Ethel's before going to work. She would take me to school, collect me in the afternoon and give me tea at her house. Then I could walk to my own house and sit on our front doorstep, watching and waiting for every tram hoping to see my Dad get off. For over two years, I sat on that doorstep, day after day, rain or shine, waiting for that moment when my Dad stepped off a tram. Then I would jump up, run towards him and leap into his outstretched arms.

Life went inexorably on. Dad was a tailor, a trade he was taught at the Catholic orphanage where he was brought up. His parents died when he was a young boy and he was sent to Buckley Hall Orphanage for Boys near Rochdale which was run by the Brothers of Charity. His sister Ethel - my auntie Ethel was brought up in a Convent. When Dad left the orphanage, they found him a job as an alteration hand with a Manchester tailoring firm, and lodgings with a Mr and Mrs Humphries, a devout childless Catholic couple who became, more or less, his adoptive parents. When war broke out in 1914 Dad joined the Manchester Regiment and was sent to France where he went though the horrors of the Battle of the Somme - four months of mindless slaughter in which over 600,000 British soldiers were killed. I often asked my Dad to tell me about his time in the army but he refused to talk about it. They called if 'The War To End All Wars' yet 21 years later, Europe was in bloody conflict again.

Although I missed my mother, I wasn't too unhappy. Coming from a Catholic background, I had lots of aunts, uncles and cousins. Dad became very friendly with a family who lived in Ashton-under-Lyne - the Hennesseys. As their name suggests, they were of Irish descent, as indeed was my late mother whose maiden name was Larkin. Dad and Michael Hennessy served together during the war and had kept in touch. After the death of my mother, Dad used to visit Michael and his two sisters, Frances and Alice, with me in tow. We'd stay the weekend and the two sisters, both of whom I called 'Auntie' made a fuss of me, which I enjoyed. They also made a fuss of my Dad, which he, too, obviously enjoyed, so much so that one weekend he asked me how I could like it if 'Auntie' Frances came to live with us. I said it would be nice, but why couldn't 'Auntie' Alice come and live with us as well? Dad looked embarrassed, hummed and hawed then told me that he and 'Auntie' Frances were going to be married and that she would be my new Mam.

I often wondered, in later years, whether 'Auntie' Alice harboured a secret love for my Dad, for she never married and died a spinster. Anyway, Dad and 'Auntie' Frances got married in our local Catholic church and we had a reception in the same upstairs room of the pub that we used two years before for the wake after my Mam's funeral.

My Dad told me that they would be going on honeymoon for a week in Blackpool, and I assumed that I would be going to Auntie Ethel's but to my surprise Dad said that I would be going with them. Blackpool was my idea of Heaven. I had been a couple of times with my Dad and loved it. It was brash, loud, vulgar and as common as muck, but for me and the thousands of people from the mill towns of Oldham, Bury, Wigan, Bolton, Salford, Preston, Blackburn, Burnley and Chorley, Blackpool with its famous tower, the pleasure beach - at that time the largest funfair in Europe - three piers and seven miles of golden beaches, was paradise. Eat your heart out Disneyworld - Blackpool was light years ahead. It had more hotels and boarding houses than any other town in Britain, sold more bottles of beer during the season than all the pubs in the rest of the country and was probably responsible for more pregnancies than anywhere else. In what other town could you visit an aquarium, a zoo, a three ring circus, a theatre, an amusement arcade, a ballroom, enjoy a three course meal in a restaurant, have your fortune told and take a trip to the top of Blackpool Tower all under one roof?

So Dad married 'Auntie' Frances. I was a pageboy and we went to Blackpool. I don't remember much of the honeymoon except for the fact that I kept calling my new Mam, 'Auntie' which resulted in my Dad getting some very strange looks from the rest of the guests.

We returned home and were a family again. We went to Mass on Sundays and entertained our relatives in the front parlour as before. I became an altar boy and at one time, after listening to a passionate and descriptive account by a visiting missionary, was filled with a consuming desire to become a missionary and convert all those heathens in Africa. Fortunately, my Dad talked me out of it. I was promoted to head altar boy which meant me leading the priest out at the start of High Mass on Sundays, carrying a large silver crucifix. Unfortunately, my role as head altar boy ended dramatically when I developed a taste for the Communion wine, and was discovered one morning before Mass, slumped in a confessional box clutching a half empty bottle and out to the world.

I got on reasonably well with my new Mam although there were times when I could have been kinder and shown more affection to her. I enjoyed school and in particular, English. The teacher used to set us essays to write on various subjects and I used to write humorous essays. I remember one - the subject we were asked to write upon was 'What I have in my pocket'. My classmates wrote things like 'What I have in my pocket is a penny, a gobstopper, a piece of chewing gum and a hankie' .

I wrote - what I have in my pocket is a hole!

That was the first piece of comedy I ever wrote. To my surprise the teacher complimented me on my imagination. The subject of the next essay we were set was 'What I did on my holidays'. I still have the exercise book in which I wrote a wholly fictitious account of a holiday. It went like this.

'For my holiday I went to Blackpool with my Mam and Dad. On the first day, we went on the sands and my Dad lay down to sunbathe and fell asleep. While he was sleeping, I buried him in sand up to his neck. He didn't find out until the tide came in and he swallowed half a gallon of seawater. The next day we went on the Pleasure Beach and I had an ice cream cornet, a bar of chocolate, a toffee apple and some candy floss. Then I asked my Mam if I could have a bottle of fizzy lemonade. 'No' she said, 'you'll be sick.' 'No I won't' I said. 'Yes you will' she said. My Dad said, 'Oh for goodness sake let him have a bottle of fizzy lemonade'. So I did. And my Mam was right. I was sick. All over my Dad!'

I handed the essay in and the following day the teacher made me read it out to the class. I did, and they laughed. And I liked the sound of their laughter. It was then I decided that, that was what I wanted to do with my life. Make people laugh.

However, my ambition wasn't to be a writer - I wanted to be a performer - a comedian. I discovered that I was a fairly good mimic and amused my classmates by imitating our teachers until one day I was overheard by the headmaster as I was imitating his slight stammer. He was not amused and I got a caning.

In 1939 three events occurred which had an effect on my future. The first was we moved house. My Dad had put a deposit on a new semi-detached house in the leafy suburb of Blackley. It was only four miles south of Miles Platting but it was another world. For a start it had a garden - in fact it had two gardens - one at the front and one at the back. It had electricity and a bathroom with an immersion heater. No more boiling up endless kettles of water to fill the tin bath on our communal bath night. We could have as many baths as we liked - when we liked. But the best feature of all in the new house was the toilet. Next to the bathroom was a separate, indoor toilet! Oh the luxury of it. Never again would I have to stave off the calls of nature for as long as possible to avoid the discomfort of sitting on a cold, dark toilet in the backyard on a bleak and wintry night. As far as I was concerned, no palace could compare with our new house. My Dad invited Auntie Ethel and Uncle Tom to tea and proudly showed them round. Dad suggested that they might like to buy a similar house on the estate but Uncle Tom shook his head. 'No, Jim' he said, 'this wouldn't do for us. I mean, it's a bit lardy-da. It's too far away from everything. There's no pub for start. And not a sign of a chippy. No - we're very happy where we are, thank you very much'. They left, privately thinking my Dad had made a mistake and had ideas far above his station and they never came to tea again.

The second event was that I passed a scholarship exam at school and won a place at St. Bede's Catholic College. It was quite an achievement for a young lad from Miles Platting and my Dad was understandably proud. I couldn't wait to go to my new school but before I could, the third event took place. Hitler invaded Poland, war was declared and I was evacuated.

I was one of thousands of schoolchildren who were evacuated from London, Manchester, Liverpool, Birmingham, Glasgow and other major cities which the Government felt to be in danger of being bombed by the

17

Germans. We were all resettled in rural areas for our safety and housed by various families who had volunteered to take in an evacuee for the duration of the war. Most of St. Bede's college went to Whalley near Preston and attended the nearby Stoneyhurst College. However, the new intake of pupils about 20 of us in all, were evacuated to Longridge, a small rural village where most of us were accommodated in farmhouses. I found myself in Hilltop Farm, which had a herd of dairy cows, about a dozen pigs, about a hundred sheep and a couple of hundred hens. We were accompanied by one priest - a Father Dempsey known irreverently to us as Wally. Our classroom was an empty hen hut, and from memory we only had lessons in the mornings. Father Dempsey, was billeted in the local pub and he preferred to spend most of his afternoons in the bar supposedly marking our homework, while we spent our afternoons running around the fields playing football or cricket.

Evacuation was a commendable scheme but by the end of the year, most of the children had returned home. I went back to our lovely house and attended St. Bede's. Our teachers were mainly priests and the college head was Monsignor Cook, who sported a beard and was known as Nittywhiskers. We had nicknames for most of our teachers - the maths teacher, a layman, we called 'Bandy' Birchall for obvious reasons, Father O'Leary who we called Holy 'Arry, a play on his name, the priest who taught history was known as 'Nigger' Bolton - don't ask me why, he was as white as we were. There was also 'Pongo' Waring, 'Jazz' Dwyer, Father Ignatius known as 'Iggy the Beak' because of his large nose and 'Wee Willie' Coulthard because of his small stature.

The war didn't touch me much apart from sweets being rationed. My Dad became an Air Raid Warden and three nights a week he went out and patrolled the neighbourhood, carrying a stirrup pump ready to extinguish any incendiary bombs the Germans might drop. Although the centre of Manchester was bombed quite heavily we escaped and the only blaze my Dad was called on to deal with was when one of our neighbour's chimneys caught fire. By one of those strange coincidences, Auntie Ethel's house was bombed and totally gutted. Fortunately she and the family were all in the

18

communal air raid shelter so nobody was injured. She and Uncle Tom moved the family into an empty house three doors away and lived there happily ever after. It was nearer the pub!

I still had ambitions of being a comedian and spent hours listening to variety programmes on the radio - or wireless as we used to call it. I heard all the great comedians of that time. Flanagan and Allen, Robb Wilton, Sandy Powell, Max Miller, Tommy Handley, Arthur Askey, Jimmy Wheeler, Tommy Trinder, Vic Oliver and Max Wall as well as some of the American comics whose radio programmes I used to tune in to on the American Forces Network - in particular Jack Benny and Bob Hope. Never in my wildest dreams did I think then that one day I would meet them in the flesh. I would memorise some of the jokes I heard on the wireless then entertain my classmates with my impressions of their acts.

One day, on my way to school. I spotted a poster on a hoarding advertising the fact that the following week, Jewell and Warriss would be appearing at the Ardwick Empire, a theatre not too far from St. Bede's. I had heard them on the wireless and was determined to go and see them, so the following day, instead of going to school, I passed a couple of hours in the Central Library reading, and then I went to the News Theatre. The News Theatre was a small cinema which specialised in showing a couple of newsreels, a travel film, a couple of cartoons such as Donald Duck and Goofy and a couple of short comedy films such as Laurel and Hardy, The Three Stooges or Charlie Chaplin. The entire programme lasted about fifty minutes and I sat through it twice. When I came out I spent some of my bus fare on two rounds of toast and a cup of tea before walking to the Ardwick Empire for the matinee performance. From memory it cost me about three old pence for a half price ticket to the topmost balcony known as the Gods. This was my first visit to a theatre and I loved it. There was a magical air of anticipation about it.

As the audience entered and took their seats an orchestra played a selection of popular tunes, then the lights dimmed, the orchestra struck up a brief overture and curtain rose on the first act, half a dozen tap dancing chorus girls. There was a magician, a juggler, a singing duo and a ventriloquist, then an interval. I could hardly wait for the curtain to rise again for the second half. The tap dancing chorus girls were on first then Jewel and Warriss came on. They were terrific and had the audience, including me, falling about with laughter. How I envied them fooling about on the stage getting waves of laughter and round after round of applause. After that initial visit I often used to play truant from school to visit the Ardwick Empire where I saw many wonderful comedians such as Ted Ray, Jimmy James, Dickie Henderson, George Formby and Gracie Fields - names that may mean nothing to those of you born in the '70s or later but in the '40s they were all famous entertainers.

However, all good things come to an end, and my theatre outings came to an end rather dramatically. To explain my various absences from school, I used to present sick notes to my teacher the day after, on which I'd forged my Dad's signature. Unfortunately, after one matinee, I was seen coming out of the theatre by the school matron who reported it to Monsignor Cook. My Dad was sent for and the matter of the forged sick notes came to light. Monsignor Cook told my Dad that it was a serious offence and in normal circumstances I would be expelled and it would be recorded on my school report. However, for some reason he relented and advised my Dad that he would give me a clean report if I left the college voluntarily. So I left of my own accord without a stain on my character, so to speak. I was 15 and I'm sure, at the time this was a big disappointment to my parents, but I was delighted.

I could now devote all of my time to achieving my ambition of becoming a comedian. But my Dad had other ideas. One of them being that I should get a job. One of the members of the parish Catholic Men's Club, of which my Dad was also a member, had a small engineering works and he agreed to take me on as an apprentice. For the first few weeks my duties were to clean the machines, make the tea and go to the nearby chip shop and collect the orders for everybody's lunch, then I was shown how to operate a lathe and began making small metal components which I was informed were used in the assembly of tank engines. I was part of the war effort - part of the vast army of people, mostly women, doing similar jobs in similar places, all over the country. The workforce consisted of two elderly men, four women - all friendly and cheerful, another young apprentice, myself, a nubile sexy young secretary with a fantastic body which the boss had already laid claim to and which taught me that, as far as the fair sex was concerned, good looks and an attractive personality were no match for a position of power and a well filled wallet. One day I would have both but that day was yet to come.

In the workshop we had a radio which was turned on all day, and as we worked we listened to programmes such as "Music While You Work" which was specifically aimed at factory workers in the belief that the music encouraged the workers to work faster. It was broadcast each day about 10.30 and each programme had a different dance band playing popular songs for an hour, to which we all sang along enthusiastically. But my favourite programme was at midday. It was called "Worker's Playtime" and was an hour long variety programme in which several popular comedians took part. Again, I listened to some of my favourite funny men and learned from them the valuable art of timing.

In the afternoon there was another sing-along session of "Music While You Work" and all in all, the days passed quite pleasantly. I became friendly with the other apprentice whose name was Kevin Patrick Anthony O'Flaherty. No prizes for guessing his nationality or his religion. Like me, he wanted to be in show business, but as a singer. He had an excellent baritone voice and I was convinced that he would make it eventually.

One day, he came into work quite excited. A talent show was to be held at the Manchester Hippodrome hosted by Carroll Levis and he was holding auditions that coming Sunday for acts to take part. His show, "Carroll Levis's Discoveries" was a big success and toured the country playing to packed houses everywhere. He would choose several acts from the auditions and put them in his show the following week inviting the audience at each performance to vote for the acts in order of popularity. At each successive performance, he would announce the number of votes cast so far for each act, and on the final show the eventual winning act would receive a cash prize of £10 - a large sum in those days - but more important - a contract to appear in a Carroll Levis Summer Show for a six week season in one of the popular seaside holiday resorts.

Kevin and I decided we would attend the audition and the following Sunday we presented ourselves at the stage door of the Manchester Hippodrome. Now, I have to let you into a secret. You have been reading this book thinking it was the autobiography of Vince Powell and in one respect it is. However, I was born and baptised Vincent Smith. When I met Kevin that day, he told me that he had decided to call himself Kevin Kelly - it sounded more theatrical than O'Flaherty. That set me thinking. What sort of a name was Vincent Smith with which to launch my career as a comedian? Vince Smith? No that didn't sound right. Vince Cassidy? No - too Irish. I racked my brains. I went through the alphabet. Vince Butler. Vince Doherty, Vince Ford, Vince Johnson, Vince Martin, Vince Ogden, Vince Powell - it tripped off the tongue. That'll do I thought. So it was as Vince Powell that I made my debut as a comedian. Some years later when I became better known as a comedy writer, I changed my name legally by deed poll from Smith to Powell.

To get back to the plot, Kevin and I gave our stage names to a stage doorkeeper and were ushered down a corridor past a row of dressing rooms, which still had the names of the previous week's performers on the doors. As you can imagine, Kevin and I were literally trembling with excitement. We eventually went through the pass door and found ourselves in the auditorium. There must have been about 40 or 50 people waiting to be auditioned and we were told to take a seat and wait until we were called.

The great man, Carroll Levis was seated in one of the boxes from where he could view and mark each act. Kevin and I waited our turn and watched fascinated as each act went into their routine - some good, some bad and some incredibly awful. There were comedians who weren't funny, singers who were tone deaf, dancers with two left feet and musicians who could only play out of tune. Each act was allowed to perform for no longer than three minutes. And some didn't even do that. A few really bad acts were cut short by Carroll Levis bellowing at them 'Thank you. That's enough. We'll let you know.' On the credit side there were a few good acts and we noticed that the good acts were asked to wait in the theatre bar after they had finished. Eventually our turn was nearing and we were moved to stand in the wings until we were called. I elected to go first and when my name was called I strode on to the stage with a confidence I was far from feeling. I'd written my own act which, from memory went something like this:

"I was walking down the street the other day - when all of a sudden I thought, I'll go to Paris. I caught a train to Dover - it was very nice. I had a private compartment. A little washbasin in the corner. A catch on the door so I wouldn't be disturbed. Smashing. When I got to Dover I jumped on a bus. I said "Driver does this bus stop at the pier?" He said "If it doesn't, we're all going to get wet through!"
I got on the ferry. I was so excited. I'd even bought a French beret to wear in Paris. But it was so rough in the channel. The boat kept going up and down, and this way and that way. I had to go and lie down in a cabin. On the bunk above me was a fellow who was even worse. Moaning and groaning. Then all of a sudden, he shouted "Look out". And I looked out. And he was sick all over my beret."

I kept waiting for Carroll Levis to shout down 'Thank you. That's enough. We'll let you know.' But he didn't so I carried on. I was encouraged by the reaction of the others still waiting to be auditioned. Some of them had actually laughed. I carried on with my patter with increasing confidence.

"I like France. I'd been learning the language for weeks. As soon as I got ashore, I rushed up to the first fellow I saw, and said "Vive la France. Ouvrez La Porte and Maurice Chevalier. He wasn't half surprised. He was a Dutchman!
I stayed at a lovely hotel in Paris. The manager took me up to my room and said 'Have you got a good memory for faces?' I said 'Yes'. He said 'That's good. There's no shaving mirror in the

bathroom!'

He went downstairs and he hadn't been gone five minutes before he was back, pounding on the door. He shouted 'Hey have you got a woman in there?' I said 'No'. He threw one in!

I went to one of those daring French night clubs where women were barefoot - right up to their necks. I met one in the bar. I asked if I could see her home. So she showed me a photograph of it.

She took me back to her flat. We sat on the settee - I'd just put my arm round her when the door opened and a big French sailor walked in. 'Oh' she said, 'meet my boy friend Hugo.' So I went. Which I'm going to do right now. Thank you for listening. Bye bye.'

As I left the stage, Kevin gave me a thumbs up. I wanted to stay in the wings and watch Kevin's performance but I was told to report to the bar. When I got there, I met Carroll Levis's tour manager who told me that there was every possibility that I would be invited to appear in the following week's show. He gave me a form and asked me to fill it in. I filled in my name, address, date of birth and handed it back to him. He glanced at it and frowned. 'Ah' he said, 'you're under 16.' 'Does that matter?' I said. 'Yes' he replied, 'you'll need your parent's permission. One of them will have to sign the form.' He handed the form back. 'Bring it to the theatre on Monday morning.'

I put the form in my pocket and went in search of Kevin but couldn't find him anywhere. I went back to the bar, spoke to the tour manager and asked about Kevin. He looked through a sheaf of papers and said 'He didn't make it.' I was gobsmacked. 'Didn't make it? But he had a fantastic voice' I said. 'I agree' replied the tour manager, 'the problem is, singers and piano players are two a penny, whereas comedy acts are few and far between. And we'd already got our quota of singers for next week's show.'

I left the theatre and looked everywhere for Kevin but couldn't find him. Eventually, I made my way home. I hadn't told my parents about the audition and was going to break it to them slowly, but I was so hyped up that I poured it all out in a torrent of words. 'I was good Dad - really good. You should have been there. The audience laughed at me and Mr Levis wants to put me in his show next week.' My Dad looked at me 'Does he now?' he said. 'Yes' I said, handing him the form. 'All you have to do is sign this form. 'Dad took the form, read it and gave it to my Mam who also read it and handed it back to him. 'Who's this Vince Powell?' he asked. 'That's me', I said. 'It's my stage name', 'Oh I see. Smith not good enough for you is it?' said my Dad. 'No - er - well - you see Dad, Powell's a better name for a comedian.' My Dad said, 'Son - I'm not going to sign this form. You've got a good job, with good prospects. Stick at it. Forget all this comic stuff.' I argued but it made no difference, my Dad was adamant and I was well and truly depressed. My big chance and I'd lost it. So I carried on doing my bit for the war effort. But unknown to me life was about to take another dramatic turn.

Shortly after my sixteenth birthday, the conscription age was lowered to 17 although by then, it looked as if the war in Europe would soon be over. Berlin was surrounded by Russian troops and Germany was overrun by British and American forces. By my seventeenth birthday Germany had surrendered and I faced the prospect of being called up in the Army or sent to work in a coal mine, a prospect which filled me with dismay.

It was a scheme initiated by Ernest Bevin who was then the Minister of Labour. Those poor unfortunate youths who were made to work in the coal mines were inevitably known as 'Bevin Boys' and I was determined not to be one of them. I prayed that the war might end soon. But fate came to my aid or was it perhaps the power of prayer? Anyway, one weekend I met up with Kevin - remember him - the singer who didn't quite make it? We had kept in touch and he called to my house bubbling with excitement. Like me, he didn't want to be called up into the Army or end up as a Bevin Boy and by chance he called into the Naval Recruiting office in Dover Street to ask if there was any chance of getting in the Royal Navy. He was told that they had a recruiting drive on and were looking for volunteers of sixteen years old or over. He volunteered and was accepted.

I talked to my Dad who fortunately, didn't want me to

become a Bevin Boy either, and agreed that I could volunteer for the Navy. I immediately jumped on a tram, got to Dover Street, volunteered, had a medical and was accepted as a probationary SBA which turned out to be an acronym for Sick Berth Attendant. One question on the form puzzled me. It asked me how many years I wanted to serve - 7, 14 or 21. I asked the recruiting officer how many years I should put in. He looked at me and said 'just write 'For the period of the present emergency.' Fate must have been kind to me that day; otherwise I would have had a totally different lifestyle. A few days later I received a railway warrant with instructions to report to HMS Drake at Plymouth. I wondered what sort of ship HMS Drake was - a destroyer, a cruiser, an aircraft carrier? To my surprise HMS Drake turned out to be a Royal Naval Shore Establishment in Devonport. Oh well I thought - better than digging for coal. A few days later, I caught a tram into Manchester and presented my railway warrant at London Road station, as it was then called, before it became Piccadilly, and settled down as the train pulled out of the station. I felt excited as we left Manchester. The train passed close to Miles Platting - I could see the gasometers opposite which I was born and wondered how long it would be before I saw them again.

Little did I know that the next couple of years would have a profound affect on the rest of my life.

Chapter Two:
THE NAVY LARK

It was dark and raining as I stepped off the train at Plymouth to be met by a Naval Petty Officer, who ticked my name off a list on a large foolscap writing pad. He directed me to where several other youths were lined up on the platform. I walked across and stood at the end of the line. Soon I was joined by half a dozen others who had been on the same train as me. The Petty Officer looked at us and shook his head.

'You poor bastards' he said pityingly. 'Follow me'. We followed him off the platform and out into the station car park where a Naval bus was waiting to take us to HMS Drake. When we arrived and disembarked we were directed to a Nissen hut containing 24 iron bunk-type bedsteads, each with a mattress, two folded blankets and a couple of pillows. Not a sheet in sight.

'Right lads', barked the Petty Officer 'choose your beds.' I quickly threw my suitcase on to a top bunk of a bed nearest the door thinking that it might be a bit claustrophobic sleeping in a lower bunk. In about five minutes, we had each claimed a bunk. The lower bunk of my bed was claimed by a cheerful looking lad. 'David Llewellyn Cadwallader' he said offering his hand, 'but you can call me Taffy.' I shook his hand and told him my name.

'Vincent Joseph Smith,' I said, 'and you can call me Vince.' I discovered that Taffy was also a budding Sick Berth Attendant and we became good friends.

The Petty Officer raised his voice. 'Right, come on. Chop chop. Look lively. You're in the Navy now. Outside - all of you. Get fell in. Double line.' We went outside and did our best to form a double row. The Petty Officer marched us off.

'Left - right - left - right - left - right.' He led us to another Nissen hut where we were told to drop our trousers and a medical officer told us to cough as he examined our testicles.

From there we went next door, where we were kitted out with our uniforms. Considering the fact that the S.A's - Store Assistants - didn't bother to measure us, most of the kit fitted remarkably well. We were marched back to our Nissen hut, told to leave our uniforms on our beds, then directed to the Mess - a naval term for canteen - where we helped ourselves to sausages, baked beans and chips, followed by jam roly-poly and custard, all washed down with sweet, milky tea.

We returned to our Nissen hut, made our beds and turned in. Not that I slept much. After sleeping on my own for so long, it was difficult to accustom myself to sleeping with 23 others, to the accompaniment of grunts, groans, snores and the occasional breaking of wind. I eventually dropped off only to be woken at the crack of dawn by the Petty Officer entering, rattling our bed heads and shouting. 'Wakey, wakey. Hands off cocks - on socks.'

I soon discovered that this was his usual 'wake-up' call, which he found quite amusing - well it **was** the first time, but after hearing it every morning, it became quite boring after a fortnight.

The first two weeks of life in the Royal Navy were spent in basic training such as marching up and down the parade ground, known as 'square bashing', taking part in route marches, going on an assault course, life-boat drill and learning how to go up and down a rope ladder - not as easy as you may think. We were then each issued with a hammock and shown how to use them as we would be sleeping in them when and if we joined a ship. At the end of our basic training we were then sent to join the particular division to undergo our specialist training for whatever branch of the Navy we had been assigned to. As I was in the medical branch I and three others were sent to the nearby Royal Naval Hospital in Stonehouse where we underwent a crash course on first aid which included how to take a pulse, how to resuscitate a patient, and how to recognise the signs and symptoms of various diseases. After a week of this, we were given a medical handbook and turned loose on a ward full of Naval patients. That most of the patients survived our ministrations was nothing less than a miracle. We did our best but we made mistakes, such as Taffy tying a tourniquet on a seaman's arm so tight that it almost cut off his circulation, and one of the others giving a constipated stoker twice the prescribed amount of liquid laxative causing him to spend most of the night on the toilet. After a fortnight of this we had a written examination, which nobody failed and were entitled to sew a badge on our sleeve. It was a red cross in a gold circle which meant we were qualified Sick Berth Attendants. The following day a list of our names was pinned up on a notice board informing us of where we would be working. Against my name was HMS Mauritius which I found to be the flagship of the Mediterranean Fleet, currently at anchor in Malta. Taffy was posted to a Naval training camp at Pwllheli in North Wales, which was fortunate for him as it happened to be where he was born. Consequently, he spent his entire Naval service living ashore at home with his parents.

I was given a rail warrant to Liverpool to join a troopship bound for Malta. It was full of soldiers, airmen and seamen all going to join their various units. It took us over a week to reach Malta through the notorious Bay of Biscay. The sea was so rough that I thought at times the ship was going to capsize. Most of the passengers were violently seasick but fortunately I wasn't affected by the constant pitching and tossing of the troopship. We eventually docked in Valletta Harbour, Malta and disembarked. The sun was shining and I was directed to a Naval launch along with two other seamen. I took in my first glimpse of a foreign country. We climbed aboard and set sail to HMS Mauritius. As we drew alongside it seemed enormous. It was a 'Colony' class cruiser with a crew of over 700. As I climbed up the gangway with my kitbag and hammock I felt so excited and proud. I paused, halfway up the gangway to look at the rest of the fleet at anchor in the harbour, which was unfortunate as it caused the sailor behind me to cannon into me. I lost my footing and reached out to steady myself by grabbing the rope banister and in doing so, let go of my hammock which fell into the sea and sank. Not a very auspicious start to my Naval career. I never recovered my hammock but when I presented myself at the Sick Bay, I found that I would be sleeping in one of the 8 beds which it held.

The sick bay staff consisted of a Medical Officer, a Petty

Officer and myself. My chief duties were to supervise the daily sick parade, fill in a report of what each sailor was suffering from before passing them on to the Medical Officer, then, when they had been examined, diagnosed and given a prescription of whatever ailed them, they were told to report to me in the dispensary where I would give them what the M.O. had prescribed. Another of my duties was to hand out condoms to those who required them. Every morning at sick parade there was a least one seaman who had contracted a dose of venereal disease and had to have a penicillin injection. One in particular had caught it three times. The M.O. was furious with him and the seaman tried to excuse himself by telling the M.O. that he thought he'd caught it from a lavatory seat. The M.O. was even more furious and bellowed at the sailor that a lavatory was a funny place to have intercourse with a girl. Actually, he was more graphic than that but I've cleaned it up a bit.

A few days after I joined the ship, we heard that we were going to leave Valletta, sail to Marseilles, and return to Malta by sailing along the French coast calling at Villefranche-sur-Mer, Genoa and Naples on the Italian coast and Palermo in Sicily. Up until then, the furthest I had ever been was Blackpool, so you can imagine how I felt at the thought of visiting all these foreign ports. We sailed through the night and tied up in the harbour at Marseilles. I was eagerly looking forward to going ashore. But fate had other ideas. As prostitution was legal in France, the military authorities took the view that they couldn't stop the troops visiting a brothel so they declared that every brothel but one was out of bounds. The odd one out was placed under military supervision with regular visits from an army doctor giving the girls injections to keep them free from disease and ensure that they wouldn't infect any of their clients. Our M.O. had come to an agreement with the Army brass that while we were in Marseilles we would take over some of the medical duties. I was summoned to the M.O's office, told to collect a supply of condoms, some cotton wool swabs, a box of slides, several doses of penicillin and a microscope and join him at the bottom of the gangway. I carried out his instructions and packed everything into a hold-all and made my way down the gangway to find him sitting in an army Jeep. A military driver took us to a nearby bar which was next door to the military brothel. We went inside to be greeted by the Madame, a large buxom lady who showed us into an office and offered us wine. I was about to say yes, but the M.O. refused.

'Sorry Madame', he said. 'We have work to do. Show the girls in one at a time, to be examined.'

The girls came in one by one and each one lifted their skirts. None of them were wearing any knickers. The M.O. took a swab from each of them, put it on a slide and examined it under the microscope. Luckily it appeared that each girl was declared clean. After the last girl left, the M.O. told me to pack everything up and he would take the hold-all back to the ship.

'I can do that sir', I said.

'No you can't,' he replied, 'you're staying here.' He handed me a large ledger, 'You must enter the name and number of every man who comes in and give him a condom.' 'And also enter the name of the lady with whom he took his pleasure. '(And I've cleaned that up too - what he actually said was much more graphic!) With that, off he went while I spent my first day in a foreign town, handing out condoms and writing names in a ledger. I was hoping that, at some point, I would be relieved and I was happy when an army medic arrived at about 18.30. However, my happiness was short lived when I discovered that the Mauritius was sailing at 21.00 that night and the last liberty boat was at 19.00. I just had time for a swift beer before I was on my way back to the ship.

We sailed through the night following the coast. Early the next morning at about 06.00 we were cruising across the Baie des Anges parallel with Nice's famous Promenade des Anglais, heading toward the natural deep water harbour of Villefranche-Sur-Mer, a small fishing port some five kilometres east of Nice.

I decided to go up on deck to look at my first view of the Cote d'Azur. The ship had just rounded the Cap de Nice and was heading into the Rade de Villefranche. I left the sick bay, climbed the companionway to the upper deck, pushed open the bulkhead door and stepped out into the bright sunlight.

31

I wasn't prepared for the sight that greeted my eyes.

Under a cloudless blue sky was a shimmering sea of purest aquamarine. I stood transfixed. Ahead I could see the peninsula of Cap Ferrat, the most expensive piece of real estate in the world. I caught brief glimpses of luxurious villas peeping out from a profusion of olive trees, pine and palm trees, with here and there flashes of orange blossoms, mimosa and bougainvillea.

On my left was the 17th century port of Villefranche-Sur-Mer, with its picturesque jumble of narrow streets, which the ravages of war had left untouched - indeed Villefranche has hardly changed during the past 400 years and even today it looks more or less the same as when I first saw it 60 years ago. I could see brightly painted fishing boats anchored to the quay, as fishermen cheerfully unloaded their catches, and above it all, rows of terracotta roofs. What a contrast to the gasworks of Miles Platting. I fell instantly in love with Villefranche - a love affair which still continues to this day.

After recovering from my culture shock, I reluctantly tore myself away from the view and went down below to seek out my two 'oppos' - naval slang for shipmates, Jock and Scouse. They were in the mess having breakfast. Jock, as usual was attacking a plate piled high with two fried eggs, three sausages, four rashers of bacon, grilled tomatoes, mushrooms, a slice of black pudding and a round of fried bread. He was a tall, lean Glaswegian who ate enormous meals, yet never put on an ounce of weight. He joined the ship in Malta, and after almost two weeks in his company, I still needed the occasional services of an interpreter to fully understand his broad Scottish accent.

Fortunately, this task was carried out for me by the other member of our trinity - Scouse - who, as his nickname implied was from Liverpool. For those of you unaware of the term, people from Liverpool were known as 'Scousers', named after a native Liverpool dish consisting of boiled mutton with potatoes and onions. That was then, and while the term Scouse is now part of history you may search in vain for a restaurant which has it on the menu, although you may still find Irish stew, a direct ancestor.

I can't recollect ever knowing Scouse's Christian name, nor

Jock's come to think of it. Christian names were a rarity in the Navy. Among our messmates we had a 'Taffy' Morgan, 'Dusty' Miller, 'Chalky' White, 'Nobby' Clarke, 'Chips' Parker, 'Sparky' Jones, 'Lofty' Green, 'Shorty' Howard and, long before racism and political correctness was an issue, there was 'Al Jolson' Reynolds and 'Gunga Din' Hussein. You were named either after your accent, colour, size or your job on board. So Jock was 'Jock' and Scouse was 'Scouse'. Me? As a Sick Berth Attendant, I was inevitably called 'Doc'.

For some reason Scouse seemed to understand every word that Jock uttered which was more than anyone else on the ship did. He himself had a thick Liverpool accent whose conversation consisted mainly of the 'F-word'. Not only was 'effing' this or 'effing' that, but he used it to break up multi-syllable words, such as fan'effing'tastic, or un'effing'believable. During this chapter, I won't pepper his conversation with expletives. It could get boring. So you'll have to mentally drop them in where you think fit.

I first met Jock and Scouse in Malta shortly after they joined the ship as we lay at anchor in Valetta Harbour. I had joined the day before and early the next morning, Jock shuffled into the Sick Bay - no, let's be honest - staggered would be a more realistic description. He looked awful. His hair was dishevelled; he was deathly pale, unshaven and could barely stand. He stood there, shaking and swaying, staring at me through bloodshot eyes.

He muttered something that sounded like "I'm Noel"; I reached for the Day Book. "Noel who?" I asked. He blinked at me then belched loudly. An almost visible cloud of stale beer-laden fumes assaulted my nostrils.

"I'm Noel" Jock repeated. I sighed, "So you said, but what's your surname?" He belched again, but this time, I was prepared and turned my head to avoid the alcoholic fumes.

"Look", I said, "I'll enter your surname later, Noel."

At this, Jock burst into a flood of incomprehensible gibberish and began weaving his arms about in an alarming way, narrowly missing sweeping several bottles of medicines off a nearby shelf.

A voice piped up from behind Jock. "Scuse me Doc". A small stocky figure pushed his way in, who I later discovered was Jock's friend, Scouse.

"Just a minute" I said irritably, "You have to take your turn. Noel was here first." Again Noel erupted into another torrent of gibberish. "I'm sorry Noel, but I can't understand a word you're saying." Scouse butted in again.

"I'm trying to tell you Doc, you've got it all wrong. His name's not Noel."

"It sounded like Noel."

"No Doc. What he said was that he's not well. No well. Get it?"

The penny dropped. "Not well - no well", I repeated

Jock nodded, and to prove the point, immediately threw up.

"I think it could be something he ate" offered Scouse.

"Don't you mean something he drank?" I said.

Scouse grinned, "Yeah, it could be that. We were celebrating his birthday."

I handed Scouse a mop. "Here. Swab that mess up and I'll see what I can do for the pride of Scotland."

While Scouse got busy with the mop, I reached for a medicine bottled labelled 'Hangover Mixture'. It was a special recipe which consisted of mixing one part of ammonia solution to five parts of water. It was given to me by a nurse at RNH Stonehouse who swore that it worked wonders for a hangover. I poured two fluid ounces into a small tumbler and handed it to Jock.

"Drink that," I said.

Jock knocked it back in a flash, then suddenly clutched at his throat, let out a strangulated cry, and threw up again, this time all over Scouse.

"You've effing poisoned him," Scouse cried. (Yes, I know I said I wouldn't but I couldn't resist it. It won't happen again. Promise!)

I sniffed at the medicine bottle, poured a drop on my finger and tasted it. With a gasp of horror, I realised that somehow when I last made up the mixture, I must have inadvertently reversed the ratio. I'd mixed five parts of ammonia solution to one part of water. The mixture was powerful enough to burn Jock's tonsils off!

Luckily for both of us, his being promptly sick had saved

him from any serious or lasting damage. And then, an amazing transformation took place. At that moment, to my astonishment, Jock stopped shaking and the colour slowly returned to his cheeks. In a flash, his hangover had disappeared.

From then on, both Jock and Scouse regarded me as a medical miracle worker and the three of us became firm friends. But I digress.

There I was, in the mess, still reeling from my first sight of the Cote d'Azur. I grabbed hold of Jock's arm.

"You've got to come up on deck - both of you."

Scouse looked up. "What for?"

"You've just got to see this view. It's absolutely fantastic."

Jock sniffed disparagingly. "The only view I'm interested in seeing is a large pint! At that moment, an announcement came over the ship's tannoy.

"Attention all crew. The ship is now at anchor and shore leave for the Port Watch will commence as of now. The first liberty boat will leave from the starboard gangway in fifteen minutes time."

There was a mad scramble as Jock, Scouse, myself and most of the off-duty watch, rushed to their lockers to change into their 'number ones' (smart uniforms) to wear ashore. We had just enough time to visit the pay office and change our money into French currency before assembling at the starboard gangway to await the arrival of the liberty boat. Because Villefranche had no docking facilities for naval ships, the Mauritius had to anchor in the bay, about five hundred yards from the shore thus necessitating the use of liberty boats to ferry the crew ashore. As we waited by the gangway I pointed to the surrounding view.

"Look Jock, Scouse - isn't that absolutely fabulous?"

Jock squinted against the sun's rays. "I canna see a bar."

"But look at the view Jock?" I said, "Don't you appreciate all that beauty?"

"I'd appreciate it more through the bottom of a pint glass."

There was an excited buzz as the liberty boat pulled alongside. We all hurried down the gangway and stepped aboard. The liberty boat was a big as a lifeboat and held nearly forty sailors. For the next thirty six hours until we set sail back to Malta, the liberty boat would shuttle to and fro between the ship and the quay, ferrying the crew ashore and back.

I stood in the bow as we headed for the tiny Port de la Sante. Several fisherwomen were squatting on the nearby Quai Courbet busily mending the nets, while their husbands weighed their catches and calculated how much money they would fetch later that day in the local fish market.

Behind them stretched a row of restaurants, nestling side by side along the Quai Amiral Courbet - Le Saint-Pierre, La Fregate, La Mere Germaine, Chez Irene and Le Corsaire. Already, waiters were bustling about laying pink tablecloths, napkins and cutlery on tables outside in the sun in readiness for lunch, while the various chefs took their pick from the newly caught fish being unloaded from the fishing boats.

I took a deep breath of the pine scented air, laced with the bracing aroma of pure ozone, and looked toward the approaching shore. Ahead, the 17th century church of St. Michel stood at the top of the steeply stepped Rue d'Eglise with its tall clock tower looming over the port like a guardian angel.

"We must go and have a look at that church", I remarked. Jock and Scouse looked at me in amazement.

"A church?" said Jock "Have ye no forgotten what we agreed last night?" I hadn't but I hoped that Jock and Scouse had.

The previous night, after a few beers in the mess, the talk had turned inevitably to girls and the three of us had owned up to being virgins. If that sounds odd to you readers living in the permissive age of the 21st century, you must remember that I am talking of events of over fifty years ago when the vast majority of teenagers only lost their virginity on their wedding night. Besides, Scouse and I were both Catholics and sexual intercourse outside marriage was a mortal sin. Not only that but think of the shame and embarrassment of having to confess to ones sexual pleasures to a priest.

However, fuelled by several cans of bitter, we agreed that the time to surrender our virginity was never better than here in France. We had been told by several of our more

36

experienced shipmates that French girls were plentiful and passionate. We made a bet that whichever one of us was the first to lose our virginity would be paid £5 each by the other two. Each of us had in our pocket, a condom appropriately referred to as a French letter.

At that moment my thoughts were interrupted by a loud cheer. We had arrived at the jetty.

No sooner did the liberty boat touch the shore than the crew were off like a flash. Scouse rushed up to a weather-beaten old fisherman who was busily painting his boat.

"Excuse me wack" he said, "where's the nearest bar?"

The fisherman shrugged. "Je ne comprends pas M'sieu."

"Bar, bar, bar" shouted Jock sounding for all the world like some demented highland sheep.

The fisherman shrugged again. Jock mimed raising a glass and drinking. At this the fisherman's weather-beaten face broke into a wide grin. He nodded and mimicked Jock's drinking gesture.

"Ah, oui M'Sieu. Bar."

Jock grinned, "I think I've got through to him."

The fisherman pointed toward a car park. "Chez Max. En face du Parking."

Jock and Scouse ran off. I stood for another moment looking across at the view of Cap Ferrat, and then followed them into the bar Chez Max.

As soon as I walked into the bar I was greeted by a smell which I soon grew to associate with any bar in any part of France. It was a subtle mixture of garlic, pastis and Gauloise cigarettes. It's a smell you never find anywhere else in the world.

I joined Jock and Scouse who were sitting at a table near the door. The atmosphere inside Chez Max was cheerful. Standing at the bar were four fishermen each with a glass containing a generous measure of cognac. On the bar in front of them were four coffees in incredibly tiny cups. They were having an animated conversation with the elderly owner; whose name we discovered later was Gerard. Where Max was, if he ever existed at all, we never found out. Scouse eyed the tiny coffee cups.

"A bit stingy with the coffee" he remarked.

"Never mind the coffee" said Jock, "let's get some beer in." He gave a piercing whistle and waved in the direction of the bar. "Beer" he called.

Gerard turned and beamed at us, displaying a mouthful of nicotine stained teeth. He moved in our direction.

"Bonjour English," he said.

Jock bridled. "No English, Scots."

"Pardon M'sieu?" said Gerard.

Jock rose and drew himself up to his full height. "Scots," he repeated "Scots!"

Gerard nodded and beamed again. "Ah oui, Scotch" He walked back to the bar, and returned clutching a bottle of Johnny Walker Black Label. "Scotch" he said proudly.

Calling upon my rather sketchy schoolboy French, I hastily intervened before Jock started World War 3. "Excusez moi M'Sieu" I explained, "vous ne comprenez pas. Mon ami est Ecosse."

A smile of understanding rippled across Gerard's face. "Ah bon. Je compris. Ecossais!" He grasped Jock's hand and shook it vigorously.

"Bonnie Prince Charlie's," he said, then produced four tumblers, opened the bottle of Johnny Walker and poured out four generous measures.

He turned to face his friends at the bar and pointed to Jock "Ecossais."

The fishermen raised their brandy glasses and said in unison "Bravo. Sante."

Gerard picked up a glass of whisky and raised it. "To brave Navy sailors." he said. The fishermen applauded. Not wishing to disillusion Gerard or his friends, I thought it best not to tell him that having only joined the Navy as the war ended, there had been no opportunity for bravery. We solemnly raised our glasses and drank. I offered to pay for the whiskies but Gerard wouldn't have it and poured out four more to finish the bottle.

"Why don't we sit outside in the sun and look at the view," I suggested. Scouse pointed out that the view from outside was of the car park and hardly worth writing home about, but we all agreed that sitting in the sunshine would be a good idea. So we rose, took our drinks and found a table outside from which we could see part of the bay and in the distance, the stern of the Mauritius rising and falling with the gentle swell of the Mediterranean Sea. It was very pleasant sitting there in the warm sunshine. We finished our whiskies and decided to order some beers. Now established as the group's official spokesman because of my schoolboy French, I was sent to order the drinks. I strode up to the bar and addressed Gerard with all the confidence I could muster.

"Trois bieres s'il vous plait M'sieu."

If I say so myself, I said the above in perfect French, which was a mistake, as Gerard immediately assumed that I spoke the language like a native and proceeded to tell me a dirty joke in French. At least I assumed it was dirty, judging from the several nods, winks, leers and gestures that accompanied the telling and the roar of raucous laughter from the fishermen. Not wishing to reveal my ignorance, I joined in the laughter, paid for the beers, put them on a tray and carried them outside before Gerard could start on another story.

As I sat down, I noticed a bus coming slowly down the hill. It stopped and turned into the car park. As we watched, about half a dozen girls alighted. They were all attractive, if perhaps a little too heavily made up and the dress of the day seemed to be extremely tight sweaters hardly able to contain their thrusting bosoms. Their skirts were so short that they hardly covered their essentials. We stared at these members of the oldest profession, for that's what they were, and watched as they made their way to the jetty awaiting the next liberty boat's arrival with it's cargo of sailors eager to take advantage of their services.

One of the girls approached our table. A shapely and voluptuous blonde, whose name I later discovered, was Annette. She smiled at me and said huskily, "Fait l'amour sailor?" I felt a stirring in my loins. I knew what she was asking but faced with this moment of truth I lost my nerve. I shook my head and mumbled "No merci."

She shrugged and walked to the bar where Gerard had poured her a coffee. Jock and Scouse were looking at me curiously.

"What did she say to you?" asked Scouse.

"Er - nothing."

"She said something about l'amour. That's love isn't it?"

"She was just being friendly."

"She fancies you Doc" said Jock.

Scouse nodded. "You missed your chance there. Why didn't you chat her up?"

"I think he's scared" said Jock.

"No I'm not."

"Well go on then" said Scouse, "dig in - fill your boots."

"I'm not in the mood."

"I told you he was scared" said Jock.

"I am not scared."

"Well go on then."

"**You** go on."

"She fancied **you** not me."

I looked across the bar where Annette was sipping her coffee. She certainly looked sexually attractive. I pictured her lying naked on a bed. She must have sensed me looking at her and turned. She smile, winked and blew me a kiss.

"Did you see that?" said Scouse, "she's practically begging for it."

"If you're not up to it Doc", said Jock, "I am."

"So am I," said Scouse.

Jock produced a coin. "We'll toss for it."

"Oh no you don't." I said.

I took a deep breath, picked up my beer, drank it and banged the empty glass firmly on the table. Jock and Scouse looked at me. I stood up. "Get those fivers ready" I said and strode purposefully to the bar.

Annette watched me approach, a knowing glint in her eyes.

"Allo Sailor," she said, "you want jig a jig wiz me?"

I suddenly felt very nervous but was conscious of Jock and Scouse looking at me.

"How much - combien?" I stammered.

"Two 'undred francs" she replied and held out her hand. I pulled some notes from my pocket and handed her two hundred francs. As I was about to put my money away, she placed a restraining hand on my arm.

"Ze 'otel is extra."

"Hotel?"

"But of course, for ze room."

I gave her another note. She took my arm and we walked out of the bar, passing Jock and Scouse who grinned and gave me the thumbs up.

"Give her one for me" said Jock coarsely.

"You can give her **two** for me" leered Scouse.

Annette took me across the road and into the Place Amelie Pollonaise, a pretty little square with a fountain in the middle, a patisserie, a couple of bars, and a gift shop. Ahead of us was the imposing entrance to the 4 star Hotel Welcome. "Good" I thought, "at least we'll be doing it in comfort." But to my surprise, Annette veered to her left, pulling me with her.

She led me to a doorway, over which was a faded sign which read Hotel Paradis. Anything less resembling Paradise. I had yet to see. Outside a dark, forbidding doorway stood a badly chipped and worn, plaster of paris palm tree, with yellowish plastic leaves. We went inside and I followed Annette up a flight of creaking stairs covered with a stained and threadbare carpet to the first floor where there was a desk on which a badly handwritten card announced that this was 'Le Reception'. Behind the desk stood a large lady with a serious case of halitosis.

She smiled at Annette who nodded and handed her a hundred franc note for which she received a key.

Annette led the way down a dimly lit corridor past several rooms. From within one of the rooms I could hear grunts, heavy breathing and other sounds of sexual activity. We stopped at a door, which Annette unlocked and we entered.

The room was small, and contained the minimum of furniture, a wardrobe, an uncomfortable looking cane chair and an even more uncomfortable looking bed. Neither of us had exchanged a word since we left the bar.

Annette started to undress.

I watched her with a growing feeling of apprehension and dread as she stepped out of her skirt and took off her bra.

"Come on Sailor", she said.

I took off my jacket, and started to unbutton my shirt. By now my former sexual desire had started to subside to be replaced by thoughts of guilt, the sixth commandment and visions of hellfire.

By now, Annette was totally naked and looking at me with more than hint of impatience as I still struggled to undo my shirt, with fumbling fingers. She shook her head and reached out to help me. As she did, her eye was caught by a medal on a chain round my neck. It was of the Virgin Mary and was inscribed 'Our Lady of Lourdes.' The medal had been given to me by a deeply religious aunt, who had it blessed by her local priest and made me promise to wear it, to keep me safe from the perils of the sea.

Annette examined the medal. "You Catholic?" she asked.

I nodded. She smiled. "Me too."

That did it. My erection swiftly vanished. I quickly grabbed my jacket, mumbled a hasty apology to Annette and fled from the room. Outside, as I made my way back to the bar to rejoin Jock and Scouse, I wondered what I would say to them, and decided to say nothing and let them assume that nature had taken its carnal course. They were still sitting there drinking as I returned. I sat down trying to look casual.

"Well," said Jock, "how did it go". I shrugged nonchalantly, "It was all right."

"All right?" said Jock. "Is that all you can say - it was all right?"

"Okay, it was bloody fantastic," I bragged.

"That's more like it," said Jock.

"You weren't gone very long" remarked Scouse.

"No well - er - they don't hang about. Time is money. And talking of which.'

Jock pulled a note from his pocket. "You're right Doc. Here's my fiver for the bet." I took it and turned to Scouse. "And a fiver from you Scouse."

He took out a five pound note and handed it over. At that moment Annette came round the corner and marched up to our table. She glared at me and put two hundred francs on the table.

"Voila" she said.

I felt myself starting to blush. Jock and Scouse looked at Annette, a puzzled look on their faces.

"Why are you giving him his money back" asked Scouse, "was he that good?"

Annette shrugged and flashed him scornful look. "Good!" she spat, "he didn't even took his trousers off!" She flounced off. Jock and Scouse stared at me accusingly.

'Bloody fantastic was it?' said Jock.

'Didn't even get your trousers off' said Scouse.

I grinned sheepishly at them, then silently handed them back their five pound notes. Vive l'amour!

I apologised to Jock and Scouse and suggested we go and visit the church. My suggestion was not met with enthusiasm.

'You visit the church' said Jock rising.

'Where are you going' I asked.

'I'm going to do what you should have done,' he said 'and this time she won't have to give me **my** money back!'

He strode purposefully toward the bar, where Annette was talking to one of the other girls. Suddenly Scouse leapt off his chair.

'Hang on Jock, he called. 'I'm coming with you!'

I watched them as they approached Annette and her friend, agreed the going rate then crossed the square and disappeared into the Hotel Paradis. That was the last time I saw them until the following morning when they insisted on giving me a blow by blow account of their amorous activities. Needless to say, it wasn't long before I too, succumbed to my carnal desires and broke the sixth commandment. We left Villefranche and continued our cruise, along the coast calling at Genoa, Naples and Sicily each of them fascinating in their own way but none of them could compare with that unforgettable first glimpse of the South of France. I had the strangest feeling that I had somehow come home - everything seemed very familiar as if I'd been there before.

When we finished our cruise and arrived back in Valetta harbour, our M.O. left the ship on compassionate grounds. We never did find out the reason although there was a rumour that his wife had left him and wanted a divorce. Anyway, he went and was replaced by another M.O. who turned out to be the M.O. from hell! He did everything by the rule book, and took forever to examine everyone who reported sick. As a consequence Sick Parade which was normally over by eleven o'clock rarely finished before one. He forbade us sleeping in the sick bay saying that the beds were for patients only and we would have to sleep in the mess on our hammocks. Luckily I had been issued with a replacement but I hated it. I was complaining about it to Scouse one day, when he suggested that I put in for a transfer. He explained that if I could find an SBA ashore or on another ship, Naval rules allowed you to swap. I sighed. 'And where am I going to find another SBA to swap with me?' I asked.

Scouse grinned. 'Funny you should say that Doc,' he said. 'one of my old mates from Liverpool is based here in Malta. He's at Manoel Island in a transit camp. He'd love to be on the ship with me. I'm having a jar with him tonight when I go ashore, why don't you join us?'

I quickly agreed, and later that night went ashore with Scouse and met up with his mate in a bar called 'The Egyptian Queen' run by a huge black homosexual. Scouse's mate was already there - with an attractive girl on his knee.

Scouse introduced us. 'Doc, meet Gerry,'

We shook hands and he indicated the girl on his knee. 'This is Rosa.'

I smiled at her. She winked at me.

Scouse explained the situation about doing a swap. Gerry immediately agreed. I asked him what the procedure was for swapping and he said all I had to do was inform my First Officer, and that he would inform **his** First Officer. We would need to sign a couple of forms, the request would go before our respective Captains, and that was it.

'Dead easy Doc.'

And it was. Two days later I was on my way to Manoel Island which was once a former leper colony. It was now a transit camp which dealt with naval personnel arriving from the UK to join a ship, or arriving from a ship to return to the UK to be demobbed. The result was that hardly anybody reported sick in case it interfered with their getting home or joining a ship. Consequently I spent most of my time on Malta exploring the island, sunbathing and swimming. Not a bad way to spend one's National Service. I spent over six happy months in Malta. However, all good things come to an end and in my case it was a notification from the Admiralty, that my term of service was nearly over and I had to return to England and be demobbed. My previous ambitions of a career in show business had been put on the back burner but as the time grew nearer for me to be demobbed; I began to think more and more what I was going to do on my return to Civvie Street. Two days later I joined the 'Ark Royal' an aircraft carrier which was returning to England with about 50 other sailors who were also being demobbed. The sun was shining as we slowly sailed out of Valetta Harbour.

Chapter Three:
CIVVIE STREET

It was raining as the Ark Royal slowly sailed into the Royal Naval dockyards at Devonport. After we had docked, all the demobees reported to the Pay Office where we each received our final pay packet plus any savings to which we were entitled. From there we went to the clothing store to collect our demob suits, a shirt, a tie, underwear, socks, shoes and a raincoat. We were given the option of changing into our civvies now and packing our uniform in our kitbags, or vice versa. I chose to keep my uniform on. We were then given a rail warrant to our nearest stations and that was it. We were civilians again. I caught the train to Manchester and as we drew closer, I saw the gasworks and my mind went back to the last time I had seen them. Such a lot had happened in the intervening years and I cast my mind back to my first glimpse of the South of France. I made a vow that one day when I had earned enough money I would go back to Villefranche again.

Naturally my Dad and stepmother were delighted that I was home and to be honest after a few days it hardly seemed that I'd been away. My Dad, who was then working as an alteration tailor at high class tailoring firm called Hector Powe, managed to get me a job as a junior salesman. But I was still anxious to make my mark as a comedian. Every week I scanned the pages of The Stage and The Performer to see if anyone wanted a comedian. Not a chance. There were plenty of ads for singers and topless showgirls but nothing for me. Then my local Catholic church put on a talent show in their school hall to raise money in order to pay to send a young girl to America for treatment that wasn't available in Britain. There would be a £5 prize for the winner, £3 for whoever came second and £1 for who came third. I entered and brushed up the script I had used for the Carroll Levis audition. I felt very confident on the night of the show. There were 8 acts - two singing sisters, a pianist, a magician, a boy soprano, an impressionist, a tap dancer, a guitar player and me. We all went on and did our acts and my jokes got a lot of laughs. Then the parish priest who acted as the compere brought us back on the stage one by one to be judged by whoever got the loudest applause. To my surprise the boy soprano came first. I later found out that he was the youngest of eight children and not only were all his family there but several cousins, aunts and uncles. The singing sisters came second and I had to be content with third place and £1. My Dad was furious.

'It's not fair son,' he said, 'you were better than any of them. That lad only won because his parents brought a coach load of relatives.' I was disappointed but it only made me more determined to break into show business. As we left the school hall, I was approached by one of the parents.

'I liked your act,' he said, 'you made me laugh'.

'Thank you' I replied.

'It was very funny. My name is Anderson. Do you do after dinners?'

I had no idea what 'after dinners' meant but before I could confess my ignorance, my Dad spoke up.

'Does he do after dinners? He does everything. Weddings, Birthdays, Business Functions the lot.'

'Are you his agent?' Anderson asked.

'No - I'm his father.'

Anderson turned to me.

'Are you free this Saturday?' he asked.

'Well - er - I - er -.' I stammered.

'My daughter's getting married on Saturday. We'd booked a comedian for the reception but he phoned me last night to say he couldn't do it as he's just had an offer from P&O to go on a comedy cruise. They're paying him five hundred pounds, and as I was only going to pay him twenty, I couldn't very well insist he does his act at my daughter's wedding could I? What do you say?'

By now, I'd managed to figure out that he was offering me a booking to entertain the guests at his daughter's wedding.

'I'll do it.' I said.

'Terrific,' he replied.

He took a card from his pocket and handed it to me.

'Here's my card. Phone me first thing in the morning and I'll give you all the details. Must dash now. My wife will wonder where I've got to. She'll be pleased when she hears about you. Don't forget to ring me tomorrow.'

He hurried off before I could reply.

'Congratulations son,' said my Dad.

'I thought you were dead against me being a comic.'

'Well I still think you should keep on with your job. Hector Powe's is a well established firm with good prospects. But when I saw you tonight, I had to admit you were good, I really did. So if you can earn a few bob making people laugh I'm all for it. But I still think you should concentrate on a proper career.'

'Don't worry Dad,' I said. 'I promise I won't hand my notice in until I'm a star.'

We made our way home. I was on cloud nine as I relived my performance, hearing again the laughter of the audience. I was convinced that I had my feet on the first rung of the ladder to fame. For the next few days, I polished up my act. I had phoned Mr Anderson and he told me that his daughter, Debbie, was marrying an Australian lad who worked behind the bar at an Aussie pub in Earl's Court. I devised a few Aussie jokes and decided I would finish on a song. The popular song of the day was 'April Showers' from the film 'The Jolson Story' which had just been released. I bought a copy of the sheet music, and learned the words off by heart. Saturday couldn't come too quickly as far as I was concerned but come it did at last. The wedding reception, a buffet do, was at the local British Legion club. I was there at least an hour before the bride and groom arrived. Mr Anderson invited me to help myself to some food but I was too nervous to eat. There was the usual toasts. To the bride, to the groom, to the bridesmaids, to the groom's parents, to the bride's parents, I thought they would never end. But they did, and I was introduced by the best man. Then came the first snag. I gave the sheet music to the pianist who told me he couldn't read music! Fortunately he knew the song and said he could cope.

I was on, I told my first joke.

'My Lords, Ladies and Gentlemen, Distinguished guests, Reverend Father, Prime Minister and just in case, Your Majesty,'

There was a few seconds of silence and I thought 'Oh heck. Not a good start.' I was about to go into my next joke, when a burst of laughter and a round of applause rang out. I was away. They laughed at everything I said. Mind you there had been a lot of toasts and a lot of champagne so they probably would have laughed at anything I said! They even laughed at my singing! Mr Anderson proposed a toast to me, and gave me an envelope containing two ten pound notes. I was kissed by four beautiful bridesmaids, several elderly ladies and an Australian homosexual! I eventually returned home well pleased with myself and more than ever convinced that my future lay in being a comedian. Twenty quid for half an hours work? A piece of cake. However I was soon brought down to earth with my next engagement. It was at a working man's club in Collyhurst called Dirty Dicks. The name itself should have warned me. I had written to the concert secretary giving him some details of myself and asked for an audition. To my surprise he phoned me and offered me a booking for the following night at the grand fee of £5.

I thought that this was a bit too low but he told me that this was the going rate for somebody who was virtually unknown. So I agreed. After all, I thought, it would be more experience and £5 was not to be sneezed at in 1949. The next night I got down to Dirty Dicks and was met by a large ugly looking man who I later found out was a bouncer. I told him who I was. He let me in and introduced me to Ted the concert secretary who told me that I was third on the bill. First on would be their resident comedian, Snowy White who also acted as compere, then it would be Jenny their resident singer then me. A local 3 piece group - piano, drums and guitar would close the first half and after an interval of about half an hour to allow the members to drink as many pints as they could, the entertainment would resume, and I would do another spot. He pointed me in the direction of the dressing rooms, or rather room. There was only one - we all had to share, that included Jenny, Snowy, the three musicians and me. He told me that as I was more or less staff, I could have two free pints during the evening. I could have one now if I wanted. I declined and said I would rather sit in the dressing room and rehearse my two spots.

He smiled at me, 'That's what I like to hear son. Dedication. If you go down well tonight I'll use you again.'

I smiled back and went to the dressing room. It was empty. I sat down and tried to decide how I could split my act in two in order to do two performances. The door opened and a thin man wearing cream trousers, a yellow shirt, a blue spotted bow tie and a vivid red jacket entered. He had a thick shock of white hair. He held out his hand.

'Howdo,' he said. 'You must be Vince. Snowy White. Welcome to Dirty Dicks.' We shook hands. 'Jenny's at the bar - why don't you go and join her?'

I muttered something about not drinking before a performance. He laughed.

'You'll need more than one drink to face this lot.'

'Why, are they difficult?'

'Difficult? I should say so. Let's put it this way. If they like you they let you live.'

I was beginning to feel uneasy.

'You'll be all right Vince. I'll warm them up for you.' He looked at his watch. 'It's time I was on. I'll switch on the tannoy so you can listen to my act.'

He reached up and operated a switch attached to a speaker. A babble of noise from the audience filled the dressing room. It was stilled by the voice of the concert secretary.

'Order, order' he shouted.

'Two pints, a voice shouted back.

There was a burst of laughter and crude remarks from the speaker. The voice of the concert secretary carried on. I listened with growing concern.

'Before we begin our cabaret. I have one or two announcements to make. It has been brought to my notice that some of our gentlemen members have been seen urinating in the car park. We have adequate toilet facilities in the club, and any member caught relieving himself in the car park will lose his membership.'

A chorus of boos and catcalls issued out from the speaker.

The concert secretary continued.

'Well, that's enough from me. I'll leave you in the capable hands of our resident funny man, the one and only - Snowy White!'

Snowy winked at me, and dashed out of the dressing room. I sat and listened to his performance coming out of the speaker. I couldn't believe what I heard. His act consisted of a string of filthy jokes covering sex, every bodily function, homosexuals, lesbians, the disabled and various animals. Judging from the sound of laughter the audience loved it. I was shocked. I had a clean act. My jokes were funny not filthy. What was I going to do? I knew that if I went onstage with the material I had I was going to die on my feet! There was only one thing I could do. I went into the club. The concert secretary was at the bar. He waved me over.

'Changed your mind about that drink Vince?'

'No', I said. 'I've got to go home. I don't feel well. I think I'm going down with the 'flu. Sorry Ted.'

Before he could answer, I ran out of the club, caught a bus home and went straight to bed thoroughly depressed. I spent the night dismally reviewing the events at Dirty Dicks. Where do I go now, I thought? Perhaps I should change my act and put in some dirty jokes and four letter words - I knew plenty from my time in the Navy. But I wanted to be more than just a club act. I wanted to appear in theatres and on the radio. My thoughts went back to when I played truant to go and watch acts at the Ardwick Empire. Those comedians didn't tell off-colour jokes or use bad language. But they were funny. And what about the funny men on the radio? Their performances bore no resemblance to Snowy White. But how did they start? Surely not in working men's clubs. I finally fell asleep just as dawn was breaking - still depressed. Perhaps my Dad was right. Maybe I should concentrate on my job and forget about being a comic.

And that's what I did. I worked hard and attended night school where I took a course on tailoring. I actually enjoyed it. Every customer became a challenge. I saw it as my duty not to let a customer leave the shop without ordering a suit. The manager complimented me on my zeal and gave me a rise. Time passed pleasantly by. I put my thoughts of show

51

business out of my mind and concentrated on my job. Life was good. I had a well paid job, and was a member of the local Catholic youth club where I made lots of friends with whom I played snooker and table tennis. It was a mixed club and we used to dance to records played on a radiogram - Glenn Miller's 'In The Mood' was a favourite.

However, fate was about to provide me with a nasty shock. My stepmother who hadn't been in the best of health for some time, collapsed one day and was rushed to hospital where it was discovered that she had Pleurisy. My Dad and I went to visit her and I couldn't help thinking back to my last visit to hospital just before my Mam died and I prayed that my stepmother would recover. She had been in hospital for almost a week when a call came through to Hector Powe asking my Dad to go to the hospital at once. I wanted to go with him, but at the time I was serving a customer. My Dad hadn't returned by the time the shop closed so I went back home to wait for him. He didn't return until late and when he did, I knew by his face that the worst had happened. He had tears in his eyes as he told me that my stepmother had been struck down with double pneumonia which, because of her weakened health proved to be fatal.

There was a Requiem Mass and my stepmother was buried in the same cemetery as my Mam. It must have been a case of déjà vu for my Dad, but he was a devout Catholic and his strong faith was a great comfort to him. We had the usual wake, went back home and started to pick up the pieces again. That great healer - Time - passed and we slowly developed a routine. My Dad and I went to work together and came back home together. We cooked for ourselves, although I must confess that, more often than not, it was fish, chips and mushy peas from the nearby chippie.

The tailor's shop had a ladies department making tailored suits, and one day they engaged a new saleslady. Her name was Pat. She was very attractive, with a nice figure, dark hair and 'come to bed' eyes, an invitation of which I very soon took advantage. We started going out together or, as it was referred to at that time, 'courting'. From the very beginning, I had a feeling that we'd met before, although I knew we hadn't. By this time Dad had left Hector Powe and was working from home. He had a sign made which he fixed to the wall outside our front door reading 'James Smith, High Class Tailor. Ladies and Gents Suits made to Measure. Alteration service available.' He was so proud of that sign. I often used to see him looking at it as if savouring the words. 'James Smith, High Class Tailor' - and why not? Not bad for an orphan. He got plenty of work - mostly from the parishioners. Meanwhile, I carried on at Hector Powe. I was still going out with Pat and I thought it was time for her to meet Dad. I arranged for the three of us to have dinner together at a restaurant in Manchester. Dad and I arrived first and went to sit at our table. We ordered drinks and waited. I saw Pat arrive and pointed her out to Dad.

Dad gasped, and almost choked on his drink.

'Are you all right Dad?' I asked anxiously.

He was staring at Pat 'Is that Pat?' he asked.

'Yes', I replied.

He watched as she made her way to our table then turned to me. He had tears in his eyes.

'She's the spitting image of your Mam when she was her age.' I was dumbfounded. So that's why I felt I knew her. Who knows? Pat arrived at the table and I introduced her to Dad who couldn't take his eyes of her. Everything went well - the meal was delicious and the wine flowed. Pat and Dad seemed to get on well together, and by the end of the meal they were both chattering away nineteen to the dozen. When we left, we walked Pat to her bus stop - she lived in Didsbury - saw her on her bus and made our way to catch our bus home.

'What did you think of her Dad?' I asked.

'I like her,' he replied, 'she's a bonny lass. You could do worse.'

For the next few weeks, Pat and I went out on a regular basis and she often came to our house for a meal. We felt comfortable with each other. One day, I took Dad out to our local pub.

'I've something to tell you Dad'

'Oh aye.'

'It's about me and Pat.'

'Oh aye,' he said again.

'I've asked her to marry me.'

He grunted. 'You took your time didn't you? I thought you'd never get round to it.'

And that was it. Pat wasn't a Catholic, but she agreed to talk to Father Anthony, one of the priests at St. Clares. He gave her a short course on Catholicism and she agreed that any children which we had would be brought up in the Catholic Faith. So we got married in a Catholic church, had a wedding reception in our local pub and went to the Isle of Man for our honeymoon. When we returned, we lived with Dad. He carried on his tailoring business and I continued at Hector Powe. Pat left the Ladies department and got a job as a Dental Secretary. We put a deposit on a semi-detached house in Wilmslow, Cheshire - no let's be honest - my Dad loaned me the money for the deposit - but that's what Dad's are for isn't it? However, to continue, life went on more or less as before until one day I bumped into Mr Anderson. Remember him? He hadn't forgotten me or my act at this daughter's wedding and he asked me how I was doing. I told him that I was now married and had a steady job. He then asked what had happened to my ambition to be a comic and I had to confess that I had put that on one side to concentrate on my job.

'A pity' he said, 'I thought you were very funny. Funnier than a lot of the so called comics I've seen or heard today.'

We parted, but I couldn't forget his words. Maybe I should give my ambition of being a comedian another go. I talked it over with Pat, who couldn't understand my enthusiasm for show business. However, she came to regard my fixation as more or less a hobby of mine which held no threat to our marriage. I decided to write to the BBC North Region Entertainment Dept in Manchester and ask for an audition. In those days the BBC was split into several regions - North, South, Midlands, Wales, Scotland etc. each responsible for their own input to the national network. So I wrote to the BBC North Region Entertainment Dept. Their Head of Entertainment was a gentleman called Ronnie Taylor. One of their popular programmes was called 'Variety Fanfare' a radio variety series featuring comedians, singers, musicians, impressionists all of whom were relatively new to radio. Out of this series, devised and produced by Ronnie Taylor came many artistes who later became famous - artistes such as Sheila Buxton, Jimmy Clitheroe, Ken Platt, Al Read, Morecambe and Wise, Les Dawson, Petula Clark and Ted Ray. To those of you reading this, some of the names will mean little but in the 50's they were big stars.

So I wrote a letter to Ronnie Taylor, told him a little about myself and that I would be grateful for the chance of an audition. I posted the letter and waited. And waited. And waited. Just when I had given up of receiving a reply, an envelope fell through our letter box. On the back of the envelope were the words 'Return Address. B.B.C. Piccadilly, Manchester.' For a few moments I just stared at those words, half afraid of opening the envelope in case it was bad news. Then I tore the envelope open and took out the letter which was inside. It was typewritten on B.B.C. headed notepaper, and only contained a few lines. It said 'Dear Mr Powell. Thank you for your letter. Mr Taylor will be happy to see you on Monday August 12 at 11:30 at the above address.' It was signed by a Pat Lamont, secretary. I could hardly wait for Monday to come round. I spent hours re-writing my script until I was happy with it. Monday came. I told my Dad about the letter from Ronnie Taylor, then changed into my best suit, caught the bus to Piccadilly and presented myself at the BBC. I was told to take the lift to the third floor where I would be met by Ronnie's secretary. I was literally trembling with a mixture of excitement and nerves as I got to the third floor where Pat Lamont was waiting for me with a welcoming smile. I followed her down a corridor and we stopped at a door marked HNR(V) which I later found out stood for Head of North Region (Variety). We went in the office. Sitting behind a desk was a stocky figure with fair hair and a smile on his face. He rose and he shook my hand.

'Welcome to the fun factory Vince,' he said.

He spoke in a quiet voice which I found comforting. He reminded me of a doctor. He had an air of confidence about him which immediately put me at ease. He asked his secretary to bring two cups of coffee, and pointed to a chair.

'Now sit down and tell me all about yourself.'

I sat down and found myself telling him my life story. He

had that effect on people. I liked him instantly. We had our coffees, and Ronnie asked me about my act, and then asked me to do it for him. I stood up and went into the act. Ronnie sat back with a smile on his face and listened. I finished and looked at him expectantly.

Ronnie smiled at me. 'Very good Vince. You've got a pleasant personality and a good confident delivery. I've heard some of jokes before, in fact I probably wrote some of them'. He sighed, 'But.' My face dropped. 'There's always a 'but' Vince. Your problem is that you are telling a lot of unrelated jokes. What you need is a hook to hang them on to. Something to link your jokes together. Look, I'll tell you what I'll do. Every Sunday we record a light entertainment programme at the BBC Playhouse. It could be the Al Read show or Variety Fanfare. I'll leave your name with the commissionaire and any time you want to go he'll let you in. It'll be good for you to watch other comics and learn from them. Try and get there about midday then you can see them rehearse'. That was typical of Ronnie. He was the most generous hearted person I have ever met. I went to the BBC Playhouse nearly every Sunday. It was a wonderful learning curve for me. One Sunday I met Ronnie at the theatre during a recording.

'How's it going Vince? Found that hook yet?' he asked.

'I'm working on it Ronnie.'

'Good.'

'I read a piece in The Stage that the BBC are going to do a talent show called 'What Makes A Star.' Do you think I should apply?

Ronnie shook his head, 'No. They're scraping the bottom of the barrel to find acts for that show. Listen Vince, I've had an idea. Have you ever thought about doing a double act?'

'No, not really.'

'Well think about it.'

I **did** think about it and the more I thought about it the more I warmed to the idea. A double act. At least I wouldn't be standing alone on stage. But wait - where would I find someone to be my straight man? Perhaps I could advertise for one. What I did was put a card in the window of our local newsagents - 'Wanted by professional comedian -

experienced straight man to form a comedy double act.' I wrote my name, address and telephone number on the card, paid a small fee to the newsagents and he put it in his window. How naïve of me to think I could find a straight man from an advert in a suburban newsagents. Now you may find what follows hard to believe but I assure you that it's perfectly true. I went back home after putting the card in the window, just had time to make a cup of tea, when there was a knock at the door. I went to answer it and there stood a young man about my age.

'Vince Powell?' he asked.

'That's me.' I replied.

'Harry Driver' he said, 'I've just seen your card in the newspaper shop. You're looking for a straight man?'

'Yes I am.' I said.

'You've found him.'

I told you you wouldn't believe me but it happened. I asked Harry in and he told me that he was married with a three year old son. He also told me that he had been doing a few clubs singing and telling humorous monologues but his experiences were the same as mine. He'd actually appeared at Dirty Dicks and was booed off the stage.

We agreed to form a double act and arranged to meet two or three nights a week to write a suitable act. As Harry worked as a trainee manager for Marks and Spencer in the city and I was also working in the city, we used to meet in Joe Lyons café, part of the Lyons Corner House chain.

We became adept at making a cup of tea last a couple of hours as we sat writing our act.

Eventually Rita, one of the waitresses became so curious of us sitting there, night after night and occasionally bursting into laughter, that she asked us what we were doing. We told her and she became so excited that she told us about several funny incidents between her and her customers. From then on, she became so interested in us that she never charged us for our tea or the occasional slice of toast or currant bun. Finally, Harry and I had a 30 minute act with which we were satisfied. We read it to Rita who laughed all the way through and insisted we give her our autographs as she was convinced that we would soon be famous.

I suggested to Harry that we phone Ronnie Taylor and ask for an audition. Ronnie was his usual affable self and invited us to his office at the BBC the following week. We spent the week going through our script and rehearsing it. We wanted to do our audition without having to read it from a script. We arrived at the BBC, and announced ourselves to the Commissionaire. He consulted a list, made a phone call and told us to take the lift to the third floor, where we would be met by Ronnie's secretary. I experienced a feeling of déjà vu as we stepped from the lift to find Pat Lamont waiting for us. We followed her to Ronnie's office. I introduced Harry to Ronnie, we chatted for a few minutes then the door opened and a dapper looking man entered. Ronnie introduced us. His name was Eric Miller, a senior Light Entertainment Producer. Ronnie asked us to go into our act. We started, rather nervously but, our confidence growing, finished with a song.

Harry and I waited as Ronnie and Eric Miller went into an adjoining office to discuss our act. Ronnie returned smiling.

'Well lads' he said, 'you've got a nice act. Eric liked it and has offered you a spot on a new radio series of a talent show called 'What Makes A Star?' He'd obviously forgotten his earlier comments that they were scraping the bottom of the barrel for acts to appear on it. Or maybe he thought we **were** the bottom of the barrel. Be that as it may, we were in no position to argue. We thanked Eric Miller and he told us to be at the BBC Playhouse the following Sunday at 4:0pm.

During that week Harry and I met every night at Joe Lyons, to go through our script and learn it off by heart. Rita was so overcome by the fact that we would actually be appearing on radio, she insisted on having her photograph taken with us and could we please get her a ticket to come to the broadcast. We got a letter from Eric Miller confirming that we would be appearing on 'What Makes A Star' and would be paid the princely sum of 7 guineas, between us! The letter also informed us that we were to do a three minute act, not a second over. He also informed us that each act would be judged by a panel of 3 judges consisting of Nelson Firth, an impressario dealing with third rate acts in fourth rate pantomimes, Bob Stokoe a television and radio critic, and a Mrs. Betty Ward, a typical Northern Housewife. They were to award points out of ten to each act. In addition the listeners were invited to send a postcard to the BBC stating which of the remaining four acts they liked the best. The act with the most number of points chosen by the judges and the act chosen by the listeners would then take part in a follow up series to be called 'Second Chance' which, in turn would be followed by a final series to be called 'Third Time Lucky.'

Harry and I met and rehearsed every night to make sure that we were word perfect. Sunday came at last, and we took a bus to the BBC Playhouse. We had asked our respective wives not to come with us, as their presence in the audience would make us too nervous.

When we arrived at the Playhouse the Commissionaire put a tick against our names on his list and wished us luck as we walked into the auditorium. We were met by Norma the production assistant, who gave us the number of our dressing room and told us that the show would begin at 6:30pm. She gave each of us a contract which we had to sign. She also handed each act a running order and we saw that we would be on second, after Linda Holroyd, a singer. We had already decided to drop our decision to finish our act with a song. As we had been told by the producer, we only had three minutes to do our act and considering that the song lasted two minutes there just wasn't enough time.

We changed into smart suits and went through our material to make sure we knew it. In no time at all, we were called and made our way back to the auditorium. All the other acts were standing around backstage trying to look confident, some of them not very successfully. Norma collected our signed contracts then Eric Miller appeared and wished us all good luck. Behind him was a pianist going though some sheets of music.

'Give it all you've got boys and girls' said Eric before leaving the stage and walking to the rear of the theatre to disappear into a glass fronted control room where he and Norma would sit with a sound engineer during recording.

By this time the audience had arrived and there was a buzz of anticipation from the auditorium.

Jack Watson, the compere of the show entered. He was a

tall, good looking man who in addition to being a BBC announcer was well known in the North of England as a comedian. He later became much better known as Elsie Tanner's boy friend, Bill Gregory, in 'Coronation Street'

'Right Jack.' we heard Eric say, 'we go in five seconds. Stand by.'

We all waited in silence. Then came a burst of recorded music, which we later found out was the programmes signature tune. A red light attached to the microphone stand flashed. It was the cue for Jack Watson to introduce the show.

'Good evening Ladies and Gentlemen and welcome to 'What Makes A Star?' a talent show in which five unknown acts will get the chance to display their talents and attempt to prove to you and the listening audience that they have what it takes to be a star. And our first act is the lovely Linda Holroyd from Rochdale. If she sings as well as she looks, we're in for a treat. Linda's chosen to sing that lovely song from 'Showboat' 'Only Make Believe'

Linda entered and started to sing. Harry, myself and the other acts watched and listened from the wings. She was good.

She finished the song and we all applauded as she came off. Harry and I just started to congratulate her when we heard Jack Watson announcing our act.

… 'Two young lads from Manchester with their own brand of humour. So settle back, relax and listen to the comedy of Powell and Driver.' We were on. Rita was sitting on the front row, clapping and waving. We both took a deep breath and started.

HARRY: Good evening Ladies and Gentlemen.
VINCE: No hang on - just a minute - I've forgotten my script.
HARRY: As I was saying, Good evening Ladies and ….
VINCE: No … just a minute …. I've forgotten my glasses. Oh no, here they are.
HARRY: (ANGRY) A fine mess you made of that.
VINCE: I'm sorry Harry.
HARRY: It's not me you should apologise to. It's the listeners.
VINCE: The listeners?
HARRY: Yes - go on - apologise.

VINCE: What now?

HARRY: Yes - now.

VINCE: (Pause) Ladies and Gentleman - listening. I'm very sorry.

HARRY: That's better. I don't know what's got into you.

VINCE: I'm nervous.

HARRY: Don't be ridiculous. There's nothing to be nervous about. Say to yourself, I'm not nervous. Go on - say it.

VINCE: I'm not nervous.

HARRY: I'm full of confidence.

VINCE: I'm full of confidence.

HARRY: I'm on top of the world.

VINCE: I'm on top of the world.

HARRY: There, don't you feel better now?

VINCE: No.

HARRY: Why not?

VINCE: I'm a liar!

HARRY: Pull yourself together. Don't you realise this is our big chance tonight.

VINCE: Is it?

HARRY: Yes. If we go down well. We could be famous.

VINCE: Fame at last.

HARRY: Our names will be up in lights.

VINCE: Like Morecambe and Wise.

HARRY: Jewel and Warris.

VINCE: Exit.

HARRY: I see beautiful women flocking around you.

VINCE: Get in a queue. You'll all get your turn.

HARRY: I see them throwing themselves at your feet.

VINCE: I like it.

HARRY: I see them begging for a kiss. I see you refusing.

VINCE: I see you need glasses!

HARRY: There you go again.

VINCE: It's not my fault. My girl friend's listening in tonight and I wanted to make a good impression.

HARRY: Vincent - I didn't know you had a girl friend.

VINCE: Oh yes, I call her my little lady of shallot.

HARRY: Why's that?

VINCE: Every time I kiss her goodnight she says 'Right, that's your lot (shallot)

HARRY: She sounds a funny woman to me.
VINCE: She's lovely. She's a combination of Marilyn Monroe, Betty Grable and
Jane Russell. There's only one thing wrong.
HARRY: What's that?
VINCE: She's lost the combination!
HARRY: Where did you meet her?
VINCE: In the park.
HARRY: How romantic.
VINCE: It was. I asked her for kiss and she told me to jump in the lake.
HARRY: And what happened?
VINCE: I got wet through!
HARRY: Have you met her parents?
VINCE: Only her mother. I'm meeting her Dad next Monday.
HARRY: Why next Monday?
VINCE: It's visiting day.
HARRY: Oh. Is he in hospital?
VINCE: No - he's in prison!
HARRY: You mean he's a criminal?
VINCE: Not really. He went to prison for something he didn't do.
HARRY: What didn't he do?
VINCE: He didn't wipe his fingerprints off the gas meter!
HARRY: He sounds very dodgy to me.
VINCE: Oh no. He comes from a military background.
HARRY: Does he?
VINCE: Yes. His grandfather fell at Waterloo.
HARRY: Really?
VINCE: Somebody pushed him off platform three.
HARRY: Tell me about your girl friend. Are you serious about her?
VINCE: Definitely. Our love affair has been fast and furious!
HARRY: Fast and furious?
VINCE: Yes. I was fast and she was furious?
HARRY: Have you asked her father for her hand in marriage?
VINCE: It's not her hand I'm interested in!
HARRY: You know very well what I mean.
VINCE: Oh yes. I said to her father, I would like to marry your daughter.
HARRY: And what did he say?

VINCE: He said 'Have you seen her mother?' I said, yes but I'd still rather marry your daughter!

HARRY: Are you sure that you can support a wife and family?

VINCE: I can support her, but I didn't know I had to support her family as well.

HARRY: Just a minute - who are you waving to?

VINCE: The producer. He's waving at us.

HARRY: So he is. I think he wants us to get off.

VINCE: Well, we'd better be off then. I'm going for an interview for a job today.

HARRY: I thought you already had a job.

VINCE: I did - but I had to leave through illness. The boss was sick of me!

HARRY: There you go again.

VINCE: Sorry. Do you want me to apologise to the audience again?

HARRY: No. Just get off. Thank you for listening Ladies and Gentleman and goodbye.

VINCE: And do be careful crossing the road. They say that a man gets run over here twice a day. And he's getting fed up with it!

HARRY: (SHOUTING) Vincent!!

We left the stage to applause, feeling quite pleased with ourselves. Jack Watson gave us an encouraging thumbs up as he passed us to introduce the next act, and we made our way back to our dressing room. As we changed into our everyday suits we listened to the rest of the show on the tannoy. The other three acts were an accordionist, a ballad singer and an impressionist. The accordionist played a medley of Scottish songs and got a reasonable amount of applause. Harry and I looked at each other.

'We did better than him,' said Harry.

I agreed.

The ballad singer sang, 'If I Had My Way' a popular song made famous by Bing Crosby. I thought he was very good and had a pleasant voice not dissimilar to Bing.

'He was good,' said Harry.

'Not bad,' I acknowledged. 'But I think we were better.'

We listened to the final act with growing dismay. He was

terrific. Not only were his impressions of Robb Wilton, Arthur Askey, Old Mother Riley, Ted Ray, Tony Hancock and even Winston Churchill spot on, he had a very funny script which got huge laughs. When he finished the applause was loud and long.

Harry signed, 'Oh well - we might as well go home now. We can't top that.'

I had to agree. However, we waited to hear the judges give their verdict. They liked Linda's 'Only Make Believe' and she got an average of 7 points. Then it was our turn. Betty Ward, the Northern Housewife liked us and gave us 9 points. Bob Stokoe complimented us on having an original script and gave us 8 points. Nelson Firth said we made him laugh but needed more experience and gave us 7 points. That gave us an average of 8 points. Harry and I cheered up. We were still in with a chance. And when the accordionist and the ballad singer got an average of 6 and 7 respectively we could hardly wait to hear how the impressionist got on. With 8 points we were in the lead. Betty Ward gave him 7 points. Bob Stokoe gave him 8 points. It was now down to Nelson Firth. Even if he gave the impressionist 9 points, we'd be joint winners. Nelson Firth praised his impressions and the script. Harry and I held our breath.

'A very professional performance from a very professional performer. 10 points!

We'd lost by one point!

Dejected, we made our way down to the auditorium. The audience had almost gone, but faithful Rita was still waiting. She told us that we were unlucky and that, in her opinion, we were the best act. She then said she would get as many of her friends at work to send the BBC a postcard, and vote for us. We thanked her and made our way to a nearby pub to join Eric Miller and his team along with our fellow contestants. He bought us all a drink said how good we all were, what a close contest it had been, then reminded us that those who lost today still had the chance of being chosen by the listeners votes to go through to appear on the next programme. Harry and I, still depressed, finished our drinks and left to catch the bus back home, to tell our respective families the news. They all took it well and told us not to be so disappointed and that we may have better luck next time. I got the feeling that my wife was secretly glad that we had lost - she'd never shown much enthusiasm about my ambition to be a comedian. I went to bed feeling even more depressed.

I was still depressed when I woke up the following morning. 'What Makes A Star' was scheduled to be broadcast that coming Saturday. That evening Harry and I met after work at our usual venue - Joe Lyons. Rita was delighted to see us, so much so that she treated us both to a free tea and a toasted teacake. Harry was as depressed as me about our chances of winning the listeners' choice. Not only that, he had a rotten cold. Rita told us to cheer up, and said that she had bought 8 postcards for all the staff in the café, asked them to fill them in, name Powell & Driver as their choice of winners and post them to the BBC. It was then that I was suddenly struck by a brilliant idea. I turned to Harry.

'I've just had a brainwave.'

'Are you sure you don't mean a brainstorm?'

'Shut up and listen. It was something Rita just said. How many people work at Marks and Spencers?'

He thought for a minute. 'I'm not sure - hundreds - maybe more - why?

'Well, Hector Powe has about twenty branches up and down the country.'

Harry frowned. 'So - what about it?'

'Well - we buy a load of postcards, put a stamp on each of them and address them to the BBC.'

Harry shook his head. 'I'm still not with you.'

'Don't you see Harry? I send a load of cards to every branch of Hector Powe, tell each of the staff to vote for us, and then post them to the BBC. At the same time you get all the staff at every branch of M & S to do the same. What do you think?'

Harry looked at me in admiration. 'I'll tell you what I think, I think you're a bloody genius.'

And that's what we did. We spent our fee and much more on postcards and stamps. In all, we sent out over 250 cards between us. The winners of the listeners' choice would be announced the following Saturday at the end of the second programme. We could hardly wait for Saturday night to come round. Harry's cold got worse. He and his wife Edith had got a baby sitter and were due to come round to my house so that they could listen to the recording with us, but when I rang him on Saturday afternoon, he sounded so rough that I told him that Pat and I would come round to his house. We got there about six o'clock and he was in bed looking very sorry for himself. His wife, Edith had brought a radio up to his room and we all sat round the bed. I asked Harry how he felt.

'Rotten', he said, 'I've got a temperature, and I'm aching all over.'

I produced a half bottle of Bell's whisky. 'Have a glass of this' I said, 'it'll make you feel better.'

Edith rose, 'I'll go and get some glasses.' She left the bedroom.

Harry called after her. 'You'd better be quick; the programme starts in a few minutes.'

As I opened the scotch, Edith returned with four glasses. I poured each of us a generous measure. Edith switched on the radio.

'I've left enough for us to raise a glass to celebrate us winning.'

'Or commiserate us losing.' said Harry.

'Drink your scotch and don't be so pessimistic.' I raised my glass. 'To the new double act of Powell and Driver. Eat your hearts out Morecambe and Wise!'

We drank and waited. From the radio came the sound of Roger Moffat, one of the BBC's senior announcers.

'This is the BBC North Region. Many famous artistes first found fame on radio, particularly in the north of England. Tonight, we present the second of a new series with the object of giving some stars of the future their chance of fame in a brand talent show 'What Makes A Star.'

We then heard the signature tune of the series, followed by the introduction by Jack Watson. We listened all the way through the five new acts, and the studio judges comments, and then waited for the results of the listener's choice from the previous week. I filled our glasses as Jack Watson made the announcement.

'Well, last week our judges voted impressionist Neil Crowther as their winner, and Neil will be back in a few weeks time in a brand new series 'Second Chance'. But did you, the listeners agree with our judges? Well, we had hundreds of postcards, but by a clear majority you voted for our comedy double act - Powell and Driver.'

We all cheered. Even Harry perked up as we knocked back our whisky's. We were so elated.

'We did it Harry' I said.

'Yes, thanks to your idea of the postcards.'

'We'll need a new script,' I said. 'You'd better get rid of that cold.'

'Don't worry Vince,' said Harry. 'If I'm no better tomorrow, I'm going to the doctors.'

'Good' I held up the bottle of whisky. 'There's just about enough for one more drink. And I think you should have it Harry - purely on medicinal grounds of course.'

I filled his glass and raised mine.

'To the future' I said clinking my glass with Harry's.

'To Powell and Driver' he replied.

We both drank.

'Well, we'll love you and leave you now,' I said. 'Get a good nights sleep Harry. I'll come round tomorrow night, and if you feel up to it, we'll make a start on the script.'

'I'll be alright tomorrow Vince. Fit as a butcher's dog.' We looked at each other and smiled.

'Goodnight Partner' I said.

'Goodnight Partner.' he replied.

We shook hands and Pat and I left. I was on such a high that I can hardly remember us getting the bus back home. I felt that this was the break we had been hoping for. When we walked in the house, Dad was waiting, with another half bottle of whisky and three glasses. He was staying the night with us.

'Congratulations son' he said, pouring us each glass. Pat said that she didn't want another drink and excused herself, saying that she had a headache and was going to bed. Dad and I sat talking about the programme and drinking the whisky. Dad eventually went to bed, and I sat on my own reliving the past few days. I was convinced that Harry and I had our feet on the first rung of the ladder to fame and fortune and that it was only a question of time before we climbed that ladder to the top.

The following morning I woke up with a dreadful headache. Naturally, I got no sympathy from Pat. 'Serves you right' was her reaction and I had to agree with her. It was my own fault. I got ready to go to work and caught the bus into town. As I sat there I looked at my fellow passengers. I felt so different to them, somehow. If only they knew they were sitting next to a future star. I passed the day in a kind of dream. At lunchtime, I went over to Joe Lyons. Rita was basking in reflected glory. She had told all the customers about Harry and me and how good we were. I felt like a star already.

Later that afternoon, my Dad phoned to say that he'd had a phone call from Ronnie Taylor at the BBC who wanted me to phone him. We weren't really allowed to make personal telephone calls but as it was from the BBC and I was now something of a celebrity the manager gave me permission. I rang the BBC's number, told them my name and asked to speak to Ronnie Taylor. I was put through at once. Ronnie came on the line.

'Ah, Vince,' he said.

'Hello Ronnie,'

'First of all, congratulations to you and Harry on being the listener's choice.'

'Thank you Ronnie' I replied.

'You won by a large majority.'

'Oh, really?'

'Yes. Quite a large majority. We had postcards voting for you and Harry from all over England. Leeds, Birmingham, Glasgow, Coventry, Great Yarmouth, Plymouth, Bristol... We even had one from the Channel Isles.'

I mentally thanked all the branches of Hector Powe who'd voted for us.

'That's marvellous Ronnie.'

'Marvellous? I'd say it was more like miraculous.'

I suddenly felt a twinge of apprehension.

'Pardon?' I stuttered. 'Miraculous?'

'Absolutely. I mean when you consider that 'What Makes A Star' was only transmitted by the BBC North Region and could only be received by listeners in that region, yet we received cards from all over the country, wouldn't you say that was something of a miracle?'

By now I was sweating. What a fool I'd been. It was obvious that I'd been cheating. Not only that, but I'd broken the twelfth Commandment 'Thou Shalt Not Be Caught Out' I didn't know what to say, so I said nothing. A hundred thoughts flashed through my mind the foremost of which was that we would be disqualified. There would be no 'Second Chance' for Powell and Driver. Goodbye Show Business! My thoughts were interrupted by Ronnie's voice on the phone.

'Hello - are you still there Vince?'

'Yes' I paused. 'Look Ronnie, I'm sorry. I didn't know. It's just that ...

Ronnie cut me short. 'I know. And I understand. And in your position I might well have done the same. But it was all a waste of time and energy. You needn't have bothered.'

'Pardon?' I said.

'Taking away all the votes that we received from outside the North Region, you and Harry still came out on top - you won by fair means not foul.'

I can't tell you how relieved I was. Ronnie went on to say that, in his opinion, we had a bright future, and there was no reason why we couldn't be successful and that he would be glad to help us.

I put down the phone. When I considered how close Harry and me had been to disqualification I broke out in a cold sweat. The rest of the day passed far too slowly but at last it was time to go. I sat on the bus on my way to Harry's looking forward to the good news I had for him. We had won the listeners choice on our own merit, we had another broadcast in a few weeks time and we had the support and encouragement of Ronnie Taylor. Stardom was just around the corner!

I got to Harry's house about 6:15. To my surprise the house was in darkness. I knocked but nobody answered. A neighbour appeared.

'Are you Vince Powell?' she asked.

I admitted that I was. She told me that she had a message for me from Harry's wife Edith. Harry's condition had worsened that morning and Edith had phoned their doctor. He arrived, checked Harry and immediately sent for an ambulance. He was now in Monsall Hospital having been diagnosed as suffering from Polio.

I immediately caught a bus to the hospital where I was directed to the appropriate ward. When I got there, Edith was talking to the Matron. She told me that early that morning Harry could hardly breathe and she phoned the doctor, who called an ambulance to take Harry to hospital. Right now, Harry was in an iron lung hovering between life and death!

Chapter Four:
HIGHS AND LOWS

I looked down at Harry. Only his head was visible. The rest of his body was encased in an airtight, oblong metal cylinder known as an iron lung from which a rubber tube led to a concertina-like pump. The pump was continuously going up and down providing artificial respiration, taking the place of Harry's weakened lungs and keeping him alive. His eyes were closed and for one brief moment, I feared the worst until the Matron explained that he had been sedated as it was essential that all his muscles were relaxed at the critical stage of the illness. I put my arm round Edith, whose face was lined with worry. Her eyes were red rimmed and tearful. She said that she would stay at the hospital until Harry woke up, even if it meant staying all night. Their neighbour had agreed to look after their son, Stephen. I offered to stay with her but she said that she would rather be alone with Harry. So I left after promising that I would return to the hospital first thing in the morning, it being a Sunday.

On the way home on the bus, my thoughts were with Harry. I couldn't get the image of him, lying there in that iron lung, out of my mind. When I got home, I told Pat and Dad about Harry. They were both as shocked as I was. We went to bed but I hardly slept, I was so worried about Harry. I got up early and went to the six o'clock Mass, where I lit a candle and prayed for his recovery before catching the bus to the hospital. When I arrived and made my way to Harry's ward, I found that Edith had gone home. The Matron told me that Harry had weathered the crisis and was now awake. She asked me not to engage him in too much conversation as it would put a strain on his weakened lungs, and told me to stay no longer than fifteen minutes. I slowly made my way to where Harry was lying in his iron lung.

'It's me Harry' I said.

We looked at each other. Harry pulled a face. 'Hello Vince.'

For a moment we said nothing. Harry nodded. 'Well this is a fine bloody mess isn't it?'

'How do you feel?' I asked.

Harry grimaced, 'I've felt better.'

'I came last night.'

'Yes, Edith told me.'

'When did it all happen?'

'Saturday. You know I was feeling rough and had all these aches and pains?'

I nodded. Harry continued.

'Well they got worse. I tried to get out of bed to spend a penny, but I could hardly stand. I fell down and Edith came running upstairs and tried to help me up but she couldn't. My legs had no feeling in them. So she phoned our doctor and he rang for an ambulance. After that, I can't remember a thing until I woke up in here. Apparently, it was touch and go whether I ever woke up again. It's polio.'

'Yes I know.'

'It's a bugger Vince. I don't think I'll be fit in time to do the next broadcast. Matron reckons it could be a few weeks before I'm on my feet again.'

'Don't worry about the broadcast. Just you concentrate on getting better.'

Harry frowned. 'Look, I've been thinking while I've been lying here. There's no reason why you shouldn't do the broadcast.'

'You mean on my own?'

'No - no. With another straight man.'

I shook my head. 'Don't talk so daft. I'm not doing it without you.'

'Why not? Be a shame to chuck the chance away.'

'Look Harry - the double act is Powell and Driver - me and you. Not me and somebody else.'

'What difference does it make? It's only for one broadcast. When I get out of this bloody iron coffin, we'll start again.'

'I'll think about it'

'Never mind, you'll think about it. Do it'

'And where am I going to find another straight man?'

'I knew you'd ask that. There's a fellow who works with me at Marks and Sparks in soft furnishings. Brian Duncan. He's a member of a local rep company. He could do it'

'I'm not sure yet that I want to do the broadcast without you.'

'Well at least, have a chat with Brian. See what you think of him. Give him a ring.'

'I'll see.'

'Never mind - I'll see' - bloody do it!'

At that moment we were interrupted by the Matron, who'd come to tell us that the specialist was on his way round and I would have to leave. I reminded Harry that I'd come and see him that evening and left. On the way home, I thought about Harry's suggestion that I go ahead with the broadcast, then decided that I'd have a chat with Brian and see what he was like.

When I arrived home I told Dad and Pat about Harry and his insistence on my doing the broadcast with another straight man. Dad thought it was a good idea, but Pat wasn't so sure. Later I caught the bus to the hospital anxious to find out what the specialist had to say. Edith was with Harry when I got there. She told me that she had spoken to the specialist but all he had said was that, until he got the results of the blood tests back, there was nothing he could really tell her. He went on to say that he should have the results by the end of the following week. Harry had told Edith of his suggestion that I do the broadcast with Brian and she agreed with him. I chatted a little to Harry then, sensing that he and Edith would like some time together, I left.

The following day, I rang M&S and spoke to Brian. I told him what had happened to Harry and arranged to meet him after work that evening in a nearby pub. I deliberately didn't make our meeting in Joe Lyons. I described what I looked like, and Brian did the same. We easily found each other and I ordered a couple of beers. He was good looking and had a confident manner. We chatted and I told him that, as soon as Harry recovered, we would be resuming our double act, and that, as far as he was concerned, his participation was purely a temporary arrangement. He understood and we shook hands. I made an arrangement for us to meet at the same place and time the following night then I went to the hospital to see Harry. I told him about my meeting with Brian, and that he had agreed to fill the breach until Harry was fit and well again. For the next few nights Harry and I met at the hospital and managed to write a script for the next broadcast.

How Harry remained cheerful enough to help write a comedy script, I'll never know. I'm sure, I couldn't have done it.

Brian and I then met every night to rehearse and I must admit, he was excellent. I phoned Ronnie Taylor to tell him what had happened to Harry and that I had a different straight man. Ronnie said that would be no problem and that he would tell Eric Millar. He said that a letter was in the post from the BBC advising us that the date of the recording of 'Second Chance' was to be on Sunday week at the Playhouse and would we reply confirming that we were available and send a copy of the script for the BBC to make sure it was fit to be transmitted.

Most evenings I went to the hospital to visit Harry. His wife Edith told me that she had spoken to the specialist about Harry's test results only to be told that they needed to do more tests, and would have some news by the following week. It was a frustrating time for everyone. The date of the broadcast came round and Brian and I met at the BBC Playhouse. Eric Millar's P.A. greeted us and went through her usual routine and gave us a copy of the running order. I groaned when I saw that the impressionist was on the same bill.

'We've had it Brian' I said. 'He's very good. He'll get the judges vote.'

We stood in the wings waiting our turn as the first act went on - two young ladies who played a duet on two pianos. Halfway during their act I turned to speak to Brian. To my surprise he was nowhere to be seen. One of the other acts told me that he saw him go into the gent's toilets backstage. Afraid that we might miss our cue, I went backstage and knocked on the toilet door.

'Hurry up Brian' I shouted, 'we're on next.'

His muffled voice came from behind the door.

'I can't do it. I'm not well. I've just been sick.'

I knew immediately that he was suffering from stage fright. I banged on the door. 'Look, if you don't open this door, I'm going to kick it down,' I heard the sound of a bolt being withdrawn, the door slowly opened and Brian peered out. He looked terrible. He was pale and trembling. I dragged him out and pulled him into the wings. The piano duet had just finished and were taking their applause. Jack Watson started to introduce us. I turned to Brian.

'Now look Brian, I don't care how bad you feel - you and me are going out on that stage even if I have to carry you on. And we are going to do our act just as we rehearsed it. It's not just for us - it's for Harry. He's depending on us.'

The orchestra went into our 'play on' music - I took Brian's hand and dragged him onstage. I turned to the audience.

'He's very shy,' I ad libbed, 'when his mother took him out in his pram, he used to hide under the blanket. I wouldn't mind but he was thirteen at the time.'

That got a laugh. Brian still looked pale. He was supposed to remark that he liked my new suit, but just stood there, too terrified to speak. So I said the line for him.

'Do you like my new suit? It's the latest style. It's call the Droop.'

Brian suddenly got with it and blurted out his line.

'The Droop? Don't you mean the Drape?'

'No,' I replied, 'there's too much droop and not enough drape.'

I breathed a sign of relief, as Brian went into the next gag.

We managed to get through our act without any more mishaps and took our applause at the end. Brian could hardly wait to get off and he fled to our dressing room. He started to apologise.

'I'm sorry Vince - I couldn't help it.'

'Don't worry about it Brian. Lots of performers suffer from nerves before they go on. It can happen to anyone.'

I turned up the tannoy so that we could hear the rest of the recording and the judges scores. I'd been right about the impressionist - he walked away with scoring maximum points. If anything he was even better than he was on 'WHAT MAKES A STAR'. We got an average of 7. So that was that. Since our ploy of arranging to send postcards from all over

Britain had been rumbled we couldn't do it again. It was up to a genuine vote from the listeners this time.

I went to see Harry the next day and told him about Brian and his stage fright and that I wasn't optimistic about winning the listener's choice. He told me that he'd just had some more tests done that morning and there was no news about his condition or when, if ever, he could expect any improvement. I could see he was really depressed and tried to cheer him up without much success.

'Come on Harry', I said, 'cheer up, you'll soon be up and about.'

'You think so?' he said, 'I've been stuck in here now for over two weeks. I can't move my arms or my legs. I wouldn't be able to breathe if it wasn't for that pump. I just wish somebody could tell me if I'm ever going to get better.'

Edith arrived and even she couldn't help him get out of his depression. I stayed, chatted to her for a few more minutes then left. The next day, I rang my own doctor and asked him about Harry. When I told him that he had Polio, his voice became concerned. He asked me to tell him everything about Harry's condition and when I told him that Harry couldn't move his arms or his legs he was even more concerned. He told me that Polio was caused by a virus which attacks the nerves of the brain and the spine, leading to paralysis of the muscles. I was stunned by his statement. However he went on to tell me that paralysis didn't happen to every case and that the tests Harry had undergone would determine whether Harry would recover or end up in a wheelchair.

When I next visited Harry I decided not to tell him what my doctor had said in case it made him more depressed. To be honest, I was extremely anxious and worried myself. The thought that Harry may be permanently disabled was too terrible to contemplate. As it happened, I found Harry in a buoyant mood.

He'd been told by the Matron, that his results would be back the next morning and that the specialist would be seeing him later in the afternoon. Harry was convinced that the news would be good.

'Look Vince', he said, 'I can move my fingers a little.' I looked through one of the plastic windows in the iron lung.

Sure enough, the fingers of his left hand started to twitch - not much, but they actually moved. Harry grinned at me.

'It's a start,' he said, 'I can't wait for Edith to get here. She'll be really chuffed.'

We chatted for a while longer, and discussed the question of how 'Second Chance' would fare when the listener's votes were counted that weekend. I promised to bring in a portable radio so that we could listen to the broadcast together. Edith then arrived and I left so that Harry could tell her about him being able to move his fingers. I didn't visit Harry the next day as Pat and I had promised to visit Dad and take him out for a meal. The next evening, when I went to the hospital I got a surprise. I found that Harry had been taken off the iron lung and was lying in a bed in another ward. Apparently, the specialist had decided that Harry's lungs were now strong enough for him to breathe on his own. He told Harry that he would be undergoing a course of physiotherapy twice every day in an effort to strengthen his weak muscles and hopefully stimulate them into some movement. This was great news and naturally all of us were delighted. That Sunday night as arranged, I took my radio with me to the hospital and Edith, Pat and I gathered round Harry's bed and listened to the broadcast. Harry admitted that Brian had given a good performance and we waited for the result of the listener's choice. To our surprise and delight, we won. We all burst into loud cheers. The night nurse came running into the ward to see what all the noise was about and we told her. Harry asked what would be the chances of him being fit enough in time for the last broadcast of the series, 'THIRD TIME LUCKY' which was due to be recorded on Saturday week. The nurse shook her head

'Sorry,' she said, 'you'll have to speak to the specialist. But, from experience, it's going to be a matter of months rather than weeks.

That put a dampener on our enthusiasm until I reminded everyone that it really didn't matter as, because it was the last programme in the series, the acts appearing on 'THIRD TIME LUCKY' wouldn't be judged by the panel, who would only offer their professional advice. In addition there would be no listener's choice. Harry said that I'd better get in touch with Brian and that Harry and I ought to work on writing the act. But I had other ideas. I told him that I would do a single act and that I'd already spoken to Brian who readily agreed. In fact, to be honest he was relieved at not having to face an audience again. Harry asked what was I going to do as a single, and I told him I'd brush up the act which I did at Mr Anderson's daughter's wedding a couple of years ago.

So I worked on the script, and the physiotherapist worked on Harry. Harry helped me with the script and I went to see him almost every other night, but there was little improvement in his condition. The recording day soon came round and I presented myself at the Playhouse for the final recording and went to find Jack Watson. I'd written an introduction to my act which involved a few lines between me and him. I showed him the script to get his approval. He liked it and agreed to do it. He complimented me on my originality and told me to give his regards to Harry when I next saw him and to tell him that, in his opinion we would go far as a double act. I handed Jack the script just before he introduced me and it went something like this.

JACK: Only half of the next act is with us tonight. Vince Powell's partner, Harry Driver is in hospital but they both agreed that this broadcast was so important to both their careers that Vince should carry on the act alone. So, with our best wishes for Harry Driver's speedy recovery let's listen to the comedy of Vince Powell.
VINCE: Thank you Mr Whatsit.
JACK: The name's Watson - Jack Watson
VINCE: Oh. Hey, I remember you. Your were here when we did 'WHAT MAKES A STAR'.
JACK: That's right.
VINCE: And you were here when we did that 'SECOND CHANCE'.
JACK: Yes.
VINCE: And now you're on 'THIRD TIME LUCKY'.
JACK: Yes.
VINCE: You're getting on all right aren't you? Were you the listeners' choice as well?
JACK: Ladies and Gentlemen - for better or for worse - I give you - and you can have him - Vince Powell.

VINCE: Thank you. I have to tell you, I've had some really bad luck recently. I opened up a chip shop - no luck. I opened up a grocer's - no luck. Then I opened up a jeweller's - I got six months.

But the judge was a funny fellow. He said Six months or a hundred pounds. I said, 'Thank you very much, I'll take the hundred pounds!'

I like being on the wireless. I bought a new suit for the occasion. I got it from a funny little tailor's shop. I went in and said, 'Show me something heavy in tweed. He showed me the manager!

I've had those drainpipe trousers - drainpipe trousers. Every time it rains my shoes get full of water!

He showed me into a fitting room and said, would you slip on the trousers. I said, I don't know about that, I've just fell over the jacket!

I had to go and have an audition for this broadcast. They treat me with respect at the BBC. As soon as the Commissionaire saw me, he jumped to his feet and rushed to the door. I thought - typical BBC courtesy. He's opening it in welcome. Then he slammed it in my face! But I didn't give up. For weeks I sat on that step. I knew that behind that door was something that belonged to me. My foot!

They finally let me in.

As soon as I stepped in the lift, I knew I'd make a big impression. I fell down the shaft!

The producer was very nice. He took me in his office, poured me out a drink and said - 'down the hatch.'

I fell down the lift shaft again!

He asked me to let him see my act. So I started with a song. I sang 'Giddy Up A Ding Dong'. He wasn't impressed. He said my Giddy was all right but he didn't like my Ding Dong!

So I played the piano for him. I played Over the Sea To Skye. I said to him, didn't that move you.

He said 'Yes. I've just been seasick!'

But you know - I've had a hard life. I was the youngest of ten children. I had to wear all their old clothes. It was very embarrassing. They were all girls!

When I got older, my Dad used to take me to school every day. Well, he had to - he was in the same class!

I didn't like the headmistress. She had a face like a tea service.

Eyes like saucers and ears like cup handles!
She said to me 'This school is noted for its sports. Do you prefer
to play cricket, rugby or football?'
I said, 'Well, if it's all the same to you, I'd rather play truant!'
Oh dear, look at the time. I must go. I have to pick my Dad up in
The Red Lion. The trouble is, every time I pick him up, he falls
down again!
Ta-ra.

I came offstage to loud applause. Jack Watson told me to get on again and take another round of applause, which I did. It was music to my ears. I thought what a pity, it's the last show - I bet I'd have got top marks from the judges. I could hardly wait to hear their comments. I stood in the wings and listened. They all said how much they had enjoyed my performance, wished Harry well and predicted a bright future for us. I joined Eric Millar and his team, Jack Watson, the judges and the other acts in the pub, to celebrate. It was too late to call and see Harry, but I'd be able to get to the hospital early the next morning and give him the good news. I stayed in the pub, basking in the congratulations of the judges and knocking back large Bell's. I could have stayed there all night, but unfortunately, pubs had to close at 10:30 in those days. I caught the bus home still on a high. My wife had gone to bed, but I was too excited to sleep. I poured myself a whisky and re-lived the events of the night. Eventually, I went to bed, looking forward to seeing Harry the following morning. I was confident that the good news would give him a boost, and that it was only a question of time before he was up and about again and we could resume our ambition to further our show business aspiration. However, fate had other ideas.

I got to the hospital bright and early. As I walked down the corridor towards Harry's ward, the Matron came out of her office.

'Excuse me Mr Powell' she said, 'could you step into the office. Mr. Dalton would like a word with you.'

I already knew that Mr. Dalton was the specialist, and wondered what he wanted to see me about. When I stepped into the office, he was looking at some X-rays.

'Ah, Mr Powell,' he said, 'come in. Sit down.' I sat down and he regarded me gravely. 'You're obviously a close friend of Mr and Mrs Driver.' I admitted that I was. He went on. 'I have some news for you. He's going to be discharged next weekend.' I was so pleased. 'That is good news Mr. Dalton. Have you told him?' He shook his head, 'No. Nor his wife. You see, we've done all we can for him here. His breathing is good but his muscles haven't responded to physiotherapy. I'm afraid he'll never be able to walk again. From the neck down, he's completely paralysed!'

What a shock to us all! I went to see Harry in hospital before he was discharged. He had taken the news quite well and was still convinced that, given enough time and further physiotherapy he would regain more movement. The person I felt most for was Edith. I tried to imagine what she must have felt like - a young woman with a three years old son to bring up and a husband who could hardly move and would need constant nursing. Everything would have to be done for him - she would have to get him up every morning and put him to bed every night. She would have to feed him, wash him, bath him, clean his teeth for him, help him with his bodily functions, and all the other basic needs which most of us take for granted. Not only that, she was now the breadwinner. How she kept going in the face of so many worries and problems, I will never know.

Friends rallied round and the Social Services arranged for a nurse to visit Harry most days to help out. When he was discharged from hospital they provided him with a wheelchair and a hoist so that he could be lifted from his bed and lowered into his wheelchair. Edith got a part time job with a ladies fashion showroom and, somehow managed to juggle all her many commitments in order to make life for her and Harry run as smoothly as possible. And I never heard her complain once.

As for Harry, he tried to make as few demands as he could on Edith. It would have been so easy for him to have given in to his illness and just lie there but he didn't. He was determined to try and bring some sort of normality into his life. I'll give you an example of his courage and tenacity. One evening as he was sitting in his wheelchair, he asked Edith if she could bring him one of her knitting needles. She frowned and asked him what it was for. 'You'll find out', he said. 'It's an idea I've had while sitting in this chair. And bring me my typewriter from the other room.'

Edith, still mystified went and got the typewriter, took off the cover and set it on the small table which was attached to the arms of the wheelchair. He then asked her to put a page of copy paper in the machine which she did.

'What is all this about?' she asked.

Harry grinned. 'Patience my love. All will be revealed. Now, fetch me two corks from the kitchen.' Edith shrugged, went into the kitchen and returned with two corks.

'Now what?' she asked.

'Push the knitting needle through the corks so that there's a cork at each end.'

Still bemused she did as Harry asked.

'Now, put one of the corks in my mouth.'

She did, and Harry gripped the cork firmly between his teeth. He moved his head up and down so that the cork fixed to the other end of the knitting needle also moved up and down.

'Now watch this'

He positioned the cork over the letter 'A' on the typewriter and pushed it down as hard as he could. The 'A' jumped forward and a perfectly readable 'A' was printed out on the copy paper. Harry was elated.

'It works', he cried, 'It works.'

He told Edith that his idea was to type an article about his catching polio and his experiences in hospital and send it to a magazine. And that's exactly what he did. Painstakingly typing out each letter he carefully wrote his article. It took him three days having to stop and rest frequently. At last, it was finished, put in an envelope and submitted to one of the many women's magazines on sale at that time. Two days later the phone rang. Edith answered it and brought the phone over to Harry. It was the features editor of the magazine. She told him that not only did she like Harry's article, but that it would appear in the next month's issue and that he would be paid £35. The next day they sent a photographer round, who took pictures of Harry at the typewriter demonstrating how he typed with the knitting needle. The article appeared, and Harry was paid. But as a boost to his morale it was priceless. He had proved that in spite of being paralysed and against all the odds he still had something to contribute to Society.

Meanwhile, I applied myself to my job with Hector Powe which pleased Pat. Naturally, I went to see Harry and Edith as often as I could, but obviously all thoughts of a career in show business were forgotten. We received a letter from Ronnie Taylor telling us that he was leaving the BBC and forming his own production company, which he christened TaylorVision. So there went our contact with the BBC. Goodbye show business. However, I was good at my job and got on well with the customers so much so that I was sent down to the Regent Street, London branch for a week with another couple of salesmen to undergo a course on how to measure a customer, how to cut out a jacket, trousers and waistcoat. At the end of the course, we were given tests, both oral and practical. We all passed and were then entitled to be called Stylists. It was a step up and more money.

As soon as I got back home, I went to see Harry. His condition was much the same. He wanted to know how I got on in London but there wasn't a lot to tell - we did the course during the day, and studied at night. But he had some news for me. His doctor had persuaded Social Services into paying for turning their garage into a bedroom with an ensuite bathroom so that Edith wouldn't have to struggle each morning and every night dragging Harry in the wheelchair up and down the stairs. They arranged for a ramp, and widened the front door to make access much easier. They also arranged for Harry to spend a week at a convalescent home near Southport while the alterations were carried out which would give them both a break. Harry asked if I could get a few days off work and go with him. We could spend the days trying to think of ideas for the BBC. I told him that although it wouldn't be a problem taking a week off, it wouldn't be very practical as he would probably have long sessions of physiotherapy. And besides I had other plans involving keeping a promise I made to myself over twenty years ago.

Chapter Five:
BIENVENUE A FRANCE

I leant on the rail of the cross channel ferry gazing at the northern coast of France. We were approaching Calais and I could make out the massive bulk of the Watch Tower which dominates the Place d'Armes. Behind this, in the distance I could see the imposing clock tower of the Town Hall, completed in 1925 and fronted by Rodin's famous statue of the six burghers of Calais.

My mind went back to the day when I leant on another ship's rail as the aircraft carrier HMS Ark Royal slowly steamed through the Straits of Gibraltar leaving the blue Mediterranean Sea and into the grey Atlantic Ocean - it really does change colour. Today, I was returning to the country I had fallen in love with so many years before - I had decided that I would take Pat and my father for a week to Villefranche. Would the magic still be there or would I be disappointed? I couldn't wait to find out. At that moment an announcement came over the ship's tannoy. 'Will all car passengers please return to their vehicles on the car deck,' and I made my way to the passenger lounge to where Dad and my wife were sitting. Pat was sipping a glass of water and looking decidedly queasy after the crossing.

My father too, was returning to France, but in his case the last time he was there was in 1918 during the 'War to end all Wars!' He was happily puffing away on his beloved pipe and reading a copy of the now defunct newspaper, the Daily Herald the official mouthpiece of the British Labour Party. To my father, a committed Socialist, it was his Bible. He believed implicitly in every printed word which appeared in its pages. If it had reported that the earth was flat or that the Pope was a serial killer he would have believed it. A second announcement blared out reminding passengers to return to their cars, and the three of us descended to the car deck and my pride and joy - a second hand pale blue Vauxhall. I had passed my driving test at the second attempt. My first test had been a disaster. I had failed on so many points - including, not stopping at a T-Junction, reversing round a corner and ending up on the pavement, attempting a three point turn which became a seven point turn, stalling several times while trying to do a hill start and hitting a parked car. I asked the examiner if I had passed.

He sighed and said, 'The only part of the test you passed was switching on the engine!'. But to continue, we made our way to the car deck got in the car and after a few minutes, the huge bow doors swung open and France lay before us.

We had left Manchester very early that morning to catch the midday ferry and, not wishing to drive too far across France on the first day, I had arranged for us to stay that night in Soissons, some two hundred kilometres south of Calais. I had booked two rooms at the Lion Rouge - strange isn't it how much more romantic the Red Lion sounds in French?

As we sped along those straight roads of Northern France lined with plane trees that might have come straight out of a painting by Corot, I happened to glance in my rear view mirror. My Dad was staring out of the window, a grim look on his face.

'Are you alright Dad?' I asked. His only reply was a long drawn out sigh.

My wife turned to him. 'Are you feeling car sick?'

He shook his head.

'Do you want to spend a penny?' I said, 'we can stop if you like.'

No it's all right Vincent,' he replied, 'I was just looking at the fields and remembering the last time I saw them. They were just acres of mud and dead soldiers - many of them my friends.' I gazed out of the car window. In a field several cows were grazing peacefully, in another a farmer was driving a threshing machine through a field of golden corn. It was hard to imagine that nearly fifty years ago; this was the scene of one of the bloodiest battles of the Great War - the Battle of the Somme in which over 600,000 allied soldiers perished. I glanced at my father again through the rear view mirror. His eyes were moist - glistening.

I turned to look at my wife. She too had tears in her eyes.

'Come on you two?' I said, 'cheer up - we're on holiday.'

My Dad sniffed, took out a handkerchief and blew his nose loudly. 'I'm all right,' he said.

We drove on in silence, each with our own thoughts.

The sun was just starting it's ritual descent below the horizon as we drove into Soissons and found our way to the Lion Rouge, an ivy clad building that had obviously been an old coaching inn. I drove through the entrance and under a stone archway into a cobbled courtyard. Along one wall hung four old metal feeding troughs which, no doubt, in the past had contained hay but were now filled with a colourful profusion of flowers. I parked the car, got our overnight luggage from the boot and we made our way into the hotel.

As we entered the foyer, I sniffed - there it was - that familiar aroma of garlic and Gauloise. I felt as if I had returned home. I crossed to the reception desk behind which stood a tall, slim elegantly dressed man who turned out to be the hotel proprietor a M'sieu Mercier. He gave me a welcoming smile.

"Bonsoir Messieurs - Madame."

I summoned up my brief knowledge of schoolboy French.

"Bonsoir Monsieur."

There was a moment of silence as M'Sieu Mercier politely waited for me to continue the conversation.

I hesitated then turned to my wife.

'Give me the French phrase book darling.'

Pat rummaged in her handbag.

'He probably speaks English' she said, handing me the book.

'He may not'. I replied, 'and anyway, it's polite to speak to people in their own language, 'I opened the phrase book and searched for some phrases which I had previously marked.

M'sieu Mercier was patiently waiting.

I cleared my throat.

'M'sieur. Je m'appelle Monsieur Powell. Je vous ecris le dernier semaine pour reservez deux chambres avec salle de bain.'

I closed my phrase book and looked at M'sieur Mercier with an expression of triumph.

He smiled, nodded and replied in perfect English.

'Ah yes Mr Powell. One double room with bath for your wife and yourself, and one single room with bath for your father.'

Pat smirked but said nothing.

I filled in the registration forms and handed over our passports as one was obliged to do in those days and in return was handed our keys. We took the lift to the second floor and went to our respective rooms to freshen up, having agreed to meet downstairs in half an hour for dinner.

Pat, still suffering from the after effects of the channel crossing plus the car journey, decided to forego dinner and have an early night. I had a quick shower and made my way downstairs to find my father in deep conversation with M'sieu Mercier. I stood nearby to listen. In common with many English tourists who did not speak the language of the particular country they were visiting, my father felt that if he spoke loudly enough, he would be understood. He also had the North Country habit of occasionally repeating certain sentences.

'Have you ever been to Manchester?' shouted my father. 'I say, have you ever been to Manchester?'

M'sieu Mercier shook his head. 'No M'sieu.'

'You don't know what you've missed. I say, you don't know what you've missed. Best place in the world. We've got everything in Manchester ' Alle Orchestra, Ship Canal and there's a chippie near us that serve the finest cod, chips and mushy peas you've ever tasted.'

I could see that M'sieu Mercier was a little confused. He smiled politely.

'I've been to London,' he offered.

'London?' said my father, 'Bloody London! I wouldn't pay you in washers to go to London. It's full of foreigners!'

I winced but M'sieu Mercier showed no reaction.

'Is your room comfortable?' he asked my father.

'Very nice. There's just one thing.'

'Yes M'sieu?'

'What's that funny little thing in the bathroom?'

M'sieu Mercier frowned and shrugged.

'It's next to the toilet. It's got two taps. I turned one on and a jet of water shot up.'

'Ah yes,' said M'sieu Mercier, 'that is the bidet.'

'Is it like a kind of drinking fountain?'

M'sieu Mercier suppressed a grin and shook his head. 'No M'sieu.'

'Well what is it for then?'

'It is - er - for washing between the legs.'

'How do you mean?'

'Well a lady or gentleman sits on it, turns on the tap and washes their - you know - private parts.'

My father gazed at M'sieu Mercier in disbelief. 'Gerraway.' he said. At this stage, I thought I'd better make my presence felt. I coughed loudly and took my fathers arm. 'Come on Dad' I said, 'let's go and eat.' My father turned.

'Hello son,' he said. You'll never guess what I've got in my bathroom.'

'Yes, I know.'

'It's for washing your ...

Fearing the worse, I dragged him away.

We entered the dining room to be greeted by an aging waiter with a drooping moustache and a melancholy expression. 'Bonsoir Messieurs' he said.

'What did he say?' asked my father.

'He said. Good evening.' I replied.

My father nodded and turned to the waiter 'Ow d'you do.'

The waiter muttered something under his breath, handed us a menu each and asked what we would like to drink. I ordered a bottle of the local wine. He nodded and shuffled off. Meanwhile my father had been looking at the menu. He shook his head and handed it to me.

'This is no good' he said. 'It's all in bloody French!'

'Yes Dad' I said patiently. 'All the menus in France are written in French.'

'Bloody silly idea' said my father.

'What have they got?'

I consulted the menu.

'Right. You can have a steak, chicken, lamb chops, grilled

sole or, if you want to be really adventurous, you could try snails or frogs legs.'

My father looked as if he was going to be sick.

'What??' he said.

'Only joking Dad' I replied.

'How can they eat muck like snails and frog's legs?'

'They're delicacies in France Dad. Frog's legs actually taste quite nice. They taste a bit like chicken.'

'There's not much meat on them though is there? You'd need a lot of frogs to make a proper meal.'

'They're not supposed to be a proper meal. They're a starter.'

At that moment, the waiter returned with the wine. He offered the cork to my father.

Dad took it. 'What am I supposed to do with this,' he said, 'stick it up my......'

'Dad!' I rapidly intervened. 'You're supposed to smell it to make sure the wine is in good condition.' I took the cork from my father, sniffed it and nodded to the waiter 'Oui m'sieur, c'est bon.'

The waiter then poured a small measure in my father's wine glass and waited. Dad picked up the glass, looked at it then looked at the waiter.

'Well fill it up then', he said

'No Dad,' I explained, that's just for you to taste. To make sure you approve of the wine.'

Dad picked up his wine glass, but rather than sip and taste, he gulped the whole lot down. I waited, the waiter waited. My father screwed up his face up as though he'd just swallowed a dose of foul tasting medicine. He looked at the waiter.

'I don't fancy that', he said, 'Have you any Guinness?'

The waiter shrugged. 'Qu'est-ce sais Guinness?'

'I don't think they have much call for Guinness in France Dad. Don't you like the wine?'

'I suppose I could get used to it,' he said grudgingly.

I nodded to the waiter. He nodded back, filled my Dad's glass and poured out a glass for me. I tasted it and smiled at the waiter. 'Tres bon.' I turned to my Dad, 'What are you having to eat Dad?'

'I don't suppose they've got fish, chips and mushy peas.'

'Not exactly', I turned to the waiter, 'Sole meuniere, pomme frites et petit pois pour deux s'il vous plait.' I turned to Dad. 'Do you want some bread?'

'Yes please.'

'Et du pain Monsieur.'

The waiter nodded, scribbled our order in his pad and moved into the kitchen. Dad took another sip of his wine.

'I think it's beginning to grow on me.'

'I thought it might.'

'Oh by the way Vincent. I can't find a radio in my room.'

'They probably haven't got one.'

He groaned. 'Oh no I'll miss 'THE ARCHERS.'

'I wouldn't worry about that Dad. You could miss it for a fortnight, and they'd still be talking about the same old things'

We sat in silence for a while until the waiter returned with a basket of bread slices cut from a baguette. He placed it on the table and left. Dad looked at the basket of bread then at me.

'What's this?'

'You said you wanted some bread.'

I meant proper bread - like Mother's Pride. You can't make chip butties with these.'

'They don't have chip butties in France Dad - and before our meal comes, they don't have mushy peas either and the fish won't be fried in batter.'

'Bloody foreigners.'

Our meal arrived. The first thing Dad did was to pick up his fork and mash his peas together. 'That's more like it,' he said. He complained about the chips not being thick enough and the sole too greasy. We finished with coffee, and the waiter brought over two large cognacs. Dad protested to the waiter.

'We never ordered these,' he said, then to me, 'you've got to watch these Froggies, putting drinks on the bill that we've never ordered.'

He handed his glass back to the waiter, who took it and put it down on the table in front of my Dad.

'Les cognacs sont un cadeau de le Maitre.' he said.

'The brandies are on the house. Compliments of the manager.'

'Oh - er - well - that's different then.' He picked up his glass. 'Cheers.'

We finished the coffee and went up to bed. Pat was asleep. I said goodnight to Dad. He started to move to his room when he stopped. 'Is true what he said?' he asked.

'Is what true?'

'That thing in the bathroom. Is it really for washing - er - you know. Your - er - how's your father?'

'Yes Dad. Goodnight Dad.'

'Goodnight Vincent' he shook his head, opened his bedroom door and I heard him mutter. 'There's nowt so queer as folk.'

The next morning, Pat was up before me and I went downstairs to find her in the dining room with Dad.

'Morning Pat - morning Dad. Did you sleep well?'

'Off and on.'

'Have you ordered breakfast?' I asked.

'There's not much to have' replied Dad. 'They don't have porridge, they don't have toast and marmalade and they don't have egg and bacon.'

'Didn't you have a croissant?'

'He had three!' said Pat.

'Three?'

'Yes well, I've got to keep my strength up somehow.' said Dad. 'What time are we setting off? '

'Well, why don't you go and fetch your overnight things down. I'll have a quick cup of coffee and a croissant, pay the bill then we'll hit the road. I'd like to get to Villefranche before it goes dark.'

Dad nodded and went up for his things. I'd already packed my things, as had Pat. I finished my breakfast and paid the bill. Dad joined us at Reception, and M'sieu Mercier insisted on shaking everybody's hand before we got in the car and set off to join the N7 laughingly nicknamed 'The Murderess' because of all the fatal accidents that occurred, many of them involving British tourists not being used to driving on the right. We made good time and were at Valence by two thirty where we stopped for lunch. As usual Dad found something to complain about.

'This steak's not cooked proper. Look - it's all bloody.'

I tried to explain to Dad that the French preferred their steaks to be bloody.

'Well I don't.' came the reply.

I called the waiter over and asked him to put Dad's steak under the grill and cook it more - 'bien, bien cuit'. The waiter looked at me in surprise, shrugged and took Dad's plate away returning in about ten minutes. He put Dad's steak on the table. Dad cut into it and nodded.

'That's much better', he said, 'Ta very much.'

The waiter stared at the steak sadly, 'Ruine' he commented.

'What did he say?' asked Dad.

'Er' - he said, 'don't mention it' I lied.

We finished our meal; I paid the bill and rose. 'Let's get moving. We've still got a fair way to go yet.'

Dad stood up. 'Where's the doings?' he said.

I sighed, 'Why didn't you go before?'

'I didn't want to go before. It's just come on me now.'

I pointed to the toilets. 'We'll see you outside Dad.'

Pat and I went out to where we'd parked the car.

'You sit in the car darling; I'll wait here for Dad.'

She sighed. 'I hope we're doing the right thing bringing Dad along. He's done nothing but complain since we left.'

'He'll be all right once we get to Villefranche' I waited by the car. Eventually Dad appeared. As he opened the car door, I noticed that his flies were undone.

'Dad.'

'Yes Vincent.'

'Your flies are undone.'

'Oh dear, so they are,' he said, zipping up his fly, 'It's my age you know. You forget things when you start getting older,' chuckling. 'Mind you, it's better to forget to zip up after you've been than forget to zip down before you go.'

I got in the car, and off we set. As I drove to rejoin the N7 I thought about what Pat had said. Maybe it was a big mistake to bring Dad along. Is he going to complain about everything for the rest of the week? I sighed. Too late now to change anything. Might as well make the best of it. I glanced in the rear mirror, Dad was fast asleep. I put my worries out of my mind and concentrated on the road ahead.

The further south we drove, the warmer the weather became. We drove through Montelimar following the river Rhone, through Orange, bypassing Avignon and Aix-en-Provence, then cutting across to avoid Marseille and Toulon then followed the coast road from St Raphael towards Nice. Pat was entranced by the scenery as I had been some twenty years before. Dad was still asleep and I decided not to wake him. We went through Cannes, Antibes, Juan-les-Pins and Nice. At every twist of the road we had wonderful glimpses of the blue Mediterranean. Eventually we descended into Villefranche and parked outside the Hotel Welcome in the Place Amelie Pollonnais. It had changed very little since I first saw it. Chez Max was still there but was now called Le Calypso. I glanced across the square. The Hotel Paradis where I lost my nerve but saved my virginity, was now a patisserie.

I called out to Dad. 'Wake up Dad - we're here.'

Dad stirred, stretched and yawned. 'Is this Villefranche then?'

'Yes, and before you start to complain ...

Dad interrupted me, 'Me? Complain? When do I ever complain?'

Pat stifled a laugh. For a moment I had an angry retort on my lips but I saw the funny side of it and laughed. I should have known. I'd lived with Dad long enough to realise that he always had the last word. We went in the Hotel, registered then took the lift to the second floor. I opened the bedroom door for Pat, and then went with Dad to his bedroom to make sure it was all right. We went inside. The shutters were closed. I opened them to reveal a marvellous view of the harbour. I stepped out on to the narrow balcony and gazed in wonder. Directly ahead was the Rade de Villefranche with a cruise liner anchored in the middle, probably in the same spot that HMS Mauritius was anchored some twenty years before. Behind the Cruise liner was the peninsula of St. Jean Cap Ferrat with it's profusion of pine trees, mimosa and bougainvillea. For an instant I was carried back to the moment so many years ago, when I first saw the Cote d'Azur, as I stood on the deck of HMS Mauritius. It was just as beautiful now as it was then. Dad came out and joined me and took in the scene.

'Well Dad, what do you think?'

'It's not got a proper beach. It's not very big - and it's all pebbles.'

'Never mind the beach - look at that view.'

'Blackpool's got seven miles of beach - and it's all sand!'

I knew I couldn't win, so I said nothing and went back to my room. Pat too was on the balcony looking at the view.

'Good isn't it?' I said.

'Breathtaking' she said.

'Let's go down to the bar and have a drink.'

'I'm all for that.'

We picked up Dad on the way and we all went downstairs and sat outside admiring the view and drinking our biere pressions - a French lager. We took a little stroll along the Promenade des Marinieres.

The week simply flew by. We had so much to see. Every day, the sun shone. We drove to Monaco, went to the Aquarium and the Palace, and watched the changing of the guard, had lunch at a restaurant overlooking the harbour, spent a day in the old town of Nice, drove up to Grasse to visit the perfume factory, and went to Eze Village, a perched village with magnificent views. To the left one could see as far as Italy, and to the right as far as St Maxime. The days just flew by and all too soon it was time for the long drive back to home and reality. I'd phoned Harry during the week. He said that the convalescent home was okay - lots of physio and good food, but he was missing Edith and would be glad to get home. He even said that he was missing me!

I paid the hotel bill, said goodbye to Villefranche and headed back to join the N7. We stopped en route at Dijon where the mustard comes from, and stopped overnight at the Hotel Victor Hugo. The following day, we started off early and got to Calais in time to catch the four o'clock ferry to Dover - fortunately for Pat, the English Channel was as calm as the proverbial millpond so she survived the crossing without being seasick. We disembarked at Dover, and by eight o'clock we were back in Manchester. And guess what? It was raining! We started to get our luggage out of the car when, to my surprise, Dad said it was the best holiday he'd ever had, in spite of the lack of sliced bread!

It was back to work at Hector Powe the next day but there was a pleasant surprise waiting for me. One of the good things about working for a large company like Hector Powe was that during the summer months I had to act as a relief stylist at some other branches when their stylist was on holiday. The following week the manager told me that I would be a holiday relief at their branch in Blackpool. I was looking forward to spending a week in Blackpool, one of my favourite places.

In the 50's it had everything. Not only did it have the famous Tower, the Pleasure Beach, a Zoo, the Winter Gardens, an open air swimming pool, and three piers, it also had eight theatres in which top entertainers appeared for the summer season. The first thing I did after checking in at my boarding house was to find out who was on and where. The bill for the Central Pier caught my eye. It was called 'The Laughter Show'. Top of the bill was Jimmy James and Company a hysterically funny comedy act, then came little Jimmy Clitheroe, a diminutive 4'3" comic whose act consisted of playing a cheeky schoolboy. Then there was Roy Castle who sang, tap-danced, did impressions and played an amazing variety of musical instruments. There was also Hylda Baker one of the funniest comediennes I have ever heard or seen.

Finally, at the bottom of the bill in small print were the names Morecambe and Wise. They were an up and coming double act who had just finished as resident comedians on a radio series called 'VARIETY FANFARE' produced by my old friend, Ronnie Taylor. I'd heard them several times and thought they were really funny. They were both from the north of England, Eric Morecambe from Lancashire and Ernie Wise from Yorkshire and their northern humour appealed to me. I went to see the show and enjoyed it - or rather - most of it. I was so disappointed in Morecambe and Wise. I'd seen them at the Ardwick Empire in Manchester a few weeks before and to my surprise they did the same act, word for word that they'd done in Manchester. I was so naïve in those days that I didn't realise that most comics did the same performance, each week, as they toured Britain's hundreds of variety theatres. The same act could last a comedian at least two years, before it needed to be changed. Indeed many comedians just kept repeating their act, year after year. For some, it lasted a lifetime. Anyway I was really disappointed - not to say annoyed - I'd paid my two shillings and sixpence or whatever the price was then, for something I'd seen already and jokes I'd heard before.

I walked round to the stage door where the stage doorkeeper sat. 'I want to see Morecambe and Wise.'

'Oh yes. And who are you?'

'My name's Vince Powell.'

He consulted a piece of paper. 'You're not on my list.'

'I'm a writer' I lied. It worked.

'Oh. They're in dressing room eight.' He pointed up. 'Up the stairs, last room on your right.

I climbed the stairs, walked along a corridor and knocked on the door.

Eric called out, 'Who is it?'

I shouted back, 'Vince Powell'

'Are you from the Inland Revenue?'

'No'

'Come in!'

I opened the door. It was a tiny dressing room with barely enough room for two people, let alone three.

Eric smiled, 'What do you want - an autograph or a signed photograph? Autographs are two and six - signed photographs five shillings.'

I soon learned that this was typical of Eric. He was always joking.

'You need some new material' I said, 'you're using all old stuff. I've heard it all before.'

'Are you a critic?' said Eric.

'No - I'm a comedy writer. You definitely need some fresh jokes.'

'Have you got any?' asked Ernie.

'Not on me. But I'll come round tomorrow night with some.'

With that, I left, went back to my boarding house and sat up all night writing jokes, some I'd written with Harry, some

I'd thought up myself and others I'd pinched from various sources. In all I filled five or six pages. The next night, before the show started I went back to the Central Pier. The stage doorkeeper waved me in, and I made my way to dressing room eight where Eric and Ernie were just getting made up. I handed Eric the pages I had written. He read them, smiled once or twice and laughed a couple of times.

'Ernie' he said, 'give him five quid.'

To my surprise Ernie took out his cheque book, wrote me out a cheque for five pounds, tore it out and handed it to me. I looked at it. It was the very first time I was paid for something I'd written. I really shouldn't have cashed it - I should have had it framed but £5 was not to be sneezed at in those days. Before I left, Eric revealed that he and Ernie were about to start their own series on BBC radio in Manchester and suggested I write to their producer, a John Ammonds as he may be looking for comedy material. I thanked them both and left. As soon as I got back to Manchester I went to see Harry told him about Eric and Ernie, and their suggestion that we get in touch with their radio producer, John Ammonds. We didn't waste any time and spent several nights writing jokes and funny routines which we sent to John Ammonds, who replied saying that although they were amusing, they weren't exactly what he was looking for. Undismayed we wrote more jokes and comedy routines and sent them off to which he replied in a similar vein.

Now you may find hard to believe what I'm going to tell you next, but it's absolutely true. A couple of days later at Hector Powe, a salesman asked me to measure a customer for a suit. He introduced the customer to me as Mr. Hammonds, but the customer corrected him by saying that his name was Ammonds. 'Hammonds without the H'aitch.' As I began to measure him, I started to wonder, Ammonds was not a particularly common name. Could this be the John Ammonds of the BBC that we'd been sending jokes for Morecambe and Wise to?

'Excuse me Mr. Ammonds, are you a BBC producer?'

'Yes as a matter of fact I am. Do I know you?'

'No - we've never met. But my partner and I have been sending you ideas and gags for Morecambe and Wise.'

'Ah - which one are you - Vince Powell or Harry Driver?'

I introduced myself and said we hoped to send him some more ideas by the end of the week and asked him if we were on the right lines. He sighed.

'Well yes, some of your stuff was quite funny. The only snag is that we already have a writer. His name's Frank Roscoe and he's written for Eric and Ernie before. The BBC have commissioned Frank to write the series.'

Another door slammed in our face!

Chapter Six:
MY NAME IS
HARRY WORTH

Harry and I were totally depressed. It seemed that our aspirations of becoming successful comedy writers had hit rock bottom. We met most evenings to try and think of ideas. We even had the idea of compiling all the jokes and comedy routines we could think of, packaging them into two volumes and advertising them in The Stage, a show business paper. We shouldn't have bothered. It cost us £20 pounds for the ad and the only reply we got was from a would be comedy writer trying to sell his jokes to us!

Things looked glum. I managed to do one or two speeches to a few Ladies Luncheon Clubs but they only paid £50. The only consolation was I got a free lunch which was invariably chicken. We rang John Ammonds but he was still involved in another radio series for Morecambe and Wise written by Frank Roscoe. However, John was encouraging. He said that he thought that we had talent and that we should persevere with our writing.

He gave us the names of some of the other light entertainment producers based at Manchester to whom we should write. Which we did. We developed the habit of meeting two nights a week to try and write all sorts of comedy routines, which we sent to every producer at the BBC. Some replied saying 'Thanks but no thanks.' Some replied just saying 'No thanks.' Some didn't even reply. We were really at a low ebb. We'd got nowhere as performers and now we were getting nowhere as writers.

Then, one Friday I got a phone call from John Ammonds. He told me that he'd now moved from radio to television and was setting up a situation comedy series for a new comedian called Harry Worth. He said they were having problems in getting suitable scripts. They had done one series written by Ronnie Taylor which hadn't really been a success, and as Ronnie was now heavily involved with his own production company, he couldn't spare the time. Would Harry Driver and I be interested in submitting a script purely on spec - he couldn't afford to commission us.

Would we??? You bet your life we would. John gave me a brief outline of Harry Worth's character - he was a likeable idiot who lived alone and was forever at odds with red tape, officialdom and bureaucracy. 'Oh, and one more thing Vince - could I have the script by Tuesday morning as I'm having lunch with Harry Worth at the BBC that day.'

Tuesday morning. It was now Friday afternoon. I rang Harry and told him. We agreed that we would have to work all day Saturday and Sunday to get the script written. We hadn't even got a plot yet. I said to Harry that as soon as I finished work that day, I would come over to his house and we would try and find an idea for Harry Worth even if it meant working all night. Edith came on the line to suggest that if we were going to be working through the night, I was welcome to snatch a couple of hours sleep on their settee.

I rang Pat to tell her the news.

When I told her that I was going straight to Harry's from work, to write a script and that I'd probably be late home, she wasn't very pleased and started to complain about putting my show business dreams ahead of concentrating on the steady job I already had. From her point of view, I suppose she was right. Anyway I assured her that I wouldn't do anything to jeopardise my job with Hector Power which she was happy with. I went round to Harry's and we started to think of a suitable plot - for Harry - Worth that is. (I think that to make things easier and less confusing I'll refer to Harry Worth as HW and Harry Driver as HD). To continue, HD and I came up with an idea of HW leaving his umbrella on a bus, and going to the Lost Property Office to see if it had been handed in. After some confusion with the clerk, HW was mistaken by a militant bus driver for a management official who was checking on the workforce which resulted in the bus drivers calling a strike. We started writing at once, with me on the typewriter and worked all through the night. Pat phoned twice to ask what time I would be coming home. The second time, Edith answered the phone and told Pat that it would be more than her life was worth to interrupt us while our creative juices were flowing so well.

We began the script with HW visiting the Lost Property Office to ask the clerk about his umbrella. A simple thing to do you would say. But not for HW as we saw him. The dialogue went something like this:

HARRY: Good morning.
CLERK: It's afternoon Sir.
HARRY: Is it really. It just shows you how time flies.
CLERK: Can I help you Sir?
HARRY: I hope so. Have you found my umbrella?
CLERK: (PRODUCING A PAD) Let me just take down a few details.
HARRY: Certainly. Well, I say it was my umbrella, but it was Aunties really.
CLERK: Yes Sir - could I have the name please?
HARRY: Prendergast.
CLERK: (WRITING) Prendergast. Christian name?
HARRY: Amelia.
CLERK: (STARTING TO WRITE THEN STOPS) Amelia?
HARRY: Yes. Mrs.
THE CLERK SIGHS - TEARS THE PAGE FROM THE PAD CRUMPLES IT UP AND THROWS IT IN A WASTE PAPER BASKET.
CLERK: Shall we try again?
HARRY; By all means. As my old headmistress used to say. If at first you don't succeed, try, try, again.
CLERK: (NOW GETTING A LITTLE IMPATIENT) Never mind that, just give me the name.
HARRY: Watkins.
CLERK: (WRITING) Watkins. Christian name?
HARRY: I don't think I ever knew her Christian name. We always called her Miss. Watkins.
THE CLERK SIGHS AGAIN. TEARS THE PAGE FROM THE PAD, CRUMPLES IT UP AND THROWS IT IN THE WASTE PAPER BASKET.

CLERK: *(ANGRILY) What is **your** name?*
HARRY: *Worth - Harry - Mr.*
CLERK: *(HEAVILY) Harry Worth. (WRITING) Thank you.*
HARRY: *(PLEASANTLY) Don't mention it.*
CLERK: *You say you've lost an umbrella Mr. Worth.*
HARRY: *Yes. I think I left it on one of your buses.*
CLERK: *Right. Could you describe it for me please?*
HARRY: *Yes. It was red.*
CLERK: *(WRITING) Red.*
HARRY: *Yes, it was definitely red. A double decker. Number 28.*
THE CLERK STARES BLEAKLY AT HARRY. HARRY
SMILES AT HIM, THEN REACHES OUT AND TEARS
THE PAGE FROM THE PAD, CRUMPLES IT UP AND
AIMS IT AT THE WASTE PAPER BASKET.
HARRY: *Missed!*

We didn't know it at the time, but that opening became a kind of blueprint for the future series. It set HW's character perfectly. However, I mustn't get ahead of myself. The next morning after writing with HD from dusk to dawn I went in to Hector Powe as usual. I yawned my way through the day, but by closing time I felt terrible. I could hardly keep my eyes open. I phoned Pat to explain that I would be late again. She was decidedly frosty. I told her how important it was and promised that when the script was finished I'd take her out for dinner at our favourite Italian restaurant. I hung up and caught the bus to HD's, bought my ticket and promptly fell asleep.

I woke up about a mile past my stop. As I walked back to HD's house, I passed a chemist's shop. I went in and told the pharmacist that I desperately needed something to keep me awake. He said that he couldn't give me anything without a doctor's prescription. I pleaded with him saying it was a matter of life and death, and promising that I wouldn't tell a soul. He hesitated then disappeared into the pharmacy, to return clutching a purple capsule. He handed it to me and told me to take it when I was feeling tired. By that time I was almost asleep on my feet. I thanked him, made my way to HD's had a cup of tea and took the capsule. To this day I've no idea what it was, but within half an hour I was wide awake and full of energy.

We stayed up all night again, writing the script. We laughed a lot at what we had written. Whether this was the effect of the purple capsule or our writing talent, was debatable. Dawn was breaking over the rooftops of Manchester when I typed 'THE END.'

I rang Hector Powe to tell them that I didn't feel well and that I wouldn't be in work that day. I also rang Pat and told her that the script was finished. Then I caught a bus into the city and called at a photocopiers where I got three copies of the script done. I couldn't help feeling nervous as I walked to the BBC's offices. In those days, writers were expected to read their scripts to the producer and virtually act them out. I just hoped that I would be able to do justice to the words. I gave my name to the Commissionaire who directed me to John Ammond's office. As I entered, he was sitting at his desk talking to a stockily built man.

John rose, 'Ah Vince, come in.' He waved a hand in the direction of the other man. 'This is Harry Worth. Harry - Vince.'

We shook hands. John went on. 'I thought it would be a good idea if Harry listened to you reading the script. You don't mind do you?'

'No.' I mumbled.

Actually I did mind. I was terrified. It was one thing reading the script to a producer, but a totally different thing reading it to the man who was going to perform it.

'Whenever you're ready Vince' said John.

I took out a copy of the script from my briefcase, cleared my throat, called upon all my previous experiences as a performer and started.

'We open on a sign which says 'Lost Property Office'. - Cut to Harry as he enters. A clerk is behind the counter. Harry smiles at him.

HARRY: Good morning.
CLERK: It's afternoon Sir.
HARRY: Is it really. It just goes to show how time flies!'

John and HW chuckled. I carried on reading. John and

HW's chuckles became loud laughter and by the time I was halfway through reading the script, they were both laughing so much that I couldn't help laughing myself. The further I read, the more we all laughed. I grew in confidence and at the end, both John and HW were practically crying with laughter. I put the script down and John and HW burst into enthusiastic applause and shook my hand.

'Marvellous' gasped John.

'Hilarious' gasped HW. He then embraced me and pressed a ten pound note in my hand.

'For you and Harry Driver' he said. 'Have a drink on me.'

John shook my hand again. 'Well done Vince. You read it so well. Come on, I'll buy you a drink. Let's go to the BBC Club.'

The BBC Club was a licensed 'members only' bar. John, who was a member, signed me and HW in. It was large Bells all round. I can't tell you how elated I felt. It was better than winning the listener's vote on 'What Makes A Star'. John told me that he would send HD and I a contract for the script. We would be paid 75 guineas - don't ask me why the BBC paid artists in guineas I didn't know then and I still don't. A guinea in those pre-decimal days was one pound one shilling. HW suggested to John that the BBC should give HD and me a contract for the entire series of six episodes and John agreed. I could hardly believe our luck. For a series of six programmes we would be paid over £400. It may not seem a lot now but in those days it was nearly as much as the average yearly wage. It seemed too good to be true. And it was. John made a proviso.

'Of course, you'll have to take time off work.'

'What do you mean John?'

'Well, you're not going to be able to write the series with you working all day and writing at night. You managed to cope with writing the first script but you couldn't keep that up.'

'John's right' said HW, 'you'd be a nervous wreck.'

'Besides,' said John, 'it's going to take you a least a couple of months to write the series, that's without allowing for any re-writes. And we need you to be rehearsals.' He shook his head. 'I'm sorry Vince, but I couldn't take a chance on giving you a contract unless I could be certain you'd be writing full time. The BBC would never agree to that. In any case, it wouldn't be fair on HW.'

'Hector Powe would never let me have two months or more off work.' I said.

'You could always hand in your notice.' said HW.

'You mean leave my job?'

'Yes.'

I was now thoroughly depressed. Only a few minutes ago I was offered the chance to write a BBC television series, and now it seemed that the chance was being snatched away. John saw how upset I was.

'Look Vince, Don't make a decision now. Go home and think about it. Talk to your wife - talk to Harry Driver. Then when you've made your mind up, give me a ring. Whatever you decide, we'll pay you for this first script.' I said nothing. My mind was in a turmoil. HW stood up.

'We ought to go John or I'll miss my train.'

John rose and turned to me. 'You'll have to excuse us Vince. I have to run Harry to the station. Get yourself another drink. Tell them to put it on my account.'

John and HW shook my hand and left. I ordered a large Bells and tried to think. What was I to do? If I left my job my wife would never forgive me. On the other hand, if I stayed on at Hector Powe, I would be throwing away the chance of being commissioned to write a TV series. And what about HD? I'd be responsible for denying him the golden opportunity of being involved with a BBC series and all that that would mean to his self respect. What was I to do? Obviously John wouldn't commission HD to write the series on his own. What a position to be in. Whichever decision I came to, I'd be in trouble. I finished my whisky and ordered another. I sat there trying to find a way out of my predicament. I could, of course lie to HD, tell him that neither John nor HW liked our script, make no mention of his offer to commission a series and leave it at that. HD would be none the wiser and I wouldn't have to tell my wife that I'd handed in my notice at Hector Powe. This would seem to be a good way out of the problem I thought.

But what about my own ambitions of a show business

career? I finally reached a decision. I would tell my wife and HD the truth and see what they had to say. I mean, I argued with myself, what if I handed in my notice and the series was a disaster? I would be out of a job, with a wife to support and no nearer achieving my ambition. On the other hand, if I did hand in my notice and the series was successful, what guarantee did I have that a further series would be commissioned by the BBC? So what was I to do? I decided that I would tell my wife and HD the truth.

I finished my scotch, and walked out of the club to catch a bus home. When I arrived at my house, Pat hadn't returned from the dental surgery and wouldn't be home for at least another two hours. So I caught another bus to HD's. When I got there he was sitting in his wheelchair anxious to hear my news. I told him everything that had happened, their enthusiastic reaction to my reading of the script and the offer of contracting us to write the series on condition that I leave Hector Powe. HD looked at me.

'So when are you handing in your notice?'

'Do you think I should Harry?'

'Of course you should. We'll never get another chance like this. This is the break we've been looking for.'

'But supposing it doesn't work? I'll be out of a job.'

'Of course it'll work. We've done one script that they liked. There's no reason we can't write the series.'

'Pat won't be pleased at me giving up my job.'

'She will when the money comes rolling in. Besides, if it doesn't work you can always get another job.'

He didn't say that he would never have a job. He didn't need to. I was only too aware of what he must have been thinking. I looked at him sitting in his wheelchair.

'You're dead right Harry. It's too big a chance to chuck it away. And as you say, if it doesn't work I can always get another job.'

'It'll work. Hey wait till I tell Edith. How much did you say that the Beeb would pay us?'

'75 guineas a script.'

HD made a quick mental calculation. '75 guineas by six. That's - er - '

'Four hundred and seventy pounds, ten shillings to be

exact. I worked it out on the bus.'

Harry was ecstatic. 'Nearly five hundred quid!' It would take me over a year to earn that much.'

'We should have a drink to celebrate.'

'Sorry Vince - we're right out of booze. We could have a cup of coffee.'

'We can do better than that Harry. I've got a ten pound note burning a hole in my pocket, that Harry Worth gave me for you and I to have a drink. We're going to the pub!

I grasped the handles of the wheelchair, pushed HD out of the house, along the road to a nearby pub. We were lucky - we just got in before closing time, which in those days was three o'clock. There was no all day drinking as we have now. Pubs used to open at twelve o'clock, close at three, open again at seven and close at half past ten. Anyway, we got a couple of scotches and drank to our success. We both felt that we were on the brink of an exciting career change. The landlord called time, we drained our glasses and I pushed HD back to his house. We agreed to wait until I had worked out my notice before starting to write the next script for HW, then I left to get the bus home.

I rang the BBC and asked for John Ammonds. When he came on the line I told him of my decision to leave Hector Powe and concentrate on writing. He was delighted and said that he would get the contracts department to send us a contract as soon as possible. I sat, happily reviewing the events of the day until Pat come home.

'Hello darling,' I said, 'I've got some terrific news. Come and sit down and I'll tell you all about it.'

She sat down and I told her about the meeting with HW and John Ammonds. I told her about me reading the script and their reaction. When I told her that John was going to commission HD and I to write a series of six programmes at a fee of just over £75 a script she was delighted.

However when I went on to tell her about the conditions attached - that I would have to leave Hector Powe and that I would be handing in my notice the next day, her delight turned to concern.

'You're not serious?'

'Yes.'

'I don't believe this. You must be mad.'

I tried to explain that Harry and I would earn over £400 for writing the scripts, and that I owed it to HD to accept John's offer but it didn't make any difference. She said I was being totally selfish. I argued that she knew it had long been my ambition to be involved in show business, first as a performer and now as a writer, but it didn't make any difference to her attitude. Just at that moment my Dad arrived and I told him the good news. The three of us sat and discussed the situation. Dad pointed out to Pat, that if I didn't go ahead and take this chance, it was something that I would regret for the rest of my life. He also told Pat that she too, would share in that regret and should have enough confidence in my talents to succeed. He also said that if it didn't work out I could always go back to Hector Powes. He revealed that he had spoken to the manager, some time ago, who assured him that, if the worst ever came to the worst there would always be a job for me. After all, they had invested a considerable amount of time and money in training me.

Pat didn't say anything for a couple of minutes, then nodded.

'You're right Dad, it's me that was being selfish not Vince.' She turned to me. 'I'm sorry Vince. You go ahead and do what you have to do.'

And that was that. I phoned HD, who by that time had a special telephone installed that he could operate by the lightest touch with a finger, and told him the news. Edith came on the line and suggested that we come to their house for dinner - fish, chips and mushy peas from their local chippie. Never one to refuse such an invitation, we readily agreed. I took a bottle of white wine and we spent a very pleasant evening looking forward to a bright future. My last week at Hector Powe passed quickly. The day I left, everyone wished me luck. That night I called at HD's and we arranged to meet the following Monday to start writing. We were eager to get going and looking forward to an enjoyable laughter-filled few days. The first thing we did when we met the next day was to think of a plot. After kicking a few ideas around we hit on a plot which involved HW discovering that his bicycle had been stolen from outside his house. He reported it to the police and we wrote a scene in his local police station, where he confused everybody. We worked hard and finished the script in just under a week. I rang John and made an appointment to go and see him with the finished script. I was really looking forward to reading it to him after what happened with the first script reading. This time I would only be reading it to John as HW was appearing at a theatre in Coventry. The day of the appointment, I got to the BBC at ten o'clock, although my meeting with John wasn't until eleven. I sat in the canteen and went through the script line by line in order to make sure that I was putting the right inflection on certain words to get the most humour from the jokes. At last it was time to go and see John. I made my way up to his office. He was sitting behind his desk puffing away on his pipe. We exchanged greetings.

'Might as well make a start,' said John.

'Right.' I opened the script. John was already smiling in anticipation. I started to read. 'It is night-time. We see a policeman approach Harry Worth's front door and ring the bell. The letter box is pushed open and we hear Harry call out.

HARRY: Who is it?
POLICEMAN(SIGHING) ... Mr. Worth.
HARRY: No you aren't - I'm Mr Worth.
John chuckled.
POLICEMAN: I'm from the station.
HARRY: Police. Fire or railway?
John laughed.
POLICEMAN: Now look Mr Worth. You telephoned us half an hour ago to report that your bicycle had been stolen. Would you please open the door?
HARRY: Just a moment. How can I be sure that you're a policeman? For all I know you could be the thief coming back to steal my bicycle clips. Would you mind poking your truncheon through the letter box and waggling it about?

John burst into laughter.
And that was the only time he laughed during my reading

of the script. It was a thirty minute script but it seemed to take me over an hour to read it. When I finished my lips were parched and my throat was dry. I looked at John. He looked at me.

'Oh dear' was all he said.

'Shall I read it again?'

John shook his head. 'I don't think I could stand to hear it again Vince. Besides, it's not going to sound any better.'

I was confused. 'It sounded very funny when we were writing it John.'

'I'm sure it did. The plot's fine but you've made the mistake that lots of inexperienced writers make. You've re-written episode one.'

I was even more confused. 'I don't know what you mean John.'

He took the script from me, started to go through it and explained. What you and HD have done is to write the same jokes - you may have changed the location and altered some of the lines but basically the jokes are the same. For example, take this scene with the policeman. It starts with the policeman saying to Harry - "now you say that your bicycle is missing Mr. Worth." and Harry replies, "Yes and it was a Christmas present from my uncle. When I woke up on Christmas day, I found it at the foot of my bed, with a little card attached. Happy Christmas it said. The policeman then says. Yes Mr. Worth, just give me the full name and address. Harry replies Ah yes the name was Santa Claus, I'm not quite sure about the address. I think it's somewhere near the North Pole."

John sighed again. 'You see Vince, that joke is a variation of the opening joke in your first script.

I had to admit that he had a point. As he went through the script he pointed out several other jokes that also bore some resemblance to our first script. I apologised profusely and told him that we would re-write the script. John agreed and asked if we could do it by the following week.

'No problem John,' I said with a confidence I was far from feeling. 'Harry and I will get cracking right away.'

'The point is Vince, the BBC will be investing quite a lot of money in the series, and they will want the scripts to be written to an acceptable standard. If they don't come up to that standard it'll be my head that will be on the block not yours.'

'Don't worry John. We won't let you down.'

I picked up the script and left. I caught the bus to HD's and sat there worried stiff. I had been so sure that our second script was as funny as our first, it never crossed my mind that there would be a problem. What if John didn't like the re-write? I'd have to eat humble pie and apply for my job back. This was when I realised that writing comedy was a very precarious occupation. There were so many obstacles to overcome on the rocky road to success. First, it would have to appeal to the producer, then his Head of Programmes in Manchester, then the Controller of Light Entertainment in London, not forgetting Harry Worth who had script approval. By the time I got to HD's I was a nervous wreck. I gave him a blow by blow account of my meeting with John. He didn't seem to be as worried as I was.

'Well. Let's look on the bright side Vince. He said that he liked the plot. All we have to do is re-write it and put some different jokes in.'

Easier said than done. We started to re-write the first scene. By nine o'clock that night we had not written a word - no I tell a lie - we'd written lots of words but we didn't think they were very funny so we ripped the pages up. We decided to call it a day. Get a good night's sleep and start again the next morning, refreshed and with renewed inspiration. We met bright and early the following day. We were certainly refreshed but devoid of any inspiration. We toiled all day, thinking of different jokes then rejecting them. By the end of the day, we were getting desperate, if not to say despondent. Nothing we thought of seemed to be funny any more. It was the same the next day and the day after.

After four days, we had not written a single line. I looked at Harry and came to a decision. "It's no good Harry. We can't go on like this. We promised John that we'd have the re-writes finished in a week and here we are without a clue of what to write. We haven't even written the first scene. We're going to have to admit to John that we can't do it.'

Harry sighed, 'You're right. I can't understand it at all. It looks as if we've dried up.'

I nodded. 'I hate to say this Harry, but ...'

'You don't have to say anything. I know exactly what's on your mind. You're going to ask for your job back.'

'It's the only thing I can do. John's not going to commission us to write any more scripts, so I haven't really any option.'

'You're right Vince - and I don't blame you.'

I felt really lousy as I made my way home. At least I had a job to go back to - Harry had nothing. I told Pat as soon as I got in. She was sympathetic but underneath she was really quite relieved. I rang Dad to tell him and went to bed feeling thoroughly depressed. I couldn't sleep and about two o'clock in the morning I got up and went downstairs and made a cup of tea. I sat at the kitchen table, got out the script I'd read to John and tried to think of some funny lines without success. It looked as it my career as a comedy writer had come to a shuddering halt. Morning came, I caught the bus into the city and got the lift up to John's office. He hadn't arrived yet, but I went in, sat down and waited. A few minutes later I heard footsteps approaching and the office door was pushed open. To my surprise, it wasn't John, it was Ronnie Taylor - remember him? We were both startled to see each other. He told me that as he was passing, he'd popped in to see John. He looked closely at me - I was red-eyed and unshaven.

'You look terrible Vince' he said.

I told him everything that had happened - the success of the first script, the chance of being commissioned to write the series, me leaving my job, the failure of the second script, our inability to re-write it and my decision to give up writing and go back to my old job. Ronnie listened intently.

'You mean to say that you and Harry sat for nearly a week and didn't write a word?'

'That's right.'

'But you must have **thought** of something.'

'Oh yes - we thought of lots of things, but we couldn't think of anything funny.'

Ronnie pointed to a typewriter on the desk at which John's secretary usually sat. 'Look Vince - there's a typewriter.' He handed my several sheets of foolscap. 'Here's some paper. Put them in the typewriter and type out what you and Harry thought of for the first scene.'

'It's a waste of time Ronnie. It wasn't funny.'

'Don't argue. Just do it. I'm going to the canteen for a coffee. I'll come back in about ten minutes.'

He went out. I put the paper in the typewriter, and started to type. It was an effort - I had to force myself to type the words. Finally, I finished. It came to about six pages. I'd just stapled them together when Ronnie returned. I gave him the pages and he went into an adjoining office to read them while I sat there feeling more and more depressed. After a few minutes, John arrived, took one look at me and said, 'You look awful. Are you allright?' I was about to tell John what I had told Ronnie when Ronnie came in waving the sheets of paper.

'John', he said, 'I've just read one of the funniest scenes ever written for Harry Worth. Listen.'

Ronnie began to read. Now I have to tell you that Ronnie was a wonderful reader - he could read the telephone directory and make it sound funny. As he read that first scene, John began to smile. Even I started to smile! By the time Ronnie had got to the end of the scene, John and I were collapsing with laughter. Ronnie Taylor had saved my career - and changed my life. He explained that, because of our inexperience and lack of confidence, Harry Driver and I had worked ourselves into a state where we couldn't see anything funny in what we wrote. He told me to go back to HD's, stop worrying, have confidence in our ability and finish re-writing the script. He rang HD and repeated to him what he had told me. I left the BBC after assuring John that he would have the re-written script in a few days. As it happened, he had it much sooner. As soon as I got back to HD's, we were so fired up by what Ronnie had said that we finished it the following day. I took it in to the BBC, read it to John who laughed most of the way through, and confirmed that we would shortly receive a contract to write the rest of the series. I phoned Ronnie to tell him the good news, and he said that we could call on him whenever we needed his help or advice, which we did frequently. Many's the time John and I waylaid Ronnie as he stepped off a plane or a train to ask him to look at a particular scene which we felt could be funnier. And he never refused no matter how late it was. I will forever be grateful to Ronnie for all his help. Many years later, he was instrumental in me writing "SURPRISE SURPRISE!" and "BLIND DATE" for Cilla Black but more of that later. HD and I finished the scripts and we started to record the shows. In those days, the BBC North Region TV studios were situated in an old church in Dickinson Road, Rusholme - a suburb of Manchester, which had formerly been a film studio known as Mancunian Films.

It was owned by John Blakeley who produced a series of low-budget British films starring such notable northern comedians as Frank Randle, George Formby, Jewel and Warris and many others. It was eventually sold to the BBC who converted it into a television studio. It must have been the smallest TV studio in Britain. It could only accommodate an audience of 60, not a lot before which to record a television situation comedy. However, John overcame this by playing back the previous week's show to each audience and recording their laughter, thus making each programme sound as if there was an audience of 120. The studio was so small that, at times, the cameramen were only inches away from the front row of the audience. They were happy days in spite of the many problems we had. It was the first ever sitcom series to be made by a BBC regional station and transmitted nationwide - in a way we were pioneers. HW was very much like his screen persona - a worrier and always at odds with life. If a door had to be pushed open he would invariably trying pulling it and vice versa. I remember on one occasion, when HW and I were having coffee in a nearby café. A lady came in and sat at a table near to us. She was carrying a cup of coffee and a plate on which were two chocolate éclairs. She ate one of the éclairs, drank her coffee, then got up and went. HW looked at the uneaten éclair, said 'Waste not - want not', rose and picked up the éclair. He had just bitten into it when the lady returned with her second cup of coffee! That could only have happened to HW.

Another equally funny incident, some years later, involved Harold Wilson, the then leader of the Labour Party and Leader of Her Majesty's Opposition. They say that everybody can remember where they were and what they were doing on that fateful day, November 22nd 1963, when John F Kennedy, the President of the USA was assassinated in Dallas, Texas. On that day we were recording an episode of "HERE'S HARRY". We had just finished supper break and the studio audience were filing in, when we heard the tragic news which presented John with a problem. Should he tell the audience about the assassination or not? If he did they certainly wouldn't be in the mood to laugh at our sitcom. John decided not to tell them, and we went ahead with the recording only telling them when we had finished. The audience left in a sombre mood. Then John got a call from the Director General of the BBC. He told John that the BBC wanted Harold Wilson to pay a tribute to President Kennedy on television. Mr Wilson was in Blackpool attending the Labour Party conference, and as Dickinson Road was the nearest TV studio to Blackpool, he was being rushed to Manchester by private car. It was John's task to direct Mr Wilson's TV tribute and transmit it down the line to the BBC's Television Centre in London. Harold Wilson duly arrived wearing his usual trademark Gannex raincoat to be told that the Prime Minister Sir Alex Douglas-Home wanted to speak with him to make sure that their tributes didn't clash.

The only telephone which afforded some privacy was in the canteen storeroom so that that the Leader of Her Majesty's Opposition had to discuss matters of State surrounded by tins of baked beans and packets of fish fingers! When Harold Wilson finished recording his tribute and left, HW was waiting at the door. By some strange coincidence, HW had a Gannex raincoat similar to that of Mr Wilson. As HW stood there with his raincoat over his arm, Mr Wilson shook his hand then, thinking that HW's raincoat was his, tried to take it away from him. Harry protested and pulled it back. For a few minutes HW and Harold Wilson were involved in a tug-of-war as each tried to claim possession of the raincoat before John intervened and order was restored. Another typical HW situation! But to get back to the first series.

Most of you who can recall the TV series of "HERE'S HARRY" will no doubt remember the opening title sequence in which HW, standing at a right angle of a shop window, raised his left arm and left leg causing his reflection to give the appearance that both arms and both legs were raised off the ground simultaneously. It was a trick which I used to do as a schoolboy. I wrote the sequence in a script which featured HW queuing to buy a jacket in a sale. When HW read the script, he didn't understand it as it wasn't easy to put into words. We were filming the sequence at my old firm Hector Powe, and I demonstrated the sequence in one of the windows. HW fell about and John said that it was so funny that we should use it as the opening film sequence for each show. Because I had devised it, the BBC paid me 7 guineas every time HW cocked his leg up!

The first series was a big success and the BBC asked us to write a second series. HW had gone on a cruise with his lovely wife Kay, an ex-dancer and we arranged to meet when they got back. It was great fun working on that first series. HW was a likeable, generous man and greatly loved by the public. The shows which we wrote were full of innocent jokes which could be enjoyed by family audiences without embarrassment. We became firm friends and I spent many happy hours in his company. He also had a wicked sense of humour as I found out to my cost one evening. He was appearing in a variety show for a week at the Bolton Grand, and as it wasn't far from Manchester, I went over to see his act. After the show, I went round to his dressing room and we started to discuss ideas for the next series. We were so engrossed in our discussions that we didn't notice the time until the stage doorkeeper arrived to tell us he was locking up the theatre.

HW asked him if he knew of anywhere we could eat at that late hour. The stage doorkeeper told us that there was a piano bar nearby which served food and was open until midnight. So off we went. It was quite a nice place with a well stocked bar and a tiny dance floor. A pianist was tinkling away on the piano. We sat down and started to study the menu. Just then, HW whispered to me 'Don't look round Vince, but there's no women in this place.'

Disregarding his advice, I looked round and he was right. It was obvious what sort of place they catered for, HW said 'Look Vince, say nothing. Let's just order our food, eat it and go.' Just then, one of the customers minced over to our table. He said 'Oh Mr Worth, I do enjoy your shows. I love it when you cock your leg up. Could I be bold and ask you for a dance?' As quick as a flash HW said 'I'd love to dance with you but Vince gets very jealous!' Thank you Harry!

The next day HD and I started to plan the next series. But we had hardly put pen to paper when the phone rang. It was from Harry Elton, a Canadian producer at Granada Television. He was looking for writers to work on a new TV series. He invited us to a meeting at Granada the following morning - a meeting which led to another big change in our lives.

Chapter Seven:
ONE FOOT ON
THE LADDER

The following morning I arrived at Harry's, wheeled him out of his house, lifted him out of his wheelchair, put him in the passenger seat, folded up his wheelchair and put it in the boot. On the way to Granada, we wondered what the series would be about - would it be a comedy or a drama? We drove into the car park at Granada; I got HD into his wheelchair and pushed him into the studios where we took the lift up to the fourth floor to Harry Elton's office. His secretary directed us to a meeting room, where we found Harry Elton and several other writers. As we were the last to arrive Harry Elton introduced them to us.

Firstly there was Tony Warren who had devised the series, which was about several Northern families who lived in the same street in a fictional northern town of Weatherfield. The street was called Florizel Street and Granada planned to produce it as a twice weekly serial which they hoped would run for six months, with a bit of luck. Tony Warren had written the first six episodes but as he couldn't possibly write two scripts every week, Harry Elton had gathered a team of writers to help keep the series running. From memory, they were H.V. Kershaw (another Harry - so far we've had Harry Driver, Harry Worth, Harry Elton, and now Harry V Kershaw. To avoid getting confused I'll stick to referring to them by their initials).

In addition to HK there was John Finch, later to find fame in devising and writing 'SAM' a long running series of his own in the early 70's which traced the life of a Yorkshireman, Sam Wilson, from boyhood to manhood. Then there was Adele Rose, an attractive Jewish girl who later went on to devise 'GIRLS ABOUT TOWN' a situation comedy, and her own long running soap, 'BYKER GROVE'. Also Mick Dynes who as far as I can remember was a bookmaker. And of course there was HD and me. Harry Elton told us that we would all be given the opportunity of writing a script each for the first series of 'FLORIZEL STREET' then frowned and said 'I hate that title - Florizel Street - it sounds like a disinfectant. Let's think of a better name'. We all put our thinking caps on. I can't now remember who came up with the eventual name but, from memory, the sequence went something like this. 'Jubilee Street' HE repeated it. 'Jubilee Street.' Not bad. Any other ideas? Someone piped up with 'Crown Street' HE thought about it 'Crown Street' Yeah, that's not bad. Another voice said 'CORONATION STREET' HE nodded 'That's it. 'Coronation Street'. And 'CORONATION STREET' it became. When the first episode was transmitted, one well known television critic wrote, 'This series is doomed from the outset - with it's dull signature tune and grim scenes of a row of terraced houses and smoking chimneys.' That was in 1960. Here we are nearly 50 years later and it's still running and as popular as ever. What is the secret of its success? It's very simple. It's about family life, with which every family can identify. It's a series about the ups and downs which every family goes through and, as such, contains moments of drama, comedy, despair and hope.

Initially, HD and I were commissioned to write the storylines for each episode and we wrote the first 500 storylines. At the same time we were faced with writing the second series for Harry Worth. We tried to juggle the two commitments, but it became impossible to fulfil our obligations to both Granada and the BBC. HD then suggested that we split our joint commitments - that I should concentrate on 'HERE'S HARRY' and he would do the same for 'CORONATION STREET'. I went in to see John Ammonds and explained the situation, while HD phoned Granada and told HE the same.

Fortunately, they both accepted our suggestion. Granada supplied HD with a secretary, to whom he could phone and dictate the storylines, and John Ammonds brought in Frank

Roscoe, a comedy writer from Blackpool who had previously written for Eric and Ernie on radio. It worked out very well. Frank and I wrote six episodes for HW and HD continued to write the storylines for 'CORONATION STREET'. By now HD had bought a car, and advertised for someone to help him - a kind of major domo who would take some of the weight off his wife. After interviewing several applicants he chose Jack Ripley. Jack was marvellous. He did everything for HD. He used to arrive at HD's house about 9am, get him out of bed, dress him and give him his breakfast. He was also proficient at shorthand, and as HD and I sat in his study, thinking of ideas and funny lines Jack would take it all down in shorthand. He was a wonderful, caring person and a godsend to HD and his wife. Things were going quite well - we were both earning a bit of money and HD and Edith moved to a modern detached bungalow in Whitefield. We still saw each other as often as we could. One day HD told me that HVK had asked him to see if I would be interested in writing some scripts for 'CORONATION STREET', Would I? Would I just? All in all, I wrote 60 episodes over the following two years, in addition to writing another two series of 'HERE'S HARRY'. I enjoyed my time working on 'THE STREET' as it was more familiarly called. They were such a great bunch of characters and entirely believable. One of my favourite actresses was the late Patricia Phoenix - Elsie Tanner to you. Yes I know that in these PC days one is not supposed to say actresses. Everyone today is referred to as an actor, no matter what sex they are - but I prefer to call ladies who act, actresses. Apart from anything else it's a much prettier word. But back to Pat Phoenix. She was a natural actress with a fiery temper and flaming red hair who instantly became the Street's sex symbol. On one occasion she revealed that, of all the writers', she preferred my scripts as she found them easy to learn. The reason for that was simple. I had the gift of writing Northern dialect with Northern speech rhythms. Pat was a larger than life character with a heart of gold who lived for a time in a modern bungalow in Sale, Cheshire. When she threw parties, which she often did, she hired the chef from Manchester's 5 star Midland hotel, to do the catering. At that time she was living with Bill Nadin, an ex-taxi driver from Blackpool. I remember one famous occasion. It happened to be Bill's birthday, but when they both awoke she made no reference to the fact. She didn't wish him a Happy Birthday and there was no Birthday card or present from her. Naturally Bill concluded that she had forgotten.

That evening, when Pat returned from the studios, she told Bill that she'd had a particularly stressful day and was going upstairs to lie down for a while. After she had been gone for about ten minutes she called downstairs and asked Bill to come up. He was still unhappy at her forgetting his birthday, but went up to see what she wanted. When he entered the bedroom, he got quite a shock. Pat was lying start naked on the bed, with a huge cellophane bow tied round her waste and a huge card with the words 'HAPPY BIRTHDAY BILL' written on it. What a woman! There will never be another like her!

Another wonderful character was the late Arthur Lowe, who played Leonard Swindley. There was a comic edge to his acting performance which made his portrayal of Swindley into a truly memorable character. He played him as a fussy, pompous know-all. He made Swindley into a very funny person so much so, that in 1965 Granada took him out of the 'STREET' and put him into his own situation comedy 'PARDON THE EXPRESSION' still as Leonard Swindley as the assistant manager of a department store, which ran for 36 episodes before he was head hunted by the BBC to play Captain Mainwaring in 'DAD'S ARMY' which he played exactly as he played Leonard Swindley. In fact he was one of those rare actors whose performances were never far away from his own persona. I remember one occasion when we were both standing outside the entrance to Granada, sheltering from a heavy downpour waiting for it to stop before going for a drink in the New Theatre Inn. I knew that Arthur had a Rolls Bentley in Granada's car park.

'Why don't you get the Bentley and drive to the pub Arthur?' He gave me a piercing look, shook his head and pursed his lips.

'No - no dear boy. No sense in both of us getting wet!'

They were happy days, and I was happy too. At last I was

doing well as a writer and starting to earn good money. However, things were not so good on the home front. Because I was still relatively inexperienced as a writer, I made mistakes and I spent many nights in an office at the BBC re-writing various scenes which HW was not entirely happy with - that, plus the fact that I had to be present at rehearsals, and still had to find time to write scripts for the 'STREET' meant that Pat and I rarely met. Pat was convinced that I was having several affairs with various girls who worked in television. To be perfectly honest I had neither the time nor the energy. Looking back now, I should have devoted more time and energy on being a better husband. But like many others before me, I was so obsessed with show business that I put it before my marriage. Gradually, Pat and I grew further and further apart. But there was never another woman. I spent more time with HD, HW, and John Ammonds than I did with my wife.

HD and I still met at least once a week. We had acquired an agent in London - Kenneth Ewing. He came up to see us and after a pleasant lunch agreed to represent us.

I carried on writing for Harry Worth and Harry continued doing the storylines for CORONATION STREET. One day I got a call from Geoff Lawrence, a BBC radio producer. He asked about Harry and whether he and I would be interested in writing a radio series for an up and coming comedian Peter Goodwright. The format was to do some short sketches interspersed by musical interludes from the Northern Dance Orchestra whose conductor was Alyn Ainsworth. I went to see Harry that evening and we decided that it would a pleasant change from what we were doing at the moment and we agreed to write it. It turned out to be very enjoyable. Peter was a funny man and also an excellent impressionist and we used his talents to good effect in the series. After we'd written one series, which was well received by the listeners, Geoff was ready to commission us to do a second series, but at a meeting with Geoff and Peter, Harry and I suggested that we do a situation comedy series based on the adventures of two Manchester lads who shared a flat. We brought in a neighbour, a dim witted character played by the excellent and very funny Joe Gladwin who was to find fame later as the voice in the Hovis commercials ... 'It were all green fields when I were a lad' ... And then as Nora Batty's husband in 'LAST OF THE SUMMER WINE'. To play Peter's flatmate, Geoff suggested a young and relatively unknown actor, Anton Rodgers. It was his first major acting role. Later he was to star in his own television series 'FRESH FIELDS' and appear in many films. The series was a lot of laughs and fun to write. We all enjoyed it immensely, the listening figures were good and the BBC pleased. I like to think it may have been the forerunner to the TV success 'THE LIKELY LADS'. A further series for Peter and Anton was planned, but unfortunately never happened. We just couldn't get everybody together at the same time. When Anton was free, Peter was away doing either a summer season or pantomime, and when Peter was free, Anton was touring in a play. However, Geoff decided he wanted to do a series starring Ray Alan, a brilliant ventriloquist, who had created a very funny character Lord Charles as his dummy, and he asked Harry and I to write it. The series was a success and led to us writing a couple of radio comedies for Billy Dainty. Billy was one of the most underrated comedians I have known. He had a wonderful sense of humour and from the moment we met, we became firm friends, so much so that he became very much a part of my life as you will read later.

So Harry and I were writing in partnership again and enjoying it. Little did we know that we would soon be writing with each other again every day which resulted in my having to give up writing for Harry Worth and Harry to step down from his involvement with 'CORONATION STREET'.

It all started with a phone call from our London agent. He told us that he had heard that Associated Television, a major broadcaster which transmitted programmes in the London area at weekends and was owned by Lew Grade, were looking for ideas for comedy programmes and advised us to phone their Head of Entertainment, Alan Tarrant. I must tell you that the Grades had a virtual monopoly as far as entertainment was concerned. They were three brothers, born in Russia whose name was Winogradski. They emigrated to England in the 20's and changed their names. Lew and Leslie Winogradski became Lew and Leslie Grade, and Bernard Winogradski became Bernard Delfont. In the 30's they all went into the entertainment business and in less than a decade they were virtually running it. Lew owned the franchise of the newly formed broadcaster, Associated Television, Bernard owned several Variety theatres including the London Palladium and Leslie had the largest theatrical agency in Britain which acted for most of Britain's major entertainers. What a marvellous set-up! But back to the plot. I phoned Alan Tarrant and asked him about Harry and I writing a sitcom for ATV. To our surprise, he said that he would be travelling down to London the following day, and could we meet him for lunch at Rules Restaurant. For those of you who are unfamiliar with Rules, it's one of the oldest restaurants in London and was established in 1798 where it became the popular haunt for writers including Charles Dickens, William Makepeace Thackeray, John Galsworthy, H G Wells, Grahame Green and many more. It was also the Prince of Wales' favourite restaurant, where he would wine and dine his mistress, the beautiful Lily Langtry. Jack drove us down to London, helped Harry from the car and I pushed him into the restaurant while Jack went to park the car. The Maitre D welcomed us and showed us to a corner table at which Alan was already seated and drinking a large Beefeaters gin - his favourite tipple. He asked us if we would like a bottle of champagne which we declined.

'No thanks Alan, I said, 'Have you seen the price on the wine list?' Alan shrugged, 'Don't worry - Lew is paying. Order what you want.'

We settled for a couple of large Bell's. Harry asked Alan what sort of comedy sitcom he was looking for, but Alan told us to forget the sitcom. He revealed that ATV had two major stars under contract and were looking for an idea for them. Naturally we wanted to know who these two stars were but Alan wouldn't reveal their identities until we had eaten.

'If I tell you now, you'll be too busy trying to think of an idea to enjoy one of the best meals you will ever have.'

Harry and I had no option but to agree. After all, we had been raised on fish and chips or sausage and mash. Who were we to argue with an obvious gourmet? Alan insisted on ordering for us. For the first course we had potted

Morecambe Bay shrimps, accompanied by a bottle of Chablis, followed by Steak and Kidney pudding with mashed potatoes accompanied by a bottle of Beaujolais Village. For desert, we had Bread and Butter pudding and Custard. By this time, Harry and I were feeling decidedly woozy so we passed on the cheese and port, and coffee and cognac. Alan, however ordered three large ports with his cheese. I protested.

'They're not for you and Harry he said. They're for me. When I present the bill to ATV accounts department they will assume that we each had a large port.'

He did the same with the cognacs, ordering three larges ones. I couldn't help but admire his capacity for alcohol. If I had drank as much as he did, I would be on the floor! Eventually, he revealed the names of the two stars for whom Lew Grade wanted us to find and idea. They were Sid James and Peggy Mount, both very experienced and talented comedy performers. Harry and I were delighted. Sid and Peggy were both big stars - South African born Sid, arrived in London on Christmas Day 1946 without a job and a wife who was pregnant. Just over a week after he arrived he landed a small part in a film. From then on, he was never out of work. With his deep throaty laugh he quickly became admired and loved by audiences. He was the only actor I have ever worked with who could turn an ordinary line into a brilliant one by adding that cheeky laugh at the end. He quickly rose to fame both on radio and television playing the straight man to Tony Hancock as well as being the principal actor in the 'CARRY ON' series.

Peggy Mount had burst on the show business scene by her storming performance as an aggressive and overbearing wife in 'SAILOR BEWARE' a stage farce, and a television sitcom 'THE LARKINS'. I assured Alan that we had already had an idea which we felt would suit both Sid and Peggy. Alan asked what it was but I said that we needed to work on it but we would phone him the next day. We excused ourselves telling him we wanted to get on road before the traffic built up. We thanked him for the meal and I pushed Harry out of the restaurant, where Jack was waiting with the car. Jack and I got Harry in the car, and off we set. Harry turned to me.

'What's this brilliant idea we've got for Sid and Peggy then?'

'I haven't got it yet. I just said that to Alan to keep him happy. I thought we might come up with an idea on the drive back to Manchester. We've got over four hours.'

And believe it or not, by the time we got to Manchester we had actually got an idea. Firstly, we decided that Sid and Peggy shouldn't be married. If they were we would lose a valuable strand of comedy, that of Sid chatting up the fair sex and being a lecherous character. If he was married he would lose a lot of sympathy with female viewers. We also dismissed them being brother and sister. We needed to find a situation to take advantage of Sid's small screen character as a randy con man. We finally hit on a situation in which Sid was a chauffeur/handyman to an elderly Colonel whose housekeeper had just left due to Sid chatting her up. He advertises for a new housekeeper and Peggy arrives and gets the job. In addition to this we added an earthy gardener. We rang Alan the following morning and he liked the set up. He cast the talented John Le Mesurier as the Colonel and the equally talented Keith Marsh to play the gardener. Harry and I decided to call it 'GEORGE AND THE DRAGON' with Sid playing George and Peggy the dragon of a housekeeper. We got down to writing a pilot script and posted it to Alan. He phoned us a couple of days later to tell us he liked the script and that, subject to the pilot being successful, would be commissioning a series of seven episodes on one condition. Could we give him a guarantee that we could write the series, given our current writing commitments to the BBC and Granada? If not they would need to bring in other writers. Harry and I had to make a decision. The script fee that ATV were offering was more than the BBC were paying for Harry Worth, and much more than Harry was receiving from Granada. So we decided to accept the contract from ATV. We told Alan of our decision. He was happy, Lew Grade was happy and we were happy ...

Pat, however, was far from happy. She still regarded my ambition to succeed as a comedy writer as a threat to our marriage. She was still convinced that I was having affairs and we argued constantly. Eventually, we agreed to separate, and I left the marital home and moved into a rented bungalow not far from Manchester Airport. I was being selfish. Perhaps I should give up writing and concentrate more on my marriage. Not only that, I was a Catholic, albeit a lapsed one. But even as I thought it, I knew I couldn't forsake what I had dreamt of for so many years. I spoke to my Dad about the situation, and whilst he was sympathetic he said he couldn't advise me either way. It was a decision that only I could make. I even spoke to a priest who told me that a separation was permitted by the Catholic Church, but divorce and re-marriage wasn't. At the time, re-marriage was the last thing I had on my mind. Surprisingly, all the emotional upset and guilt feelings didn't affect my work. When I was writing with Harry, everything else went out of my head.

The pilot of 'GEORGE AND THE DRAGON' went well, and ATV commissioned us to write the series. Part of the show's success was due to the casting and the continuing battle of wits between Sid and Peggy. It all worked beautifully. No sooner had we finished recording that first series than ATV commissioned a second. We were both still involved with the 'STREET' and one day we were called in to a meeting with Derek Granger who was then producing the 'STREET'. When we arrived, he was in another meeting and Harry and I decided to ring Kenneth Ewing our agent in London to tell him how well 'GEORGE AND THE DRAGON' had done and that ATV were planning a second series. He was pleased and why not? He was on ten percent! He mentioned to me that the BBC were planning a series of six half hours and were looking for ideas. I said we'd try and think of something. After I hung up I told Harry about the BBC looking for ideas and we put on our thinking caps. I thought back to when my father was working at Hector Powe. There was an Irish alteration hand also working there who had a fondness for Irish whisky and I wondered if there was an idea about a couple of tailors in partnership, one a trouser maker and the other a coat maker. Each needed the other to exist. Then I had the idea of the coat maker being Jewish and the trouser maker an Irish Catholic. Harry thought it was a terrific idea so I phoned our agent again to tell him. He also thought it was a good idea and suggested that we phone the BBC and run it past Frank Muir, who was then the joint Head of Comedy with Denis Norden. So I phoned the BBC and asked to be put through to Frank Muir. His languid voice came on the line.

'Yes. Hello Vince.'

'Hi Frank - Harry and I have got a great idea for a situation comedy'.

'Yes'

'It's about two tailors who work together - a Jewish coat maker and an Irish Catholic trouser maker.'

'Yes'

'Well that's if Frank. What do you think?'

'I'm afraid I need much more than that. Why don't you send me an outline? About six pages will do - oh, and a character breakdown.'

I bit my tongue to stop myself from swearing at him and hung up. Harry looked at me questioningly.

'Call's himself a Head of Comedy. Huh! He can't see a good comedy when it's staring him in the face.'

The trouble was, of course that Harry and I could see so many possibilities in the idea. The clash of personalities - not to mention the clash of religions. I picked up the phone again.

'Who are you ringing now?' asked Harry.

'Lloyd Shirley.'

Lloyd was the Head of Drama at ABC Television who I'd met a couple of times. He was a cheerful, bearded Canadian and was producing a series of plays with the title of 'ARMCHAIR THEATRE'. I told the switchboard my name and asked to be put through to Lloyd.

'Hi - Vince. How are you doing?'

'Fine. Listen Lloyd, Harry and I have got a marvellous idea for an 'ARMCHAIR THEATRE'.

'Great - what is it?'

I said the same words that I'd said to Frank Muir.

'It's about two tailors who work together - a Jewish coat maker and an Irish Catholic trouser maker.'

There was a pause, and then Lloyd said. 'Terrific - I'll buy it.'

For a moment I was dumbstruck. 'Don't you want to see an outline or something?'

'Listen Vince, do you boys want to write it or not?'

'Of course we do.'

'Okay. I'll ring contracts department and get them to sort out a fee with your agent.'

'Yes but ...'

'End of conversation. You're wasting valuable writing time.'

With that, he hung up. And that was how 'NEVER MIND THE QUALITY FEEL THE WIDTH' was born - as a 60 minute 'ARMCHAIR THEATRE'. It was directed by Patrick Dromgoole and they cast Frank Finlay as the Irishman and John Bluthal as the Jewish coat maker. Lots of people who were intrigued by the title asked me where it came from and I explained that one of the salesmen at Hector Powe had a habit of saying it to prospective customers as he showed them a length of cloth. It really meant nothing but it impressed the customers.

Because Harry Driver and I were still committed to Harry Worth and Coronation Street, we hadn't time to attend the rehearsals of 'NEVER MIND THE QUALITY, FEEL THE WIDTH' which took place at ABC's studios in Teddington, but Lloyd Shirley phoned me and said it was going well. The show was recorded and a transmission date fixed. When it went out I watched it with Harry and Edith and a few friends. When it ended they all applauded saying how funny it was. Harry and I looked at each other in dismay. We both realised that it should have been a situation comedy and as such it would have run for several series. And we'd wasted it on one 60 minute 'ARMCHAIR THEATRE'. The following day I spent all morning on the telephone. First I rang Alan Tarrant at ATV and asked him whether he'd watched our 'ARMCHAIR THEATRE'. He hadn't but a couple of other directors had seen it and gave him a glowing report. Encouraged by this I suggested to Alan that perhaps ATV might like us to write a sitcom series based on the idea. His reply wasn't good news. He explained that we would be wasting our time as he didn't think that Lew Grade would ever agree to do a Jewish comedy, that could be seen as making fun of Jews.

I then rang Philip Jones who was the Controller of Light Entertainment for ABC Television who transmitted on weekends in the North-West and Midlands area. He had actually seen the 'ARMCHAIR THEATRE' and thought that it was excellent. I then suggested that the format could make a successful long-running sitcom series. Phillip agreed, but then revealed that the Drama Department and the Entertainment Department were two separate entities and rarely took ideas from each other. I tried to persuade him otherwise but he wouldn't budge. So there we were - Harry and I - with a potential hit on our hands and nobody wanting to buy it. We felt that we couldn't offer it to the BBC, as there was no way the BBC would take a project which started on commercial television. As for Granada, they weren't doing any new sitcoms. We were so depressed that we went to the pub to drown our sorrows. Unfortunately, far from drowning them, the more we drank the more depressed we became. We weaved our way back to Harry's house and sat staring at each other.

'There's a bottle of sherry in the kitchen' Harry said.

'Good,' I replied, went in search of it, and brought the bottle into the lounge. I poured us out two glasses into one of which I put a straw for Harry - we had recently discovered that this was the best method for Harry to drink as it saved all the bother of getting up and holding a glass for him to drink from.

'Cheers', I said, sitting on the settee.

'The same to you' said Harry.

As I took a mouthful, I suddenly remembered that I didn't really like sherry, but by then it was too late - my glass was nearly empty. I can just remember having another glass and asking Harry if he wanted another. He replied with a loud snore. I had one more drink then fell asleep myself. And that was how Edith found us when she got back from work a couple of hours later. I awoke the following morning still on the settee. There was no sign of Harry. Edith entered the room and glared at me.

'Good morning,' I croaked.

'I'm not speaking to you,' she said.

'You've just spoken to me' I pointed out.

'Don't you ever let my husband drink so much again.'

'I'm sorry Edith.'

'It's all right you saying you're sorry. I had to get him out of bed four times during the night. Twice for him to spend a penny and twice for him to be sick!'

With that, she left to take her son Stephen to nursery school. I went to Harry's bedroom but he was fast asleep, so I crept out and went back to my rented bungalow. The next day we rang Granada's Controller of Entertainment to try and sell him the idea of doing a series based on the 'ARMCHAIR THEATRE' but without much success so we bowed to the inevitable and tried to think of another idea for a sitcom series. By this time Harry had been provided with a hands free telephone system which enabled him to make and receive calls.

The next day, was incredible and will remain in my memory forever. It began with a telephone call from a Stuart Allen from the BBC. We had known Stuart for some time as he was John Ammonds assistant at the start of the HARRY WORTH series. He eventually a became producer/director in his own right and moved to the BBC Television Centre in London. We wondered why he was ringing and he revealed that he had watched the 'ARMCHAIR THEATRE' and liked it. Not only that but had persuaded Frank Muir into letting him do a series of six thirty minute episodes on BBC2. We could hardly believe it but he told me that Frank Muir had seen the show and liked it. Naturally, Harry and I were overjoyed. A sitcom series transmitted on BBC2 would be automatically repeated on BBC1 which meant that we would get two script fees. We rang our agent, told him the news and asked him if ABC Television had any copyright claim on the idea. He told us that the copyright remained with us. He did say though that, as a matter of courtesy, we should phone Lloyd Shirley to acquaint him of the facts.

We immediately phoned Lloyd who congratulated us and confirmed that there was no copyright problem. We were just debating whether we should go and have a celebratory drink at the pub when the phone range. It was Alan Tarrant.

'Great news lads' he said. 'I've just come out of a meeting with Lew Grade and he wants you to write six episodes of 'NEVER MIND THE QUALITY, FEEL THE WIDTH' for ATV, and he wants Topol to play the Jewish tailor.'

In case you don't know, Topol became famous for his role of Tevye the milkman in the movie version of the successful award winning Broadway play 'FIDDLER ON THE ROOF.'

I stood there without speaking, the phone glued to my ear. Harry was equally dumbstruck. Alan's voice shook me out of my silence.

'Hello - Vince - Harry - are you there?'

'Did you hear what I just said? Lew wants you and Harry to write 'NEVER MIND THE QUALITY, FEEL THE WIDTH' with Topol as the Jewish tailor.'

'Yes Alan we heard you,' I replied - still in shock.

'Well don't you think that's marvellous?'

'Er - yes.' I stammered. 'Marvellous.'

'Vince - have you been drinking?'

'Not yet, but I will be later.'

'You don't seem very excited at the news.'

Harry spoke, 'Yes we are Alan - very excited. It's great news.'

'Listen, boys, I've got to go now. I'm expecting a call from Topol's agent. I'll phone you later.'

Harry and I looked at each other.

'What are we going to do Harry?'

'Don't ask me.'

'If we do it for ATV with Topol in it, it's bound to be a big success.'

'Yes but on the other hand, we practically said 'yes' to Stuart Allen. And remember, it'll be shown on BBC2 and repeated on BBC1. What are we going to do?'

We both thought about it, then Harry said, 'I know what we should do.'

I felt a sense of relief. 'Good old Harry,' I thought. It'll be his decision not mine.

'Okay Harry - tell me. What should we do?

'Phone our agent and let him decide.'

I had to admit that it was a good idea. After all, that's what agents are for. Let him earn his ten percent. I picked up the phone and dialled his number. When he came on the line we told him what had happened.

He told us to ignore the offer from ATV and went on to explain that BBC2 was regarded as an up market channel.

He reminded us of the repeat fees, and that the BBC had been the first broadcaster to offer us a series. We agreed with him and hung up. We decided to phone Frank Muir and confirm that we would be writing the series for BBC2 but before I could pick up the phone, it rang. I picked up the receiver. The operator asked if I was Vince Powell. I said I was and she said 'I have Philip Jones for you.' Harry operated his hands free apparatus. Then Philip came on the line.

'Hello Vince.'

'Hi Philip - Harry's on the line too.'

His next words gave me the shock of my life.

'Vince - Harry - I will match any offer that either the BBC or ATV make to you for the rights of 'NEVER MIND THE QUALITY, FEEL THE WIDTH' I almost dropped the phone.

'What did you say Philip?'

'I've just been speaking to Lloyd Shirley and your agent. I understand that you've had offers from both the BBC and ATV for the rights to 'NEVER MIND THE QUALITY, FEEL THE WIDTH'

'Well - er - we - er - '

Philip carried on speaking.

'I am prepared to better any script fee you have been offered by the BBC or ATV to write the series for us here at ABC. You won't regret it.'

I decided to stall for time.

'Ah - yes - well - Philip. Nothing is definite you understand and we need to discuss the situation.'

'Of course you do. Talk it over with Harry. Talk to your agent. Take you time. And ring me tomorrow.'

'Yes - yes - I will Philip.'

'Just remember this Vince. It was ABC television which had enough faith in your idea to commission it - albeit the Drama department. I've just watched a playback of 'ARMCHAIR THEATRE' and it would make a very funny situation comedy series.'

'Yes Philip.'

'Well, I'll leave you now to discuss it with Harry and your agent. Don't forget to ring me in the morning with your decision. I'll be in the office from ten o'clock. Cheerio Vince - cheerio Harry.'

I put down the phone and looked at Harry who was shaking his head in disbelief. Now I have to tell you that, on the surface it might seem as if we were in a strong position. We had three major broadcasters, each willing to commission a series of 'NEVER MIND THE QUALITY, FEEL THE WIDTH'

It was a 'win, win' situation. We couldn't lose. But wait a minute. If you think about it carefully, whichever broadcaster with whom we decided to do the series, meant that we would be turning down two other major broadcasters, who may not take too kindly at our decision. What should we do for the best? We decided to phone our agent again. I got through to Kenneth and put him in the picture. He listened carefully to what I said and told me that he needed to think about it and would phone us back in half an hour. It was the longest half hour in our lives. Finally the phone rang. It was Kenneth.

'Vince, Harry, I've thought about the situation and talked it over with my colleagues. And this is what we all agree you should do. Our unanimous opinion is that you should do the series with BBC2. After all, they made their offer before either ATV or ABC came into the picture. ATV are only interested in the possibility of signing a big name like Topol. And as for ABC they're not really interested - they're just jumping on the band wagon. It's our considered opinion that you should write it for the BBC.'

With that he hung up. I turned to Harry.

'What do you think Harry?'

He shrugged 'I think we should stick with the BBC like Kenneth said.'

'I suppose you're right. But I'm worried about how ATV and ABC will react when we tell them. They're not going to like it. It could affect our relationship with them in the future.'

Harry shrugged again. 'Too bad. As they say. 'That's show business!'

Suddenly I had a brainwave.

'Hang on Harry. I've just had a great idea. What if I drive down to London at the crack of dawn tomorrow, call on Alan

Tarrant at ATV, Frank Muir at the BBC Television Centre, Shepherds Bush and Philip Jones at ABC in Teddington and tell each of them, face to face about our decision. What do you think?'

'I think you're barmy.'

'I may be, but at least I can explain to each of them in person why we've decided to do 'NEVER MIND THE QUALITY, FEEL THE WIDTH' with BBC2.'

'It's up to you Vince.'

'Right.' I picked up the phone and dialled Kenneth's number. His secretary answered and told me I'd just missed him. He'd gone out for lunch. I gave her the message and she promised to give it to him as soon as he got back. I left Harry, and drove back to my bungalow, stopping on the way to fill the car with petrol. In those days the M1 hadn't been completed and it could take about four hours or more to drive to London from Manchester so I decided to have an early night. My alarm clock woke me at 4:00am. I had a quick cup of coffee then set off. Luckily, there wasn't much traffic at that time in the morning so I was able to stop at a transport café for a plate of eggs, bacon and sausage. I had checked on the road map and had decided that the ATV studios at Borehamwood would be my first port of call, then the BBC Television Centre at Shepherd's Bush and finally ABC's Television Studios at Teddington. I got to ATV's studios about 8:45am, parked the car and made my way up to Alan's office to wait for him. At about 9:15am the door opened and Alan came in. If he was surprised to see me, he didn't show it.

'Good morning Vince,' he said cheerfully.

I cleared my throat and bowled right in.

'Alan - I'm afraid Harry and I have made a bit of a cock up about 'NEVER MIND THE QUALITY, FEEL THE WIDTH'

I told him the whole story from the beginning. To my amazement, when I got to the end he burst out laughing.

'You needn't have driven all this way, just to tell me that. A phone call would have done.'

I explained about me wanting to give the facts to him, Frank Muir and Philip Jones personally and hoped that Lew Grade wouldn't be too upset.'

'Don't worry about Lew,' he said. 'Your agent was right about one thing. Lew is more interested in getting Topol under contract than acquiring the rights to 'NEVER MIND THE QUALITY, FEEL THE WIDTH' If you and Harry can come up with another idea for Topol, Lew will be very happy.'

'Well, as a matter of fact Alan, I thought of an idea while I was driving down here. It's about a synagogue in the East End. Their Rabbi has decided to retire and live in Israel. A new Rabbi is appointed - it's Topol, whose unorthodox attitudes lead to conflict between him and the Chief Rabbi, and several important members of his congregation.'

'I like it' said Alan. 'As a matter of fact I think it's a better idea for Topol than 'NEVER MIND THE QUALITY, FEEL THE WIDTH'. Why don't you and Harry send me a brief outline and I'll run it past Lew.'

I breathed a sigh of relief. So far so good. One down - two to go.

'Come on Vince,' said Alan, 'let's go to the canteen, I'll buy you a cup of coffee.'

I declined his offer explaining that I was on my way to see Frank Muir and Philip Jones. He wished me the best of luck and I left. On the way out, I decided to phone Harry and Kenneth to put them in the picture. They were both pleased at the idea for Topol and Kenneth reiterated that in his opinion Philip Jones wasn't really interested in 'NEVER MIND THE QUALITY, FEEL THE WIDTH'. I drove to the BBC Television Centre, parked the car and went in reception where I asked to see Frank Muir. I was told that nobody in the Light Entertainment department was available. A casting director had died the week before and the entire Light Entertainment personnel were attending his funeral and wouldn't be back until later that afternoon.

'Ah well' I thought, 'it's not imperative that I speak to Frank today. We're doing it for BBC2. I'll phone him tomorrow.'

I returned to my car and drove to Teddington Studios. After parking, I presented myself to a receptionist and gave her my name.

'Ah Mr Powell,' she said, 'Mr Jones is expecting you. Go through the double doors on your left and take the lift to the second floor where Mr Jones' secretary will meet you.'

I followed her instructions but when I stepped out of the lift, I was surprised to be greeted by Philip himself.

'Vince', he said, shaking my hand. 'Welcome to Teddington luvvie. Come into my office.'

I followed him into his office overlooking the River Thames where he invited me to sit down. He looked at me with a worried frown on his face.

'Howard Thomas is not happy,' he said mournfully.

Howard Thomas was the Managing Director of ABC Television. I wasn't quite sure why Howard Thomas wasn't happy but some sixth sense warned me it had something to do with 'NEVER MIND THE QUALITY, FEEL THE WIDTH'. Philip went on.

'You see luvvie, the new television franchises are due to be announced at the end of the week. ABC has applied for the extremely profitable weekday London area Monday to Friday, but it's not going to look very good to the Independent Television Authority if a project which was first developed and shown by ABC Television were to be snapped up by a rival independent contractor or, even worse, the BBC. It could seriously jeopardize our application.'

As he spoke I was becoming more and more concerned. What had originally started out as a simple public relations exercise was now taking on a totally different aspect. I could see what Philip meant. If Harry and I kept to our original decision to accept the offer to go with BBC2, it could result in ABC not only losing it's franchise application for the coveted London Weekday area, and being forced to continue with it's current and less profitable area or even not being awarded any new franchise at all and virtually going out of business altogether. My mind was spinning - what should I do? I asked Philip if I could phone Harry.

Philip rose from his chair. 'Sit here at my desk Vince. I'm going to the canteen for a cup of coffee. There's the phone. Ring Harry - ring your agent.' He moved to a cabinet and opened the doors to reveal a well stocked cocktail cabinet.

'Help yourself to a drink. Have whatever you like. I'll be back in about half an hour, then we'll have lunch - I've booked a table in the Executive Restaurant.' He made as if to go then stopped. 'Obviously we would like you and Harry to do the series here with ABC - but whatever decision you come to, I hope that you and Harry will bear us in mind for any new ideas you may have in the future. I'll be back in half an hour.'

With that, be left. My mind was in a turmoil. I went to the cocktail cabinet and poured myself a large scotch which I knocked back in one swift gulp. I went back to sit in Philip's chair and tried to think. I liked Philip. We'd only met a couple of times, but he was always very pleasant. He'd built a highly experienced and talented team of technicians around him, and was well thought of in the industry. He ran his Light Entertainment department smoothly and efficiently yet with an air of friendliness. What a difference between his attitude and Frank Muir's reaction when I first talked to him about 'NEVER MIND THE QUALITY, FEEL THE WIDTH'. What was I to do? I rose, went to the cocktail cabinet and poured myself another scotch, then sat down, picked up the phone and asked to be put through to Lloyd Shirley office. I told him about our situation and Lloyd said that Philip was the best Controller of Light Entertainment he'd every worked with and that we wouldn't regret doing 'NEVER MIND THE QUALITY, FEEL THE WIDTH' for ABC. I thanked him and dialled Harry's number. I told him about my conversation with Philip and what Lloyd had said and that I had a gut feeling that, no matter what our agent said, we should go with ABC. Harry said, 'It's up to you Vince - whatever you decide I'll go along with.'

We chatted a bit more then I rang off. I was still confused, and torn between the BBC's offer and the knowledge that the series would be repeated on BBC1. We would be getting two script fees for each script. Could we afford to turn their offer down? Just then Philip came back. Before I could speak, he held up a hand.

'Before you say anything Vince, let's wait until after we've had lunch. We might as well enjoy a good meal without worrying about your decision.'

'I agree Philip, but we'll both enjoy lunch so much more if a I tell you that Harry and I have agreed to write 'NEVER MIND THE QUALITY, FEEL THE WIDTH' for ABC.'

The relief on Philip's face was palpable. He shook my hand.

'You won't regret it luvvie' he said. He opened a bottle of champagne, and we drank to the success of the series. During the lunch I learnt a little of Philip's background. He had started his career as a radio producer with Radio Luxembourg and was so successful that he was head hunted by Tyne-Tees Television to develop their Light Entertainment department. This he did so well that his output caught the eye of Brian Tesler, then the Controller of ABC Television. Brian was so impressed with Philip's ability and expertise in producing a weekly schedule of popular and enjoyable light entertainment programmes with a limited budget that he offered Philip the job as Director of Light Entertainment at ABC Television.

Philip accepted and became the most successful Light Entertainment Head of British Television with many of his shows appearing in the top ten television ratings. After a good lunch, I left Teddington in an alcoholic haze and drove back Manchester. Luckily, I managed to avoid being stopped by the police and by the time I arrived home I was relatively sober.

It was quite late when I got to Manchester, but I called at Harry's house and gave him a blow by blow account of my meeting with Philip Jones. We then phoned Stuart Allen and told him of our decision. He was disappointed naturally, but he understood and said he would tell Frank Muir. We also rang our agent but he was out of the office so we left a message with his secretary. I then went home and to bed.

The following morning, I was awakened by the telephone ringing. I looked at my watch. It was almost ten thirty.

'Hello', I muttered into the phone.

'Vince, it's Stuart. I hope I haven't woken you up.'

'No', I lied.

'I told Frank, about your decision with 'NEVER MIND THE QUALITY'. He wasn't best pleased'.

'What did he say?'

'He said that you and Harry would never work for the BBC ever again!'

'You're joking aren't you?'

'I'm not - I'm deadly serious Vince. I've never seen him so

139

angry.'

For a moment I was shattered. My worst fears had been realised. We had alienated the Head of Comedy at the BBC, the largest television company in the country - larger than all the commercial companies added together. Not only that but we had gone against the advice of our London agent who might decide not to represent us in the future. I said a hurried goodbye to Stuart, and put down the telephone.

I lay there feeling so depressed. Then I had a thought. What was I worried about? We may have upset the BBC but we'd already decided against doing the series with them. We still had the idea for Topol for ATV and 'NEVER MIND THE QUALITY' for ABC. The telephone rang - it was Harry. We both started to speak at once. I shouted him down and told him about Frank Muir's statement that we would never work for the BBC again.

'I know all about that.' said Harry. 'Stuart rang me before he rang you.'

'Cheer up Harry. We've still got ATV and ABC.'

'Correction. We've only got ABC.'

'What do you mean?'

'Alan Tarrant phoned me earlier. Topol's not available. He's gone to America to appear in a Broadway play.'

'Well, we could get somebody else. There's plenty of good Jewish actors around.'

'Exactly what I said to Alan. He said that Lew Grade was dead set on Topol and that now he wasn't available, Lew had gone off the idea.'

'Never mind Harry. I've got a feeling that 'NEVER MIND THE QUALITY' will turn out to be a big success on ABC.'

'I hope so. But what if ABC's franchise application is turned down? You know what they say - trouble always comes in threes.'

'Don't be so pessimistic. Everything's going to work out just fine. I can feel it in my water. I'll come round to your house later and we'll talk about it.'

I drove round to Harry's and reminded him of Philip's offer for us to think of a comedy series for ABC, even if they did lose their franchise application. We spoke to our agent, who told us that we were mad to have spurned the BBC.

However, he agreed to still represent us. We still had the second series of 'GEORGE AND THE DRAGON' to write for ATV, and we spent the next couple of days thinking of suitable plots.   Weekend came and went. On Monday morning, the new television franchises were announced by the Independent Television Authority. To our delight ABC was awarded the new franchise for the London Weekday area and ordered to merge with REDIFFUSION TELEVISION. A new company was formed under the title of THAMES TELEVISION to commence broadcasting the following year. Philip, true to his word, commissioned Harry and I to write the first series of 'NEVER MIND THE QUALITY'. Ronnie Baxter, one of ABC's experienced directors was chosen by Philip to produce and direct the series. Ronnie was a Mancunian, an accomplished musician and a Manchester United supporter - we couldn't have wished for a better director. There was just one snag. Frank Finlay, the actor who played the Irish tailor in the ARMCHAIR THEATRE didn't want to do a situation comedy series. He felt that there was a danger of him becoming typecast and he would rather be known as a drama actor not a comedy actor. We went to see Iris Frederick; ABC's casting director whose daughter Lynne later married Peter Sellers. Iris suggested Joe Lynch, an Irish actor she had seen in a comedy play at Dublin's Abbey Theatre. We arranged to meet him at Teddington Studios and sent him one of the scenes from the ARMCHAIR THEATRE production so that he could read for us. When he arrived we discovered that not only had he learned his part but that he'd learned everybody else's part. He was excellent and he got the job immediately. It was a terrific series and we had lots of fun doing it. The other regular characters were Cyril Shaps as Rabbi Levy and Eamon Kelly as Father Ryan. Both John Bluthal and Joe Lynch kept us laughing with Jewish and Irish jokes. This was before political correctness was ever thought of. We introduced a Jewish character called Lewtas who had a workshop on the same premises and dealt in belts, buckles, buttons and trimmings. The part was played by Bernard Spear, who started his career on radio as a comedian, under the name of Loopy Lou and he eventually rose to fame on the West End stage as Sancho Panza in the musical 'MAN OF LA MANCHA.' He also appeared in many films and television plays, among them Jack Rosenthal's award winning play 'BAR MITZVAH BOY.' There were many amusing incidents during the series, but one in particular which comes to mind concerns the Jewish dietary laws. As you are probably aware, Jews are forbidden to eat pork. In this episode, the Irish character Patrick has bought two pies for lunch, a pork pie for him and a chicken pie for his Jewish partner, Manny. In the script, while Patrick is out, Rabbi Levy calls to try on his new suit. Manny offers him a cup of lemon tea and a piece of chicken pie, but inadvertently gives him a piece of pork pie which the Rabbi eats. The mistake is discovered when Patrick returns and the Rabbi is shocked. Patrick tries to console him by saying. 'Don't worry Rabbi. There's not much pork in those pies - mostly gristle,' to which the Rabbi replies, 'I'm not so much worried about eating pork - what's more worrying is that I liked it!' We thought it was a funny piece of business but to our surprise, Cyril Shaps refused to do it. We reassured him that he wouldn't really be eating a pork pie - we'd make sure it was a kosher meat pie, but he was adamant. 'I'm playing a Rabbi - many of our viewers are Jewish and will be offended if they see me eating pork. Even if it isn't pork, they may think it is.' It looked as if we would have to cut that routine out, when up spoke Bernard Spear. 'I'll do it. It may not be as effective as a Rabbi eating a pork pie, but it's still funny.' So we switched the lines and it stayed in. During the run of the series, the director, Ronnie Baxter, cast several well known stars in supporting roles.

Rupert Davies, who had starred in 'MAIGRET', a series of BBC dramas with Rupert as George Simenon's pipe smoking detective, appeared in one episode playing a Bishop. Dennis Price, star of countless British films and that resoundingly successful 60's TV series 'THE WORLD OF WOOSTER' created by P G Wodehouse was tempted out of semi-retirement in the Channel Isles to appear as a Saville Row salesman.

The truth was, the series was so popular with the acting fraternity that many actors were delighted to appear - during its four year run several well known names took part in single episodes, among them, David Kossof (appearing as himself), Dick Bentley, England and Chelsea footballer Peter Osgood, Yootha Joyce, David Kelly and Fred Emney, a particular favourite of mine. Fred was a larger than life character, both as an actor and a person. A huge, rotund figure of a man with his ever present large cigar and monocle. And a sharp, cutting-edge wit. I remember when we were rehearsing the episode in which he appeared, there was a moment in the script when Fred had the last line in one scene in an office and the first line in the following scene in a shop.

Ronnie took him to one side. 'Fred, after delivering your line in this scene, can you nip round the back of the office set so that you're ready to say your line in the shop?'

Fred paused, took a puff at his cigar, adjusted his monocle, looked at Ronnie and said 'You'll send a car will you?'

On another occasion when he was appearing in 'WHEN WE ARE MARRIED' a north country play written by J.B. Priestley, the company had been informed by the theatre manager that, the great man would attend the final dress rehearsal. Priestley duly arrived, took a seat on the front row of the empty theatre and sat through the performance. Naturally, the cast expected him to say a few words of encouragement to them at the end, but Priestley got up and started to make his way out without speaking. Fred stepped towards the footlights and called out after him.

'If you didn't like it, you shouldn't have bloody well written it!'

I can honestly say that the series of 'NEVER MIND THE QUALITY' ... Was the one which I enjoyed the most. It was a joy to write, the actors were brilliant and the television audiences enjoyed it - even the television critics liked! One episode was singled out by The World Council of Churches to be shown at their annual synod as an example of ecumenicism

But the moment I will never forget was during one Sunday Mass at Saint Clare's, my parish church. In the series, I had referred to Father Ryan's church as Saint Clare's, and in the middle of the Mass just as the parish priest, Father Ignatious, was reading the parish notices, he happened to spot me sitting in the congregation. He nodded to me and announced.

'Saint Clares's is a very famous church which has been seen on television in that wonderful series, 'NEVER MIND THE QUALITY, FEEL THE WIDTH'. It's written by Vince Powell who is one of our parishioners, and you can see it on your television every Friday night at half past seven on ITV. Vince is here at Mass, sitting over there.'

He pointed to where I was sitting, and all heads turned to look at me.

Father Ignatious called out from the altar.

'Stand up Vince so we can all see you.'

Reluctantly, I got to my feet, when, to my surprise the whole congregation started to applaud. How's that for a plug?

At that time, I had met and was going out with an extremely pretty girl who worked at Granada. Her name was Judi and she worked as a secretary to Cecil Bernstein, who, with his brother Sidney owned Granada Television. By now, I had virtually no contact with Pat although I still had moments of guilt brought about by my strict Catholic upbringing.

Work was good and our writing careers seemed to be going well. We were writing a situation comedy series for two major broadcasters, ATV and Thames and life was very pleasant. However, we grew tired of having to travel from Manchester to London and back twice a week. So we decided that we would move to London. After a few weeks, during which Edith house hunted for Harry and I, we found suitable premises and prepared to move. Edith had found a bungalow for her, Harry and their son Stephen in Weybridge whilst I bought a flat in nearby Kingston Upon Thames. There was only one drawback, Harry's assistant, Jack, was reluctant to move from Manchester but agreed to stay on until a suitable replacement had been found. An ad was placed in the local newspapers and after interviewing several applicants, Harry eventually engaged Eric Tilley, who was a trained male nurse working at a local hospital and was ideal for the position. An agreement was made whereby Eric worked Monday to Friday and Jack would work week-ends.

We had finished writing the second series of 'GEORGE AND THE DRAGON' which had gone exceptionally well and were waiting to hear from Philip Jones about a further series of 'NEVER MIND THE QUALITY ...' We drove over to ATV at Elstree for a meeting with Shaun O'Riordan who had replaced Alan Tarrant as Head of Comedy, Alan having decided to go freelance. We were sitting in the bar - where else? - We got most of our best ideas sitting in a bar - when I suddenly had a brainwave. I turned to Harry. I've had a thought. What about doing a comedy series about the Home Guard?' For those of you who may be too young to remember, the Home Guard was a voluntary organisation of elderly British Citizens formed during World War 2, with the objective of repelling any German soldiers foolish enough to invade our country. We kicked the idea around over a couple of large scotches and agreed it had the makings of a very funny series. Shaun arrived, gratefully accepted our offer of a large gin and tonic and we told him about the Home Guard idea. He liked it but told us that Lew Grade was considering doing another series of 'GEORGE AND THE DRAGON' and we would have to wait. A few weeks later, David Croft and Jimmy Perry presented a pilot script to the BBC called 'DAD'S ARMY' - all about the Home Guard! Sometimes that's the way the cookie crumbles.

However, we weren't down in the dumps for long. We got a call from Philip Jones to meet him in his office at the newly formed Thames Television where he not only made us an offer we couldn't refuse, but which led to our most productive and prolific period in our careers - a period which is now referred to as The Golden Age Of Comedy.

Chapter Eight
IT WAS A VERY GOOD YEAR

Eric Tilley picked me up in Harry's Jaguar for our appointment with Philip Jones. Harry was sitting in the passenger seat. We drove through Hampton Court, across the bridge spanning the Thames on which, even at this early hour pleasure launches were sailing, packed with tourists. We drove past the imposing Hampton Court Palace, steeped in history and through Bushey Park, one of the Royal Parks with herds of deer roaming freely around - a very pleasant change from the usual monotonous drive from Manchester. I thought to myself 'I think I'm going to like living down South.' We eventually arrived at the studios, unloaded Harry and got him into his wheelchair. Eric went to park the car and I pushed Harry to Philip's office where he was waiting for us with a pot of freshly brewed coffee.

'Come in lads. Help yourself to coffee. There's a plate of biscuits if you want any.'

I poured the coffee for Harry and I. Philip sat back and smiled at us.

'I expect you're both wondering why I've sent for you.'

'You're going to tell us that it's all been a terrible mistake. Brian Tesler hates 'NEVER MIND THE QUALITY ...' and is cancelling the series.' joked Harry.

Philip grinned. 'On the contrary Harry, Brian loves it and we'll be doing some more. But, strangely enough Brian and I were discussing the pair of you yesterday. In a few weeks' time, the new company, Thames Television will be officially launched on air and we would like to commission you both to write the first new situation comedy to go out under the Thames banner. How do you feel about that?'

Naturally, Harry and I were delighted and flattered. I was

just about to reply when Philip held up his hand. 'I haven't finished yet. Brian and I would like to give you a two year contract to write a minimum of thirteen situation comedies a year for Thames Television.'

Harry and I were speechless. Thirteen shows a year for two years, meant security - well, at least for two years. We shook hands with Philip and suggested we celebrate with a drink. Philip nodded. 'I thought you might say that so I took the precaution of making sure I had a bottle of Bells in my cocktail cabinet.'

We drank to our forthcoming contract and Philip said that he looked forward to it resulting in a long and successful association between Thames and Harry and I. He invited us to stay for lunch but we said we'd rather get back home and start thinking about an idea for the new series. I finished my drink rose and sat down again. 'However Philip, we might just force ourselves to have another scotch before we leave!'

If it occurs to you that we did quite a bit of drinking in those days, you would be right. It was customary - one could say - obligatory, particularly in show business! Come to think of it, I don't think it's changed much.

We got back to Harry's and told Edith the good news about our contract. To celebrate the occasion Harry, who had been thinking of changing his car, went to his local car showrooms to trade his Jaguar in for a newer model, while I decided to call in to a couple of estate agents to look for a house nearer to Harry and Edith in Weybridge and put my flat in Kingston Upon Thames on the market. To everyone's surprise Harry returned home to announce that he had exchanged his Jaguar, not for another Jaguar, but for a second hand pale blue Rolls Royce Corniche! It was ideal for Harry - the doors were much wider, making it far easier for him to be lifted in and out, and it had a much larger boot which could accommodate the wheelchair and, at a pinch, the portable hoist. All right, it was expensive but we all felt that Harry deserved a bit of luxury, considering what he'd gone through.

As for my house hunting, in less than a week, I had found a four bedroom house about a ten minute walk from Harry's bungalow and sold my flat at a good profit. I rang Judi. Our affair had gone from strength to strength, and I begged her to come and live with me. I needn't have begged - she was just as keen as I was. There was only one small snag. How would her parents and my father react to us living together? It may seem odd to those of you, living in this more modern society, but over thirty years ago, it was still considered sinful for a man and woman to live together as husband and wife without being married. In those days, the term 'partner' invariably referred to a business associate. However, we decided to go ahead and pretend that Judi would be staying with Harry and Edith. I am sure her parents and my Dad weren't fooled for a minute but they were content to live with our subterfuge. It did cause some problems later on, when either Judi's parents or my Dad came down to visit and we had to hurriedly remove any traces of Judi living with me and transfer them to Harry and Edith's. We needn't have bothered as on one occasion when Dad came down for the weekend, he asked which bedroom did Judi and I sleep in!

Harry and I spent several long days trying to think of a suitable idea for the launch of Thames Television, without success. We went through every conceivable situation and subject but none of them seemed to inspire us. Then, when the right idea finally came it was a pure accident. Harry's accountant in those days was Joel Barnett, who later became the labour Member of Parliament for Heywood in the 1964 General Election, rose to become the Chief Secretary to the Treasury and was eventually knighted to become Lord Barnett. I can claim a modest part in his success, as I helped to canvass support for him in 1964. Anyway, Joel arranged for Harry to visit the Stranger's Gallery during a sitting of the House. I didn't go, and when Harry returned he told me all about it. He said the MP's called each other names and behaved like overgrown schoolchildren. . . 'Honestly Vince, it was like a comedy show!' I suddenly had one of those rare flashes of inspiration.

'That's it Harry - that's the idea we've been looking for.'

Harry frowned. 'What do you mean?'

'We'll do a sitcom set in the House of Commons. Two MP's - one labour, one conservative who share an office in Westminster. We'll call it 'THE BEST OF ENEMIES'. What do you think?'

Harry immediately saw the comic possibilities in the idea. We phoned Philip Jones and told him about our idea. Philip was enthusiastic and told us to go ahead and write seven episodes which would be transmitted as the first situation comedy series from the newly formed company. He told us that the series would be produced and directed by Malcolm Morris; one of ABC's experienced light entertainment directors and arranged for us all to meet at the studios the following week. Harry and I drafted out a plot for the first episode and discussed who we thought would be ideal to play the 2 MP's. We decided that the Conservative MP should be middle-aged, pompous and bit of a windbag who's been an MP for several years and that the Labour MP should be a young, newly elected member, keen and conscientious but rather naïve. On researching the subject, we discovered that the House of Commons employed several messengers whose duties included looking after the member's wants and needs. We both agreed that Deryck Guyler would be perfect. Deryck was one of Britain's most experienced and funniest character actors. Those of you, who are old enough, may recall that he created the Liverpudlian character Frisby Dyke. He later went on to appear in 'PLEASE SIR' as Potter, the caretaker and Corky the policeman in the Eric Sykes series. The following week, we met the producer, Malcolm Morris at the studios. Not only did he approve of our choice of Deryck Guyler, he had a choice of his own to play the part of the Conservative MP - Robert Coote, an experienced and talented actor who had recently been part of the original London cast of 'MY FAIR LADY' playing Colonel Pickering to Rex Harrison's Professor Higgins. We both looked at Malcolm.

'You won't get him Malcolm,' I said, 'he's a big star in films and the theatre. He'll never agree to do a television situation comedy.'

Malcolm grinned, 'I wouldn't bet on it Vince. I've already spoken to his agent who said that Robert likes the idea and would love to do it providing he likes the script. So it's all down to you boys. You'd better make sure the script is a good one.'

Harry chipped in, 'Don't worry Malcolm. It'll be the best script we've ever written. He'll love it.'

We were then joined by Iris Fredericks, the casting director for Thames Television who suggested a young but talented actor called Tim Barrett to play the part of the Labour MP. As none of us were familiar with his work, we arranged for him to come in to the studios and audition for the part. That concluded our business for the day so we did what we normally do. We retired to the bar!

For the next few days, Harry and I worked hard on the script. We sent copies to Philip and Malcolm and waited. For a writer, this is one of the worst periods in his or her life. Every writer expects an immediate response. If one is not forthcoming, the doubts set in. 'They don't like it.' 'They hate it.' We read through the script again and again to see where we may have gone wrong and find ways in which we could improve it.

Finally, the call came.

'Hello luvvies.'

It was Philip.

'Are you free tomorrow?'

We said we were.

'Good. Ten o'clock in my office then. Okay? See you both tomorrow. Bye.'

He hung up. Harry and I looked at each other.

'What do you think Harry? Did he like it?'

Harry shrugged. 'I haven't a clue.'

'He didn't say he didn't like it.'

'That's true. We'll just have to wait until tomorrow.'

And that's what we did. We waited in an agony of uncertainty and doubt. If only television executives and producers realised how writers are riddled with insecurities, perhaps they might endeavour to reply to submissions a little quicker. As I write this autobiography in the 21st century, I am still awaiting acknowledgements and responses from several major broadcasters to whom I submitted scripts several weeks ago.

Anyway, Harry and I duly presented ourselves at Teddington Studios the following day. We were a little late in arriving and were directed, not to Philips office, but to a meeting room. Seated at a long table were Philip Jones, Malcolm Morris, Iris Frederick, Robert Coote, Tim Barrett and Deryck Guyler. I pushed Harry in and introductions were made by Philip. Malcolm rose but before he could speak, Robert Coote cut in.

'I would like to say a huge thank you to Vince and Harry for writing a funny and original script which I look forward to performing.' Both Deryck Guyler and Tim Barrett echoed Roberts comments, and then Malcolm suggested we all have a cup of coffee before settling down to read the script. Harry and I had deliberately written the first script to involve only the three main characters, apart from a couple of minor supporting characters who weren't needed at the first read through. We all finished our coffee and started to read the script, with Malcolm reading the stage directions and the minor parts. It went very well and at the end, Philip rose, announced that he was pleased and confident that the series would be a success then returned to his office. Usually, at this stage there would be discussions between the director and the cast as to whether any of the lines needed to be re-written, and the writers sent away to re-write them. Fortunately, everyone seemed to be happy with the script, so Harry and I left to go back home and start to write the next script. The schedule was that there would be an official read through the following week, then after a week's rehearsal the first script would be recorded at the weekend after which, the series would be recorded weekly. This meant that Harry and I would have to virtually write and deliver a script a week for the next six weeks - a formidable, but not impossible task.

During the rehearsals of the first script, Harry and I spent every day, thinking of plots for the rest of the series and by the time the recording day arrived, we had six funny plots worked out. All we had to do was write them!

On the day of the recording, Harry, Edith, Judi and I went to the studios and watched the show being recorded, not from the studio floor as one would expect, but on a TV monitor in Philip's office. Philip preferred to watch recordings exactly as the viewers would eventually see them and without the distractions of cameras and a studio audience. Philip opened his drinks cabinet, it couldn't have gone better. Nobody forgot their lines or fell over the furniture and the audience laughed in all the right places. Harry and I looked at each other and grinned. Philip congratulated us and we all made our way to the Executive Restaurant where Philip had laid on a cold buffet and drinks for the cast and crew who joined us shortly. It was congratulations all round.

'Great show Vince.'

'Well done Tim'

'Terrific script Harry'

'Super performance Robert love.'

'Beautifully shot Malcolm.'

Etcetera, etcetera, etcetera.

It's moments like this that all show business people live for. It makes all those hours of rehearsing - of learning and remembering the lines - worth while.

Harry and I drank it all in. For us too, it was a reward for all our hard work in writing the script and in particular for Harry who had overcome his own personal tragedy. We enjoyed our moment of success and went our separate ways home looking forward to writing the rest of the series.

However, as we were shortly to discover, Fate had other ideas!

For the next few days we worked on the script for the next episode. We finished it and sent if off to Philip to await his reactions. Harry's wife, Edith was going back up to Manchester the next day to stay with and visit old friends which would leave Harry and I free to concentrate on writing. We couldn't wait to start. Then it happened. We couldn't understand it why we hadn't heard back from Philip with his reactions to the second script. We rang his office but his line was engaged so we left a message for him to ring us. About ten minutes later, the phone rang. I snatched up the receiver.

'Hello Philip.'

But it wasn't Philip. It was Deryck Guyler.

'Hello Vince. Bad news isn't it?'

'Is it?'

'About the series.'

I was mystified. 'What about the series?'

Having a rattling good time

Mother and child

Father and son

An alter boy with a taste for communion wine

Above 1: With Mam and Dad in Blackpool

Above 2: My cousin and I outside my house in Miles Platting. I'm in the driving seat

HMS MAURITIUS at anchor in Villefranche.
The start of my love affair with the Cote d'Azur

Dad and step-mother outside
our house in Blackley

Land ahoy! I'm the one with the cap on.

My first wife Pat and
I on Blackpool pier

An early publicity photo during
my stand up comedy days

Left: A boozy night ashore in Trieste. Sitting next to me is my old friend Jock

Fellow writer Frank
Roscoe and I trying
to think of something
funny in our office
at the BBC Manchester

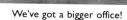

We've got a bigger office!

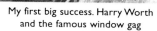

My first big success. Harry Worth
and the famous window gag

Harry Worth, Writer/Producer
Mike Craig and I, fooling about

With two Manchester United legends, Sir Bobby
Charlton & Pat Crerand at a Man United function

Jim Bowie ex-thames senior
manager of entertainment in
our office overlooking the river

George Evan and I preparing our creative
writing correspondence course

Miss Ten Percent, my
former agent Jill Foster

Sign on the dotted line ... my second wife Judi

Wedding guests from left to right - Jimmy
Jewel, the bride's father, actor Joe Lynch.

Rehearsing 'Proper Charlie' with Jack Smethurst
for BBC Radio Manchester

I think we've both had enough Dad

Three generations. Me, my son Dominic and my Dad

Mike and Bernie Winters
rehearsing with producer/director
Stuart Allen at Thames Television

Left: Recording 'Proper Charlie' with,
from left to right, John Jardine, David
Ross and Jack Smethurst. The series
was produced by Mike Craig.

Below: Jimmy Jewel and Ben Warris
at the height of their career

Producer/director Ronnie Baxter with
actor John Bluthal filming an episode
of 'Never Mind the Quality, Feel the
Width' on location in Whitechapel

One of Harry Driver's and my successes

Harry and I in his garden
before our Paris trip

Harry and I outside the Sacre Coeur in Paris

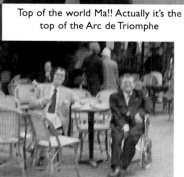

Top of the world Ma!! Actually it's the
top of the Arc de Triomphe

Aperitifs on the champs-Elysees

Harry and Eric on the Bateau Mouche, Paris

Running repairs to writer
Carla Lane's dress.

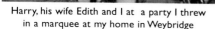

Harry, his wife Edith and I at a party I threw
in a marquee at my home in Weybridge

A serious discussion with
Billy Dainty, Harry Worth
and Harry Driver

Cabaret time with Victoria Spinetti, Billy Dainty,
Harry Worth and Ernie Wise

My Gold Rolls Bentley

Too funny for words. Billy, Harry and Ernie

My favourite view. Villefranche Sur Mer
on the French Riviera

Julliet Grimm my co-deviser
of 'Give us a Clue'

My second Rolls Royce, with my step-sister
Ivy and her partner, Tommy

Africa Plage in Beaulieu Sur Mer. From left to
right - Moi, Julliet and Tony Parker. Kneeling,
Producer/director Nick Hurran

Phillip Jones and I in what Phillip
described as 'Cloud Cuckoo Land'

Tony Parker and I discussing a script

Restaurant Chez Bidou in Villefranche

Play it again Bidou

Bidou and I

Charlie trying to sell me cheap
carpet on Africa Plage

Tony Parker and I, in the Hotel Versailles

Outside David Niven's house
on Cap-Ferrat

'Betty's Bar' in Villefranche. Betty's
the one with the blonde hair

On Lyle McCabe's yacht in Middle Harbour,
Sydney. Jack Smethurst can be seen in
the mirror taking the photo

Outside the Jermyn Street theatre
before my one man show

The cast of 'Mind your Language'

Jack and I 'Down Under'

Owzat!

The location I found to shoot
'*Love Thy Neighbour*' in Australia

Panning for gold at Sovereign Hill

Michael Mills and his children on board his yacht

Dominic and I in Sydney

With Anna Karen, Rudolph Walker and Jack Smethurst at a book launch. In the background are Lionel Blair and John Inman

Michael Mills making a point to John Bluthal on location in Sydney

With Su Pollard in her dressing room

Writer Charlie Stamp, brother of actor Terence Stamp, and I at a party at his house in Oz

Across a crowded room. My first meeting with my future wife Geraldine

Put me among the girls. From left to right - Geraldine, Tricia Colgan, me, Elyse (Kerry Jewel's wife) and Valerie Leon (Michael's wife)

A familiar sight Down Under

Geraldine on our honeymoon in the
South of France - Where else?

My favourite picture of my children, Anthony,
Dominic and Genevieve

A family meal in Beaulieu

Ready when you are Cilla

On location in Miami for a Cilla Black special

Left: Miami Beach - Take One

Cilla and Bobby in Miami. No he's
not spending a penny!

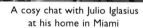

A cosy chat with Julio Iglasius
at his home in Miami

Two antique, antique dealers, Sir Donald
Sinden and Windsor Davies in 'Never the Twain'

With the Bee Gees in
their Miami studio

The 'Blind Date' team in the studio

Allan Randall and I onstage
rehearsing the George Formby
play 'Turned Out Nice Again'

On location in Lourdes with camera operator Caren
Moy and sound engineer John Marchbank during the
filming of 'A Journey to Lourdes'

The Grotto in Lourdes where Bernette
had her vision of the Virgin Mary

Cruising with - from left to right -
Lorraine Chase, Jean Fergusson, Danny La Rue
and Johnny Casson. In front - on his knees as
usual is Mike Craig

Presenting Cardinal Hume with a
cheque for £700 with Jim Bowie and
Moira Lister

Tom O'Connor, Mike Craig and I relaxing
in some port or other

John Ammonds and I at Gatwick
setting out on another trip to Beaulieu

Petit Dejeuner

Left: With Remy, owner of La Mere
Germaine in Villefranche

Below: At the Auberge de La
Madone with - from left to right:
Marie-Jose, Moi, Carrine, her
husband Christian, owner
hotel/restaurant and John Ammonds

The beach at Juanles Pins the
morning after I scattered Jimmy
Jewel's ashes. If you look closely
at the bottom middle of the
picture, you can make out a silver
trail going up to the debris near the
top. That's Jimmy Jewel.

I'm in there somewhere!

'Haven't you heard? It's been shelved.'

'You're joking.'

'No. I've just had a call from my agent. Thames Television are on strike.'

I couldn't believe what I was hearing. 'Look, Deryck - I'll ring you back. Okay?' I put the phone down and it immediately rang. This time it was Philip.

'Bad news Luvvie.'

I motioned for Harry to get on the line with me. 'Go on Philip, but I think I know what you're going to say. I've just had Deryck Guyler on the line.'

We listened as Philip explained. Due to certain problems with the recent merger between ABC and Rediffusion regarding pay structure and working practices, negotiations have been ongoing between the Thames Management and the union ACTT - Association of Cinematograph, Television and Allied Technicians. The union general secretary, Alan Sapper, had called his members out on strike as from the coming weekend which means that the second recording of 'BEST OF ENEMIES' was cancelled. As the strike looked likely to go on for some time, this had led to a revision of recording schedules and our series had been shelved until such time as the strike had been resolved which, knowing the usual intransigence of the left wing union, could be several weeks. Philip said how sorry he was. 'We will be going ahead with the series later this year, but as far as you and Harry are concerned, the pressure's off for the moment. Look, I have to go - I'm late for a meeting. Ring me in a couple of days and we'll fix up a lunch.'

He hung up. Harry and I looked at each other. After the euphoria of the previous week, we both felt deflated. Harry swore several times - something which he didn't normally do - and I sought solace in a very large scotch, before going back home to tell Judi the news. She was out shopping so I tried phoning Dad to tell him but he wasn't in either. I sat there, feeling very sorry for myself when the phone rang. It was Harry.

'Look, I've spoken to Edith. She's in Manchester visiting friends, but I don't fancy staying in tonight with just Eric for company. How do you feel about us all going out for a nosh?

We could go to that authentic French restaurant in the village that you like - Chez Antoine's. You reckon the food's good, and let's face it, it's probably the nearest I'll ever get to France. What do you say?'

'Leave it to me Harry. I'll book a table for four. See you there about half past seven.'

I immediately felt better. I really enjoyed Chez Antoines. Antoine, the patron, was from Marseilles and quite a character. I remember on one occasion when I was dining there, two elderly ladies had ordered Entrecote Bordelaise. One of the ladies complained about the Bordelaise sauce.

'You've put too much gravy on the steak' she said.

Antoine stared at her. 'Gravy?' he said, 'gravy?' He then took her plate and that of her companion away. 'You are not fit to eat in my restaurant.' He advised them to go to the nearby fish and chip shop and ushered them out. On another occasion when I was eating there, the restaurant was only half full, when in came half a dozen bikers, all in their black leather jackets, pierced ears and tattoos. Antoine took one look at them and said, 'I'm sorry. We are full M'sieu'. One of the bikers glanced round at the empty tables.

'What about these?'

'They are all reserved.'

The bikers left and the empty tables remained empty for the rest of the night. What a character. But I liked him. I phoned and booked a table, but I kept thinking of something Harry had said. 'It's probably the nearest I'll ever get to France.' An idea was beginning to take shape in my mind.

Later that day, I spent a couple of hours on the phone making certain arrangements. Judi returned home and I told her the news about the series being shelved. She was as disappointed as I was, but she pointed out that as it was only being postponed it wasn't the end of the world. I told her that we would be going out to eat at Chez Antoine's later with Harry and Eric which pleased her. Eric picked us up just after seven. He would be driving which meant that Judi and I could have a few drinks. When we got to the restaurant, we got Harry seated then I took Eric aside and asked him if Harry had a valid passport. Eric said that Harry still had a 10 year passport from before he caught polio. I asked him if he, too, had a passport and he said he had. He looked at me puzzled, and asked me what this was all about.

I said, 'Eric, tomorrow morning, I want you to get Harry up at six o'clock and have him shaved, showered, dressed and ready to leave the house by seven.'

He looked confused. 'What's going on?'

'I'll tell you what's going on', I said. 'We're going to Paris. The three of us. Me, you and Harry.'

I went on to explain. Harry's remark about being in Chez Antoine's was the nearest he would ever get to France had set me thinking. I phoned a friend of mine who ran a travel agency and he arranged flights and a hotel in Paris for the three of us. We would be staying for five days and would be back before Edith returned from Manchester. I hadn't mentioned it to her and wanted it to be a surprise for Harry, so I told Eric that we would tell Harry that we were meeting an American TV producer at Heathrow who was flying in that morning from Los Angeles. Judi would drive the three of us to the airport. Eric was both surprised and delighted and immediately agreed to enter into the conspiracy. We returned to the restaurant and had a superb meal. The conversation was all about France with Harry saying he'd love to go there one day and Eric, Judi and I trying hard not to give our secret away.

The following morning, Judi drove me to Harry's. Harry was up, dressed and waiting, complaining the fact that we had to travel to the airport in my Jaguar rather than his Roller. We couldn't tell him the real reason was that we wouldn't be returning and we didn't want his Rolls to be in the airport car park for five days. We got Harry into the car and Eric managed to load a suitcase in the boot without Harry seeing, and then set off for the airport. At Heathrow, we got Harry into his wheelchair and Eric pushed him inside the arrivals concourse. We arranged to meet in one of the many coffee outlets. I made the excuse that I would accompany Judi to park the car, and then I collected Harry's suitcase and mine then ran to the check-in desk in departures. I had our three passports, flight tickets and a letter from Harry's doctor confirming that he was fit to fly. I checked in and received our boarding cards then made my way to the coffee shop where Harry and Eric were waiting. Never one to pass up an opportunity to ham it up, I faced Harry, struck a dramatic pose and in a passable imitation of Eamonn Andrews, (the celebrated TV announcer) said, 'Harry Driver. You think you're here at London Airport to meet an American TV producer but you're not. Today, this is your flight!' With a flourish I produced the tickets and waved them in front of his eyes.

It took a minute for it to sink in. He stared at the tickets, looked at Eric who was broadly grinning then at me.

'You pair of conniving sods!'

I told him of how I'd planned this and that even Edith didn't know about it. We phoned her there and then to tell her. When she'd got over the shock she wished us a safe journey and told us to enjoy ourselves.

Harry was still in a daze when we pushed him through Passport Control and into the departure lounge. We made for the nearest bar and sat there with Harry happily taking everything in until our flight was called. There was a surprise waiting for me when we boarded the plane. Thanks to the friendly travel agent, we had been upgraded to First Class. We put Harry in the window seat, and accepted a complimentary glass of champagne, courtesy of BEA (British European Airways) as BA was called then. Harry was thrilled and excited as the engines revved up, backed out of departure gate and took our place on the runway. It was all a new and still quite unbelievable adventure for him. We took off. Harry gazed out of the window at the ground as the plane rose in the air. I pointed out Windsor Castle to him and in no time we were high in the air and crossing the English coast with the English Channel below us. Harry couldn't take his eyes from the window. He was seeing views that he never thought he would ever see given his physical condition. We were served a snack and another glass of champagne,

Then, all too soon we began our descent to Paris. We were booked in to stay at the Hotel Montalembert on the left bank and took a taxi from the airport. On the journey, Harry took in the unfamiliar sights and sounds of Paris. I'd never seen him so animated and happy. I made the decision that, during our stay we'd take Harry to as many of the major tourist attractions as we could, no matter how difficult. And that's what we did. After checking in at the hotel and making sure that our rooms were okay, we set off. We crossed the River Seine by the Pont Royal, then through the Tuileries and the Place de la Concorde and up the Champs Elysees. We stopped at one of Paris's celebrated eating and watering holes, Fouquet's for a drink and a sandwich, then carried on until we came to the Arc de Triomphe, taking it in turns to push Harry. We crossed the Place de l'Etoile and spent a few minutes looking at the Tomb of the Unknown Soldier. I looked at Eric.

'Are you ready for this Eric?' I asked.

'Ready for what?'

I pointed to the top of the Arc de Triomphe. 'You see those people right at the top there?' He nodded. 'Well, us three are going to join them!'

Harry and Eric suddenly looked nervous as we made our way to a doorway in the arch. Ahead of us stretching upwards was a narrow flight of stairs.

'Right - come on Eric.'

Eric grabbed hold of the wheelchair handles, and I took hold of the front wheels. We manhandled Harry up that flight of stairs with its twists and turns until we reached the top. When we burst through, into the sunlight there was a gasp of amazement from the crowd of tourists who saw us, then to our surprise many of them burst into applause. It was worth our effort to see Harry's face as he sat on top of the Arc de Triomphe gazing at the incredible view of the Champs Elysee far below. However, we had to get back down again, and it wasn't any easier going down than it had been on the way up. But we made it, and started the journey back to our hotel. It was now late afternoon, and I suggested that we stop for a meal. I could see that all the excitement had tired Harry out, and pushing him in the wheelchair hadn't done much for Eric and I either. So we ate at a restaurant on the Rue de Rivoli before crossing the Pont Royal and arriving back at our hotel. What a day - we were all shattered. And each day was the same. We did as much as we could in the time that we had. We rose early, had our coffee and croissants, and were out of the hotel by nine o'clock. One day we took a taxi to the

Eiffel Tower and stood in a long queue of tourists waiting for one of the lifts, to the relief of Harry and Eric who, for one awful moment thought we might have to walk to the top. As we were waiting, a uniformed attendant spotted us, and then beckoned us to the head of the queue. 'Priorite pour l'homme infirme' he cried. I paid for the tickets, he ushered us into the lift and up we went. Another day we visited the Sacre Coeur and ate in the Place du Tertre. We blessed ourselves with holy water and lit candles in Notre Dame. We sat on the Quai Du Louvre sharing a baguette, ripe camembert and a bottle of red wine. The day before we left we had lunch on a Bateaux Mouche, one of the several river boats on which you could eat a four course meal and enjoy a vintage bottle of wine for a couple of hours while sailing up and down through Paris. It was a wonderful five days. The following day, we flew home to reality.

The technicians strike was still on at Thames and there was no sign of it ending. We spoke to Philip who said he had no news of when, if ever, 'BEST OF ENEMIES' would be rescheduled but that we should carry on writing the other scripts and we would be paid for them.

On the strength of that, I decided to buy a new car. I went to the showrooms where Harry had bought his Rolls Corniche and half an hour later was the proud owner of a second hand gold Rolls Bentley. It had everything - automatic, power steering, central locking, cruise control and a sun roof. Harry thought it as a bit flash and maybe it was but I loved it.

The following week, we got a phone call from the BBC who wanted to know if Harry and I would like to write an episode to be included in their next series of Comedy Playhouse. Comedy Playhouse was a brilliant idea in which several comedy writers were invited to write a half hour situation comedy from which, hopefully, one of more could be developed into a series. From the first series, transmitted in 1961, one such episode was made into one of the BBC's most successful comedy series - 'STEPTOE AND SON'. Later comedy series spawned by Comedy Playhouse included 'MEET THE WIFE', 'TILL DEATH US DO PART' and 'ALL GAS AND GAITERS'.

Harry and I thought back to Frank Muir and his declaration that Vince Powell and Harry Driver would never write for the BBC again. But Frank had now left the BBC and was the Head of Entertainment for London Weekend Television, a new company which had been awarded the franchise for weekends in the London area. Evidently the BBC had forgiven us for the 'NEVER MIND THE QUALITY' episode. When we heard that our old friend, Stuart Allen would produce and direct the COMEDY PLAYHOUSE, Harry and I agreed to write an episode and came up with an idea about industrial relations in a small engineering company, in which a militant, left wing shop steward had called a strike. The idea had echoes of the current ongoing situation at Thames and we called it 'SPANNER IN THE WORKS'. Stuart liked the script and told us that he had cast Jimmy Jewel to play the shop steward. We immediately objected. We knew that Jimmy, years before, had been part of the successful double act with his partner Ben Warris, but since the act had split up, he had not done much work. We felt that the part of the shop steward should be played by an experienced comedy actor rather than a Music Hall comedian. But Stuart disagreed with us and insisted that Jimmy should play the part. We were so disappointed that we even discussed not going to the recording of the show. However, we did and to our surprise and astonishment, Jimmy was marvellous. He gave a very professional performance and we apologised profusely to Stuart. We congratulated Jimmy who insisted on taking us all out for dinner. From that day, Jimmy and his family became firm friends of Harry and me, and was eventually to play a large part in both our lives.

Although Stuart, Harry and I were pleased with 'SPANNER IN THE WORKS', the BBC weren't enthusiastic and it never became a series. So Harry and I concentrated on writing the rest of the scripts for 'BEST OF ENEMIES'. We heard from Philip that the strike could be over in a couple of days but there was still no news of any more recording dates. We rang Shaun O'Riordan at ATV to ask if there was any news about a new series of 'GEORGE AND THE DRAGON' but Shaun said that Lew Grade hadn't made his mind up yet.

We spent most of our days between sitting in Harry's garden, or watching Wimbledon and the test matches on television with the occasional pub lunch at one of the local hostelries. To tell the truth, we were bored. We wanted to sit and write - to feel those creative juices flowing as we sat and bounced comic ideas and lines back and forth. We wrote well together, Harry and I. We both had the same northern sense of humour. There were times when we would be sitting in Harry's study, when we would both simultaneously come out with the same comic line. It was almost like telepathy, the way we thought along the same lines.

After several days of doing nothing, apart from getting on each other's nerves to say nothing of Edith's and Judi's we decided that we would endeavour to think of a brand new idea for a situation comedy and try and sell it to a broadcaster. We agreed that it should be a northern comedy set in the Lancashire industrial town of Colne, and that it should be about a brother and sister, who lived with their elderly widower father, who owned a pickle factory, the daughter acted as housekeeper to her father, and the son, a womaniser, acted as the factory manager. Both disliked each other but even more so, hated the smell of pickles and vinegar which they had to endure every day. Their father passed away in his sleep, and left everything - the house and the factory to his two children, equally, between them - on one condition. They had to live in the house and continue to run the pickle factory. Those readers of a mature age may have an inkling of what the eventual series became. We liked the idea as it had plenty of comic possibilities. We worked out the plot and were just about to start to write the script when the phone rang. It was from Granada Television. Peter Eckersley who had been a writer, then producer of CORONATION STREET, and was now their Head of Entertainment, had taken a leaf out of the BBC's book and was mounting a series of six half hour comedies, under the title of COMEDY SHOWCASE. Would Harry and I be interested in writing one? What an amazing coincidence! We accepted his offer, wrote the script about the pickle factory which we called 'THICKER THEN WATER' and sent it off to him. We suggested Jimmy Jewel to play the brother and

Hylda Baker to play his sister. Hylda was a variety artiste and had a very funny act with a stooge who never spoke during the entire act. The stooge was a man, dressed as a woman and went under the name of Cynthia. The part was played by several different performers - at one time by Matthew Kelly. I had seen Hylda play a straight role in an earlier episode of 'Z-CARS' a police series set in Liverpool and was impressed by her acting ability. Peter liked the script, but not the title, which he changed to 'NEAREST AND DEAREST', and made plans to record a pilot programme at Granada studios up in Manchester.

The following day we heard from Philip. The strike was over and he was trying to arrange new dates to record the rest of the 'BEST OF ENEMIES'. He asked us to come in and see him as he had some other news for us. Eric drove us to Teddington, and I pushed Harry up to Philip's office. As usual he had coffee waiting. He asked me to sit down and his secretary poured us each a cup. As she left, Philip told her not to put any calls through for the next half hour. Harry and I looked at each other. Something serious was going on. Philip spoke.

'I hear you've written a Comedy Playhouse for the BBC, and a sitcom for Granada.' Harry and I reacted. 'Don't look so surprised luvvies. News gets around in this business.'

I began to worry that we might have jeopardised our contract with Thames and explained that the BBC were not going to develop our Comedy Playhouse idea into a series and that the sitcom for Granada for Granada was just a one-off.

Philip nodded, 'Yes I was aware of that Vince. I spoke to Brian Tesler last night about the situation.'

My heart sank. I feared the worst.

Philip went on. 'We know that you're both still waiting for news from ATV about the possibility of doing a further series of 'GEORGE AND THE DRAGON' , and Brian and I are concerned that you and Harry may find yourself so committed that you may not be able to fulfil your contract with us to write thirteen comedy scripts a year.'

I looked at Harry. He was slumped in his chair a glum look on his face.

Philip cleared his throat. 'So we have a proposition to put to you both.'

We waited.

'We would like to extend our existing contract with you to write 13 scripts a year from two years to five, and offer you an exclusivity contract to you both for five years so that you would only write for Thames Television during that period. In addition we would like you to act as our Comedy Advisers - in other words to help find and develop scripts by other writers. Naturally, we'll pay you an exclusivity fee and an extra fee for being our Comedy Advisers, and we'll talk to your agent about that. What do you say?'

I couldn't say anything. My mind was in a whirl. Thirteen scripts a year for five years was a total of sixty-five scripts. The money we would earn would be a small fortune. I glanced at Harry and saw that he was a stunned as I was. We were both at a loss for words.

Philip broke the silence. 'Would you like to ring your agent?'

I shook my head. 'No Philip. I'm sure Harry will agree that your offer is too good for us to refuse.' Harry nodded his agreement. Philip smiled and said he would have the contracts drawn up as soon as possible and would we like to join him for lunch. We accepted and made our way up to the executive restaurant. Philip said that he had a couple of phone calls to make, but that he would be with us soon. Harry and I were still in a state of shock and could hardly believe our good fortune. We both agreed that we'd made the right decision to tie ourselves to Thames for the next five years. Philip arrived in the restaurant with more good news. We had been allocated an office overlooking the Thames where we could sit and work. There would also be a desk for Eric. And that wasn't all. We had been given two parking spaces for our cars. That was the icing on the cake. Parking spaces were like gold dust. We finished lunch and Eric drove us back to Harry's house dropping me off at my place on the way. Edith and Judi were as pleased as we were about our good fortune which was more than our agent was when we rang him later. He felt it wasn't wise for us to be exclusive to only one broadcaster. We told him that we had agreed the deal and that was it. If he didn't like it, we'd find another agent. He eventually agreed to carry on representing us. However, events of the next two days made us wonder whether if he had been right and our exclusivity deal had been such a wise decision after all.

The first thing that occurred was a telephone call from Peter Eckersley at Granada. He told us that he had changed his mind about doing the Comedy Showcase idea of six separate sitcoms and decided to do an entire series of six 'NEAREST AND DEAREST's' which he presumed we would write. We had to tell him that we were now exclusive to Thames Television and couldn't write for Granada. What a blow!

The second event was a telephone call from Sid James.

'Hello Vince. Hi Harry. Terrific news. Just had a call from Shaun. Lew wants to do another series of 'GEORGE AND THE DRAGON'. Thirteen programmes. Isn't that great?'

We just couldn't believe it. In the space of two days we had been offered to write nineteen sitcoms, which, because of our contract with Thames, we couldn't accept. I told Sid about Harry and I being exclusive to Thames. Sid asked if we'd signed a contract.

Harry, who was on the line replied 'Well, not yet Sid. It's still being sorted out between our agent and Thames.'

'Don't sign it,' he said, 'you'd be better off here with Lew Grade. He's bigger than Philip Jones. He's bigger than anyone. He's Mister Show Business!'

Harry and I looked at each other.

I replied. 'I'll tell you what Sid, we'll ring you back in half an hour. Okay?'

I hung up and turned to Harry. 'What are we going to do?'

He shook his head. 'I don't know. We haven't signed the contract with Thames yet.'

We discussed the situation and the options open to us. We could tell Philip we didn't want to sign the exclusivity contract which would leave us free to write the series for both Granada and ATV. But if we did, would Thames still want us to write for them? We eventually decided to do the honourable thing and stay with Thames. After all, we had given our word to Philip, and in spite of Samuel Goldwyn's view that 'A verbal contract isn't worth the paper it's printed on' we felt that our word was our bond.

We rang Sid and told him of our decision. After wishing us the best of luck and telling us to keep in touch, he rang off. The following morning Harry and I drove into Teddington, parked in our allotted spaces and went to our new office overlooking the river. We sent Eric to the bar to buy a bottle of Bell's and rang Philip's office to ask him to join us. When he arrived, I poured out four whiskies and we drank to christen the office. We told Philip about the phone calls of the previous day from Peter Eckersley and Sid. Philip was sympathetic and generously told us that he would allow us to write three more episodes for Granada, but that he couldn't allow us to write 'GEORGE AND THE DRAGON' for ATV. At that moment, our phone rang. The first call we had received in our new office I picked up the receiver. It was Sid James.

'Hello Vince. Listen - I've been thinking. If you and Harry can't write for ATV, think of a new sitcom for me and I'll come to Thames.'

For a moment, I was at a loss for words. What a tremendous compliment this was to Harry and I. Not many comedy actors recognised that a great deal of their success was due to their writers. I told Sid that Philip was with us in the office and would he tell him what he had just said to me, then handed the phone to Philip. As Philip and Sid talked, I explained the situation to Harry. When Philip put the phone down he was grinning like a Cheshire cat. To have secured the services of such a talented and celebrated star such as Sid James for Thames Television was a coup. He immediately told Brian Tesler who talked to Sid's agent, Michael Sullivan to work out a deal, then arranged for us all to have lunch on the 'boat'. The boat in question was the 'MV IRIS' which was permanently moored on the Thames adjacent to the studios. It had a famous history, being one of the small ships which took part in the heroic evacuation of the British Army from Dunkirk in 1940. After the war the IRIS became a pleasure boat until it was acquired by ABC Television, and then Thames. It was completely refurbished and used by the TV Companies as a floating restaurant to which potential stars and investors were invited. It had a top London chef who was responsible for gourmet meals and a superb wine list.

Anyway a lunch was arranged for Sid and his lovely wife Valerie, Sid's agent, Philip and his equally lovely wife Florence, Brian Tesler, Harry and I. We all had a wonderful time.

Sid agreed in principal to sign a contract to work for Thames and his agent and Brian Tesler arranged to meet later in the week to iron out the financial details. All that remained was for Harry and I to come up with a suitable idea for a situation comedy series. No worries, we both thought.

We met the next day in our office and confidently put on our thinking caps. But for some reason, we couldn't think of a thing. We decided that staring out of our office window at the river and the passing river traffic was interfering with our thought processes, and that it might be better if we worked at home in Harry's study.

It made no difference. We sat in that study, day after day, desperately trying to find that elusive idea for Sid without success. Our well of inspiration appeared to have run dry. Then out of the blue came another of those coincidences, with which we seem to have been blessed from time to time.

Chapter Nine:
HAPPY DAYS

One morning, after spending another couple of fruitless and unproductive hours thinking of nothing, we decided to have a change of scene and go to our local pub for a drink and a ploughman's. When we arrived there was a little party going on. It appeared that one of their customers, who worked as a car mechanic at a nearby garage was leaving his job and that this was his leaving party. Harry and I knew him as we both had our cars serviced at the garage for whom he worked. We joined his party to wish him well.

'I hear you're leaving the garage Ted'. I said.

'Yes' he replied, 'can't wait to get away.'

'Come up on the pools have you Ted?' said Harry.

Ted grinned. 'Chance would be a fine thing. No. I just got fed up of working indoors, and coming home every night covered in oil and dirt. From next week, I shall be my own boss working outside in the fresh air.'

'Doing what?'

'I've bought a little smallholding in Sussex. Only fifty acres with a couple of hundred poultry, a few geese, half a dozen pigs and two goats. I might not make a fortune, but I'll have a much better lifestyle.

Harry and I suddenly reacted simultaneously each struck by the same thought. The telepathy was working again. There was the idea that we had been searching for. We sat down, borrowed a couple of napkins from the landlord to make notes on and by the time we'd finished our ploughman's, we had the basis of an idea.

We saw Sid and a colleague, fed up with the daily monotony of working in an accounts office, suddenly rebelling, handing in their notice and buying a small farm. The comic possibilities of two men who didn't even know how to milk a cow trying to cope with all the problems of running a farm seemed to be ideal for Sid. We gave it the title of 'TWO IN CLOVER' with the farm called Clover Farm. We talked it over with Sid, who loved the basic premise, as did Philip at Thames. The only cloud on the horizon was who do we cast to play Sid's mate in the series. Thames casting director, Iris Fredericks suggested a brilliant Welsh actor called Victor Spinetti - yes I know he doesn't sound Welsh, but he was born in Cwm, Wales, of an Italian father and Welsh mother. Victor was a highly successful actor, writer and director who first found fame with Joan Littlewood's Theatre Workshop, with which he did 'OH WHAT A LOVELY WAR', and then later directed The Beatles movies. Sid was very enthusiastic about working with Victor and Philip contacted Victor's agent but he told us that Victor was in Paris doing a movie. To my surprise, Philip arranged for me to fly to Paris, meet Victor at his hotel, tell him about the proposed series and hopefully get his approval to star in it. Fortunately Victor was a great admirer of Sid James and agreed like a shot.

During the flight back, I thought, not for the first time, how lucky I was to be working in an industry in which I met so many famous celebrities, many of whom later became my friends. One of the reasons I formed so many close friendships with the stars with whom I worked was that, having written a script, I used to attend every rehearsal during which I worked closely with the director and the actors, fine tuning the script and adding extra bits of visual comedy, whereas many writers just sent their scripts in and took the money.

Anyway, Victor returned from Paris and we went into production with 'TWO IN CLOVER'. Philip had decided to dispense with a pilot programme and go straight into a series of six. We had been lucky to get Alan Tarrant, who had worked with Sid on 'GEORGE AND THE DRAGON' to produce and direct the series and Alan came up with the idea that we would have the set of the farm built in the studio, including a cowshed and a barn. He arranged to hire a couple of cows to be tethered in the cowshed and half a dozen hens to be in the barn. To make sure the hens didn't wander away, a few handfuls of corn were to be scattered on the barn floor. It was going to look so authentic and real. We were all excited and couldn't wait to record the first episode. We rehearsed during the day without the livestock, the studio audience arrived, was seated and the cows led in. The audience was fascinated. Some handfuls of corn were scattered on the barn floor, and the hens released. They immediately began pecking at the corn. Everything seemed to be working perfectly. Alan Tarrant was just about to start the recording, when disaster struck.

One of the cows began to urinate all over the studio floor. This startled the hens who scattered into the audience. The other cow then decided to evacuate it's bowels! It was pandemonium.

Two of the camera crew, slipped on the wet floor, one of them ending up in a pile of steaming manure. Naturally, the audience found everything highly amusing and roared with laughter. Alan apologised to them and cancelled the recording. Sid and Victor came out and made several jokes most of which were highly lavatorial and the audience left, a few of them with the added bonus of looking forward to a chicken dinner - we never recovered any of the hens.

At a subsequent meeting, the following day it was decided that, in future, any scenes involving animals would be shot on location at a nearby farm. The series eventually got under way, was well received by the public and a second series was recorded the following year. Unfortunately, the second series wasn't as popular and the audience ratings dropped. Because of the expense involved in filming on location, Thames decided not to continue with another series. We were back to square one - trying to think of an idea for Sid. Fortunately, Sid was committed to appearing in a stage play and a film so the pressure was off for the time being.

But not for long. Philip reminded us of our contract to write 13 sitcoms a year for Thames and asked us to think of another idea for a series. We agreed to start thinking, but before we got very far we got a telephone call from Peter Eckersley at Granada to tell us that they were recording the first episode of 'NEAREST AND DEAREST' the following week and could one of us come to the recording. As it was more convenient for me to travel, I went, leaving Harry to think of an idea for a new sitcom.

I drove up the day before the recording and stayed at my Dad's house where he insisted that we went to the St. Clares Catholic Men's Club associated with the church of which my Dad was chairman. I wasn't too enthusiastic, but to please my Dad, I went. He phoned the club to tell them that we would be there later and to make sure they had a supply of Bell's whisky. I drove us to the club. For some reason Dad seemed to be in a state of suppressed excitement. I found out why when we got to the club. I parked the car and we walked to the entrance. I opened the door to be greeted with the signature tune of 'NEVER MIND THE QUALITY ...' being played on a piano. The club was packed and everyone applauded as I entered. The parish priest, Father Ignatious made a speech and handed me a large Bells. I was a celebrity in my own backyard. I looked at my Dad - he was so full of pride and I felt grateful that he was able to share in my achievements. I went over to him and we embraced. I realised that he had organised this especially for me. We had a wonderful night and I didn't have to pay for a drink. Several of my old school chums were there and we went down memory lane together. All too soon it was closing time and we had to go home. I was in no fit state to drive and Dad didn't know how to, but one of the parishioners who lived not far from Dad volunteered to drive us home in my car.

The following morning, very much hungover, I drove into Granada. My first stop was the canteen for a mug of hot black coffee. Peter Eckersley joined me and together we went to the studios where Jimmy Jewel and Hylda Baker were waiting. After renewing my acquaintance with Jimmy, I chatted to Hylda until it was time to go into the studio and start the camera rehearsal. Up until then, they had just rehearsed in a rehearsal room, without the camera crew. With the crew present came the laughs. There was one scene in which Jimmy was in bed pretending to be ill in order to avoid stocktaking. He was drinking whisky, smoking and reading the sports page trying to pick a winner at Newmarket. From time to time, Hylda entered and Jimmy had to hide his cigarette and drink and try to look ill. This went on for a while and the crew found it very funny. Hylda was not best pleased.

'Just a minute' she said, 'I'm in an out of this scene like a fart in a colander.'

Peter looked concerned. 'Have you a problem Hylda?' he asked.

'Yes' she replied and pointed to Jimmy. 'He's getting all the laughs. I'm getting now't.

I tried to butt in. 'It's a very funny scene Hylda.' I said.

Hylda glared at me. 'I'm glad you think so. I think its rubbish. You'll have to re-write it and give me a few laughs or I'm not going to do it.'

At this, Jimmy got out of bed. 'Right' he said, 'I shall be in my dressing room until you sort this out. And if I don't like the re-written script, I won't bloody do it!' And with a vitriolic look at Hylda, he strode out.

What a start to the series! Peter sent the crew to the canteen, Hylda retired to her dressing room and Peter and I started to re-write the offending scene. I put in a few funny lines for Hylda, we ran it past Jimmy who reluctantly agreed to do it, and we carried on with the camera rehearsal. From then on, Jimmy's attitude to Hylda changed. They hardly spoke to each other for the rest of the day and sat at separate tables for lunch in the canteen. In spite of that, the rehearsals went well and we eventually broke to let the audience in. When they had all settled in their seats, Peter appeared, welcomed them to Granada and introduced the cast. In addition to Jimmy and Hylda were their neighbours Walter and Lily played by Eddie Malin and Madge Hindle, later to find fame as Renee Roberts in Coronation Street. Also in the cast was that brilliant character actor Joe Gladwin. Taking a leaf out of Hylda's past variety performances, Harry and I decided that Walter would never speak and that Lily would speak on his behalf. Consequently, Eddie Malin had one of the most enviable roles on television. During the five years that the series ran, he never had to learn or remember a line of dialogue, but just sit and smile and nod occasionally.

The recording started and went exceptionally well. The studio audience laughed in all the right places - Peter and I were smiling as we went into the end of the final scene, which was a close up shot of Jimmy. Hylda, who was obviously unaware of this, glanced up at a studio monitor and went berserk. She stepped out in front of the cameras and waved her hands.

'Stop the show', she said. 'I'm not having this. I'm the star of the show, not him. It's me that should be in that last shot. You'll have to change it.'

Peter came rushing down from the gallery and Jimmy fled to his dressing room. Peter addressed the audience, told them that there was a technical fault and that the recording was over. The audience, slightly bemused, left. Peter was furious with Hylda but she was unrepentant insisting that she be included in final shot. Peter finally said that he would edit the shot so that both Jimmy and she would be on the screen together.

From that day on, it was open warfare between Hylda and Jimmy. For the next five years during the run of the series, they barely exchanged a word, save for the ones which were written for them in the script. There was one occasion when, after rehearsing for the day. Jimmy was driving back to the Midland Hotel where he and Hylda were both staying, he noticed Hylda walking back to the hotel, in the pouring rain. He stopped the car wound down the window and called to her. 'Get in Hylda,' he said. 'I'll run you to the hotel.' Hylda started at him balefully, with the rain dripping down her face and said two words, the second of which was off!

In spite of their continuing enmity the series was a huge ratings success, and some years later, Granada asked Harry and I to write a stage version of the show for a summer season at Blackpool, but more of that later.

I returned home to find that Harry had come up with a good idea for a new sitcom about a couple falling in love. What made it different was that the couple in question were both in their 60's he Walter, a widower and she, Ada, a widow who lived with her daughter and son-in-law neither of whom approved of this geriatric love affair.

We made Walter a grave digger, who had actually buried Ada's husband. They met in the cemetery, when Ada went to put flowers on her husband's grave and their friendship blossomed into romance.

We went to see Philip with the idea. He thought it was an interesting concept, but wondered if it was right for a situation comedy. Would audiences laugh at a love affair between two elderly characters, he asked. Perhaps it should be a drama, he suggested. We understood his concerns as the idea was a break from the recognised sitcom formula which depended on getting big laughs from the viewer, but we persuaded Philip to withhold judgement until we had written the script. He agreed and within a week we handed him a finished script which we had called 'FOR THE LOVE OF ADA' and told him that we had thought of Beryl Reid to play the part of Ada. We felt that with her vast experience as a comedy performer, she would be ideal to make the most of our script and get lots of laughs from our lines. We told Philip that we were aware that we were breaking new ground, but that we were both confident that a series would be a success with the public. Almost two weeks went by as we waited for his verdict. Eventually he sent for us.

We went in his office. The script was on his deck. For a moment nobody spoke. I thought to myself, he doesn't like it. Then Philip cleared his throat.

'I've read the script lads and I have to say, it's beautifully written. It's warm and gentle and parts of if are quite touching.'

I breathed a sign of relief.

Philip continued. 'However, I felt that I should get a second opinion so I gave it to Bill Stewart and asked him to read it and tell me what he thought.'

Bill Stewart - or to give him his full name William G Stewart - was an experienced Light Entertainment producer, later to achieve fame as the creator and presenter of the popular television quiz 'FIFTEEN TO ONE'.

'What did he say Philip?' I asked.

'He said he thought it might make a half hour drama, but as far as a sitcom was concerned he didn't think there was a laugh in it'.

My heart sank. But there was worse to come as Philip went on.

'I also sent the script to Beryl Reid,' he said.

'Don't tell us Philip,' Harry said. 'She hated it.'

'Well, actually she didn't express an opinion except to say that she didn't want to play a sixty year old pensioner.

Harry groaned. 'Looks like we've had it Vince,' he said, 'and it seemed such a good idea when I thought of it.'

'Cheer up Harry', said Philip, 'you've just heard the bad news. Now are you ready for the good news?'

Harry and I looked at Philip.

'Is there any?' I asked.

Philip nodded. 'I gave the script to Ronnie Baxter and he loves it.'

Ronnie Baxter, as you may recall, produced and directed our series of 'NEVER MIND THE QUALITY FEEL THE WIDTH.' I have to say, he was the best director I have ever worked with. He had a flair for comedy and for getting the best out of actors to say nothing of the writers. Most writers hate doing re-writes to their scripts and Harry and I were no exception. Many directors with whom I have worked during my career have phoned me on receiving one of our scripts, and the conversation has usually gone something like this.

'Hello Vince - Harry. Got the script this morning. There are a few lines on page two needs looking at. Scene three needs to be funnier. The end of scene five needs a bigger laugh and I'm not too happy with the tag of the show.'

Not a word about the overall content of the script, Ronnie's reaction to a script was totally different.

'Hello Vince - Harry. Got the script. Terrific. Well done. Very funny. A lot of laughs. Loved the first scene. Just a couple of small points you might like to look at.'

By this time, we would have re-written the entire script if he'd have asked us to.

'Are we going ahead with a pilot then Philip?' I asked.

'Yes luvvie,' he replied, 'I still have reservations but I trust your judgement.'

That's what made Philip Jones the best Head of Light Entertainment in television, and Thames Television the most successful company in terms of variety and sitcoms. Philip trusted the people who worked for him, respected their talent, and gave them their head even when, at times, he may have had doubt about a particular project.

At that moment, Ronnie Baxter entered Philip's office, nodded to me and Harry and said to Philip, 'She's here Philip. She's waiting downstairs in reception.'

'Good' said Philip, 'we'd better put Harry and Vince in the picture. Would you like to do that Ronnie?'

Ronnie explained that, after reading the script the previous day, he was convinced that the part would be perfect for an elderly actress whom he'd always admired and that he had telephoned her and invited her to Thames for lunch. He'd had a copy of the script biked over to her house in London and arranged for a car to pick her up the following morning and bring her to the studios.

'Yes Ronnie', I said impatiently, 'but who is this wonderful actress who'd be perfect to play Ada?'

Ronnie took a deep breath. 'Irene Handl' he said proudly. Harry and I reacted with disbelief. Irene was a delightful character actress who had taken up acting in her mid thirties, but quickly made her mark in films, television and the theatre, working with many top film and TV stars, both in Britain and America.

'What do you think lads?' asked Ronnie.

Harry was the first to speak. 'What a brilliant idea Ronnie. You're right. She'd be perfect for Ada.'

'I agree,' I said, 'but would she agree to do it? She's such a wonderful performer with a great track record. She might not want to do a sitcom.'

'Well we'll soon find out,' said Philip, 'she's on her way up.'

As if on cue, the door opened and Philip's secretary poked her head in.

'Miss Irene Handl' she announced and Irene entered. At first glance, it appeared that she was carrying a couple of fur stoles under each arm, but on closer inspection they turned out to be two Chihuahuas, Irene's pet dogs who she took with her everywhere. Ronnie introduced Philip, Harry and I to Irene. Philip offered her a chair, opened the drinks cabinet asked her if she would like a drink.

Irene shook her head. 'No thank you. I don't drink - but I'm sure Beulah would like one.'

We all looked round for whoever Beulah might be. Irene indicated one of her dogs.

'This is Beulah. And the other one is Quetzel.'

Philip nodded. 'Would - er - Quetzel like a drink as well?' he asked.

Irene shook her head. 'Oh no. She doesn't drink.'

Philip picked up the telephone and spoke to his secretary. 'Darling', he said, 'could you bring in a saucer of water for one of Miss Handl's dogs'

Irene shook her head 'No no. Beulah would prefer something stronger. Have you a bottle of beer?'

Philip produced a bottle of beer, and we watched in amazement as he opened it poured the contents into a glass dish and put it on the floor. Irene put Beulah down next to the dish and the tiny dog lapped up the beer.

We discussed the script and with Beryl Reid in mind, I asked Irene if she would be happy to play an old age pensioner.

She smiled at me, and with a twinkle in her eye said, 'My dear Vince - I *am* an old age pensioner!'

She asked us if we had anybody in mind for the rest of the cast, particularly who would be playing Walter, but we hadn't any thoughts. Irene then suggested an actress called Barbara Mitchell to play her daughter. We all knew Barbara's work and immediately agreed. Ronnie then suggested an old friend of mine, Jack Smethurst to play Irene's son-in'-law, which Harry and I seconded. Jack and I were old friends and had a lot in common. We went to the same Catholic school and our lives had followed a similar pattern. When I was working in the tailoring trade, I attended a tailoring course at the College of Domestic Science in Manchester. To my surprise, one of my fellow students was Jack. After we'd completed our course, we lost touch until some years later, when I was writing the Harry Worth series. I was leafing through Spotlight, which is the Actors and Actresses Directory, when I noticed a familiar face. It was Jack. Unknown to me he had attended LAMDA, the London Academy of Music and Dramatic Art and become an actor. Life is full of strange coincidences. John Ammonds the producer of the Harry Worth series was looking for an actor to play a window cleaner in one of the episodes. I showed Jack's photograph to John and he immediately booked him for the part. Several months later, when I was writing 'NEVER MIND THE QUALITY....' which Ronnie Baxter was directing, I recommended Jack for a part in one of the episodes. Ronnie cast Jack to play the part of a mild mannered, rather meek character which was totally opposite to the aggressive roles he usually played. Ronnie remembered his performance and as a result, cast him to play Irene Handl's son-in-law in 'FOR THE LOVE OF ADA' a weak and ineffectual man with a domineering wife. So far, so good. All we now had to do was find someone to play the part of Walter Bingley the elderly grave-digger. Easier said than done. We scoured the pages of Spotlight and spoke to several agents who sent us details of various elderly actors whom they represented, all to no avail. Try as we did, we couldn't find anyone who we felt would be suitable for the part.

Then one morning I was driving to Teddington Studios and listening to the car radio. The Morning Story was just about to start. It was an adaptation of Hindle Wakes a North Country play which was being serialised over the next few weeks. It was being read by Wilfred Pickles. Wilfred was a blunt Yorkshireman, who for some years, together with his wife Mabel hosted an extremely popular radio series 'HAVE A GO'. They visited various small villages around the country, took over the local village hall and chatted to several of the local inhabitants from all walks of life about their jobs, their hobbies and their hopes and ambitions. Built into the programme was a simple quiz with prizes attached, usually some local produce such as a jar of home made jam, a hand knitted scarf or a set of cushion covers plus a small cash prize. The series spawned a couple of catchphrases which may be remembered by those of you who are old enough, such as 'What's on the table Mabel?' and 'Give him the money Barney,' Barney being the BBC Producer, Barney Colehan. There was also a musical quiz in which the piano was played by Violet Carson who later found fame as the curmudgeonly battleaxe Ena Sharples in CORONATION STREET.

I sat in my car listening to those rich and fruity Yorkshire tones of Wilfred then drove to the nearest telephone box (mobile phones were still to be invented). I rang Ronnie Baxter and told him to find a radio and listen to the Morning Story. I gave him the number of the telephone from which I was ringing, put down the receiver and waited. Ten minutes later the phone rang. It was Ronnie. He was jubilant.

'That's it Vince', he enthused, 'we've found our grave-digger.'

I then rang Harry Driver only to find that he, too, had been listening to the Morning Story and had been trying to phone me.

Wilfred was just right for the part. His warm Yorkshire accent complemented Irene's cockney accent perfectly. They went together like fish and chips. We recorded a pilot programme which went so well with the studio audience that as soon as the recording finished Philip announced that we would immediately go into a series of six. This gentle story of a tender love affair was an instant success with the viewers and went on to become one of ITV's biggest hits, resulting in a feature film being made. Like most Yorkshiremen, Wilfred had a dry sense of humour and also, like most Yorkshiremen, he was very careful with money. There is one wonderful story about him which I know to be true. During the radio series of 'HAVE A GO' when he and Mabel were touring the country, they used to stay at small local pubs which catered for Bed and Breakfast. Wilfred had his own specially printed chequebooks much larger than normal. Each cheque had 'HAVE A GO' printed on it in large letters. When the time came for Wilfred to pay the bill, he would ask the landlord how much it came to. On being told, and as he was writing out the cheque, he would casually say 'You know, a lot of landlords never cash these cheques. They have them framed and hang them behind the bar!' As a consequence, his cheques were rarely cashed. What a clever and crafty move.

But on one memorable occasion, Wilfred surpassed himself. He was writing a cheque out for twenty five pounds, and telling the landlord his usual story of his cheques being framed and hung behind the bar when the landlord said, 'What a good idea Mr. Pickles - I'll do that myself.'

As quick as a flash Wilfred said, 'Oh well in that case, if I make the cheque out for fifty pounds, can you give me twenty five pounds in cash?'

What an opportunist. That's a true Yorkshireman!

Having completed recording the first series of 'FOR THE LOVE OF ADA', Harry and I were looking forward to a well earned rest but fate decided otherwise. We got a call from our agent who told us that he had received a letter from a film company who were anxious to commission Harry and I to write a screenplay based on our sitcom series 'NEVER MIND THE QUALITY....' Some months earlier, Ronnie Woolfe and Ronald Chesney, the creators and writers of the successful sitcom series 'ON THE BUSES' were commissioned by Hammer Films to write the screenplay for a movie version. It was produced and shot on a shoestring budget and to everybody's surprise made a huge profit for Hammer.

Our agent revealed that the film company interested in 'NEVER MIND THE QUALITY ....' was none other than M.G.M! M.G.M! Metro Goldwyn Mayer! One of Hollywood's biggest moviemakers. Visions of Oscar nominations and winning the Academy Award followed by a glittering career as famous Hollywood screenwriters filled our imaginations. However, the truth, as so often happens in real life was very far removed from those dreams.

We wrote a screenplay which we sent to Ronnie Baxter who had been commissioned by M.G.M. to direct the film. Ronnie liked the screenplay and forwarded it to M.G.M's UK representative at their London office. Locations were found, and sets built at Pinewood Film Studios in Iver Heath. The principal parts were cast with John Bluthal and Joe Lynch playing their original television roles of Manny Cohen and Patrick Kelly. Eventually, we all met up in a rehearsal room at Pinewood to read through the screenplay. It read extremely well with lots of laughs, after which we all went to the bar for several celebratory drinks.

The following morning we began filming the first scene which took place in Cohen and Kelly's workroom. After a couple of hours we stopped for coffee break during which Ronnie received a phone from M.G.M's London office. A new Executive Producer had been appointed and had just arrived from Los Angeles. He told Ronnie that he had read the screenplay and was not happy with it.

Ronnie tried to explain that we had already started filming and that M.G.M. had had the screenplay for several weeks. Why was the Executive Producer querying it at such a late date? The Executive Producer whose name was Jerry - something or other, brushed Ronnie's protests aside and informed him that a car was on its way to Pinewood to pick him up, together with the writers and take us to attend a script meeting at the London office. I rang Harry who was at home, gave him the news and told him that I'd ring him after the meeting.

A car duly arrived, Ronnie dismissed the cast for the rest of the day and he and I were driven into London. We were shown into the Executive Producer's office. He was in his shirtsleeves sitting behind a huge desk. Two chairs were placed in front of the desk. Ronnie and I sat down and waited, Jerry picked up a copy of the screenplay.

'This script stinks', he said.

Ronnie and I looked at each other in shocked silence.

Ronnie was the first to reply. 'I thought it was very funny.'

Jerry pulled a face. 'It's too tame. It's got no balls.'

Ronnie reacted. 'I don't know what you mean.'

Jerry sighed. 'It's very simple. Nobody screws anybody in this movie.'

'Have you seen the television series?' I asked.

Jerry shook his head. 'Nope.'

'It's about the relationship between a Jewish coat maker and an Irish Catholic trouser maker and their different faiths. They are both devout God fearing men.'

Jerry scowled at me. 'Listen Buster, I got news for you. Jews screw - Catholics screw. Sex sells movies and we gotta have some sex in this movie.'

I couldn't believe what I was hearing. I glared furiously at Jerry. 'You can't be serious.'

'Oh but I am, 'he replied. 'As a matter of fact, I've been thinking of bringing in another writer to spice up the script.'

At that I stood up. 'That's the first sensible thing you've said since we got here. Bring in another writer by all means, and while you're doing it, take my name and Harry Driver's name off the screenplay. This is no longer the movie we set out to write.'

I turned to Ronnie who was sitting there in a state of shock. 'Sorry Ronnie. I've heard enough. I'm going home. I'll ring you tonight.' I strode out of the office, and caught a taxi to

Waterloo Station, where I rang Harry and gave him a blow by blow account of the meeting. He totally agreed with my actions. I then phoned our agent to put him in the picture and he assured me that, whatever the consequences of the meeting, and having signed our contract with M.G.M. we would receive our full fee for the screenplay. I then caught a train to Weybridge where, to my surprise, I was met by Judi outside the station, sitting in my car.

'Thank goodness you're back,' she said, as I climbed into the car, 'the phone's been going mad. Ronnie's been trying to get you and so have John Bluthal and Joe Lynch.

As we arrived at the house I could hear the phone ringing. I ran in and picked up the receiver. It was Ronnie.

'Vince. I've been trying to get you for ages.'

'Hi Ronnie. Are you still at M.G.M?'

'No, I'm at home. I left shortly after you went.'

'Why - what happened?'

'Jerry wanted more than half the script re-written and some nude scenes put in, including a sequence where Manny and Patrick pick up a couple of prostitutes. So I told him I didn't agree and I quit. I'm now no longer the director.'

I tried to tell him not to be so hasty but he was adamant. I suggested that Harry and I should drive over to his house that evening and discuss the situation and he agreed. No sooner had I put the receiver down than the phone rang again. It was John Bluthal. He told me that he and his co-star Joe were in the bar at Pinewood and had heard a rumour that Ronnie, Harry and I were no longer on the film. I confirmed that this was true and told him the reasons. John asked me to hold the line while he spoke to Joe. After a few minutes John came back and told me that, after speaking to Joe, he and Joe had agreed to resign from the film. So much for our dreams of Hollywood and the Academy Awards. All shattered within the space of a couple of hours.

That evening, when Harry and I arrived at Ronnie's house, we found him in deep conversation with a middle-aged gentleman who Ronnie introduced as Peter Whitehead. Peter told us that he was the new Executive Producer on the film, and that, after the meeting at M.G.M's offices, Jerry had been summoned back to L.A. and that he, Peter, was now in charge of the production. He then told us that shooting would resume again at Pinewood the following day, with the original script, cast and director and assured us that there would be no more talk of anybody screwing anybody. In the final event it was Jerry who ended up being screwed, as when he got back to L.A. he was promptly fired! They certainly don't mess about, these Hollywood film moguls!

And so filming proceeded and the film got made. Harry and I didn't win an Oscar, but it was a moderately successful film and at least Harry and I could list among our achievements that we had written a screenplay for Metro-Goldwyn-Mayer.

Meanwhile, the series of 'BEST OF ENEMIES' went into production. Harry and I went to every recording and felt that the series had all the signs of being a success. How wrong we were. The viewing public didn't like it and switched off in their droves. To this day, I still don't understand why. The scripts were well written, the actors excellent yet, for some reason it didn't appeal to the viewers. Maybe they weren't ready yet for a political situation comedy - who knows? Some you win - some you lose.

In spite of the failure of 'BEST OF ENEMIES', life was good. Thames was a great company to work for and by far the most successful of the Independent companies. There was always two or three shows being recorded each week - a drama in Studio 1, a sitcom in Studio 2 and a game show or quiz in Studio 3. One could go in the bar any lunchtime and rub shoulders with famous stars such as Edward Woodward, Leo McKern, George Cole, Michael Caine, Tommy Cooper, Benny Hill, Max Bygraves, Joan Collins and Wendy Craig to name but a few. It was a wonderful time to be alive and be part of show business.

Harry and I were still committed to finding a new idea for Sid James who was still involved in a theatre tour and another Carry On Film so we decided to have a break from writing sitcoms and turn our talents to writing a sketch show. We had long been admirers of Mike and Bernie Winters, a successful comedy double act and suggested to Philip that we write a show for them. Philip was no stranger to Mike and Bernie and had helped to set them on their television career by inviting them to host ABC's weekly variety series, 'BIG NIGHT OUT' followed by 'BLACKPOOL NIGHT OUT' in 1963 and 1965. We met with Peter Frazer-Jones who had produced and directed their last two stand-up sketch shows and suggested that, rather do a conventional sketch show we do a sixty minute spectacular with a storyline running through it. Mike and Bernie would play themselves who had been given the chance of doing their own TV show providing they could arrange for several famous celebrities to appear in it. During the programme, they would call on their old friend Lionel Blair to help them. Lionel suggested Des O'Connor and Mike and Bernie went to Des's house where they became involved in a domestic situation between Des and his wife - played by the lovely Joan Collins. Des then suggested the French singer Sacha Distel. Mike and Bernie caught a plane to Paris. They caused havoc on the plane and more havoc in Paris which led to them being arrested and spending the night in a French prison cell. Finally, the show was ready to go into production. Des sang a couple of songs, Lionel choreographed a couple of dance routines, one of which featured Mike and Bernie dancing with Joan Collins and the show finished with Sacha singing his latest release. It was a good show and Phillip immediately suggested we follow it up with another. This time, Harry and I again decided to give the boys a storyline which was a kind of biopic - The Mike and Bernie Story. There were no big stars. All the other parts were played by actors, one of which was Lynda Baron who had been somewhat out of the limelight for some time. Her appearance with Mike and Bernie led eventually to her appearance in 'OPEN ALL HOURS' as Nurse Gladys Emmannuel.

This again was well received and, in turn, led to Harry and I writing a sitcom series in which Mike and Bernie were cast as a pair of starving, unsuccessful, unemployed comedians. It was okay, but not brilliant and the boys decided to return to their more familiar formula of stand-up comedy and sketches and over the next couple of years did several more successful shows until 1978 when the act broke up acrimoniously. Mike emigrated to America and Bernie found a new partner in the shape of a huge St Bernard dog named Schnorbitz with whom he did several series. I was very fond of Bernie. He was a lovely man and sadly died in 1991 at the young age of 58.

Meanwhile, Harry and I returned to trying to think of a new sitcom idea for Sid James. His theatre tour was coming to an end and Philip was anxious to go into production with a new TV series as soon as possible before another broadcaster came up with an offer.

Sid's agent had phoned Philip to remind him that Sid was under contract to Thames to make another 13 shows, and under the terms of that contract, would have to be paid his fee for those shows whether or not he actually made them.

Harry and I were desperate. We both wondered if we had hit that dreaded barrier, the Writer's Block. It was a condition experienced by many writers in which the mind becomes a total blank. Philip gave us an ultimatum. If we couldn't think of a suitable idea by the end of the month, he would have to call in other writers.

Chapter Ten:
BUSINESS AS
USUAL

A week went by and Harry and I were no nearer finding an idea for Sid James. Our creative juices had dried up. Then Sid's agent, Mike Sullivan, threw us a lifeline. He rang and told us that another of his clients, Jimmy Logan, a Scottish comedian was appearing in a comedy play at the New Metropole Theatre, in Glasgow, which he owned and that it would be an ideal vehicle as a TV sitcom for Sid. I rang Sid and we arranged to fly up to Glasgow the following morning, see a matinee of the show and fly back that evening. It was arranged that Jimmy Logan would pick Sid and I up from Glasgow airport.

Jimmy Logan was one of Scotland's foremost comedians. Although virtually unknown south of the border, he was lionised in Scotland, particularly in his native Glasgow. I didn't realise how popular he was until we landed at the airport and there, waiting for us at the foot of the gangway was a silver Rolls Royce with the number plate JL 1 and the smiling face of Jimmy Logan behind the steering wheel.

Sid and I disembarked from the plane, and climbed into the Rolls where Sid introduced me to Jimmy who then drove off, out of the airport and toward the theatre. It was an incredible journey. As we drove through the streets of Glasgow, people, recognising the car, started waving and cheering at Jimmy, who waved back to them regally. Sid and I were amazed at the reception Jimmy was getting, then, entering into the spirit of the thing, we began to wave back to the crowds ourselves. We felt like royalty sitting there. We finally got to the theatre, and Jimmy led us to his dressing room, where we met his father, Jack Short who himself had been a variety artist along with his wife May and their five children known as The Logan Family - a real show business troupe.

The first thing Jack did was to ask us if we wanted a 'wee dram'. Sid declined but I, not wishing to appear unsociable, accepted. Jack began to pour me out a tumbler of whisky. As he kept pouring, I called out, 'That's enough. You've hardly left enough room for water.'

Jack reacted as if I had physically struck him.

'Water?', he said, 'water!! Ye'll no put water in this. It's fifty years old!'

With that, he filled the tumbler to the brim, handed it to me and poured a similar measure for himself. He raised the glass said 'Cheers' and drank the lot in one swallow. I sipped cautiously at mine until it was time for Sid and I to take our seats in the theatre. I gulped the rest of my whisky down and went with Sid. Jimmy had reserved a box for the two of us and we read the programme while we waited for the curtain to go up. The play was about a left wing trade union shop steward and his many confrontations with his employers. The lights dimmed, the curtain rose, I settled in my seat and within minutes I was fast asleep! I slept through the whole performance - even the interval. Sid later confessed that he hadn't the heart to wake me up. It was the applause from the audience at the final curtain which eventually woke me. We made our way back to Jimmy's dressing room which was packed with his friends and well wishers all congratulating him on his performance. We managed to add our congratulations to Jimmy, then left to catch a taxi back to the airport and our flight back to London. I tried to apologise to Sid, blaming my falling asleep on the large whisky, but he told me I hadn't missed anything, that he didn't like the play and it wouldn't have been suitable as a TV sitcom for him. C'est la vie!

The following morning I went to the studios to see Philip. I'd phoned Harry the previous evening and put him in the picture. Philip was already in the picture - Sid had phoned his agent who, in turn, had phoned Philip.

'Back to square one,' I thought. But not quite. Philip told me that he had telephoned several writer's agents, informed them that Thames were looking for a sitcom idea for Sid, and if any of their clients could come up with a suitable idea, would they send it to Philip as soon as possible. I felt as though Harry and I had let Philip down and began to apologise, but he quickly stopped me.

'You've nothing to apologise for Vince,' he said, 'you and Harry have written some great comedies for us and I'm sure you'll write many more in future. This is just a temporary blip and you'll both get over it. Just forget about it for now'.

Philip's remarks cheered me up so much that I drove over to Harry's house, picked him up and we went for lunch at Chez Antoine's. I told him what Philip had said and over a delicious Sole Meuniere and an excellent bottle of Chablis, we decided to take Philip's advice and put Sid James out of our minds for the next few days. But it didn't last long. The following week Philip called us in for a meeting. He had received several ideas for the sitcom series for Sid from various writers and wanted to discuss them with us. When we arrived at his office, we found Sid and his agent Mike already there drinking coffee with Philip. There was an air of anticipation in the room which I, for some reason, didn't share. Sid revealed that he was looking forward to hearing the ideas and was anxious to be involved in another TV series.

'To tell you the truth, I'll be glad to get out of the house. The wife's got me doing all sorts of odd jobs, and the kids are driving me up the wall. Kids of today - honestly - I just don't understand them.'

Philip nodded sympathetically. 'It's a different generation Sid. It happens all the time. My father could never understand me.'

'Well let's hope one of these ideas is a cracker,' said Mike.

'Hear, hear,' said Philip, picking up a sheaf of papers. 'I've got six ideas here for us to choose from. I'll read them out one by one. I suggest that we wait till I've read them all then we can choose which we feel has the most promise.'

Philip began to read the ideas out loud. The first had Sid as the landlord of an East End pub coping with the all the problems entailed in running a pub helped by a succession of busty barmaids.

The second had Sid running a betting shop. In the third he

was a boxing promoter, hoping that one of his young protégés training in his gym will turn out to be a world beater. The fourth idea was Sid as a small time unsuccessful crook, the fifth was Sid as a bouncer at a late night drinking club and the last idea was Sid as a barrow boy on the market.

As Philip went through the list of ideas, I got more and more depressed. I looked at Harry who pulled a face and shook his head.

'Well luvvies,' said Philip cheerfully, 'lots of possibilities there. What do you think Sid? Which one do you fancy?'

Sid frowned. 'Well to be honest Philip, I don't fancy any of them. How about you Mike?'

'I quite like the pub idea.'

Philip nodded, 'Yes so do I. I think it has lots of possibilities for comedy.'

Sid looked doubtful. 'Let's ask the writers. What do you think Harry?'

'I'm with you Sid. I wasn't wild about any of them.'

Everybody turned to look at me.

'Well Vince', said Philip, 'what do you think?'

I took a deep breath. 'I'll tell you what I think. For a start, any of those ideas which you've read out, given the right treatment could work as a sitcom. But they're all much of a much-ness. Not one of them expands Sid's TV persona. I've got an idea that I think will work. It was something you said earlier Sid that started me thinking. I think Sid should be happily married, with two kids - a 16 year old daughter and an 18 year old son. The kids don't understand their parents and parents don't understand their kids.'

For a moment, nobody spoke. Then Mike glared at me and said, 'Are you mad Vince? Are you trying to ruin Sid's career? It's taken him years to build up his television character as a bird pulling Jack the Lad and here you are trying to destroy it.'

'With respect Mike,' I replied, 'look at Sid.' Everybody looked at Sid. I carried on. 'He's no spring chicken. If he continues to play a bird pulling Jack the Lad much longer, he'll soon be accused of being a dirty old man!'

There was a stunned silence. Then Sid spoke up.

'I think Vince is absolutely right.'

'So do I', said Harry, 'I think it's a cracking idea and it's absolutely right for Sid.'

And that's how 'BLESS THIS HOUSE' was born.

We cast the lovely and talented actress Diana Coupland to play Sid's wife, Robin Stewart to play their son and Sally Geeson to play their daughter. It was an immediate success and turned out to be one of the longest running sitcoms on British television. It was never out of the top ten TV ratings. More than 70 episodes were made between 1971 and Sid's sudden and unexpected death on stage in 1976.

He was appearing at the Sunderland Empire in a tour of THE MATING SEASON. Sid was standing in the wings waiting for his cue to go on stage. It was the opening night and the first few minutes had gone well. His cue comes and he makes his entrance to tumultuous applause. He is followed on stage by actress Olga Lowe who delivers her opening line to which Sid has to reply. The reply never comes. He steps back and sits on a sofa, clutching his chest. An announcement is made for a doctor, but it is too late. Sid had suffered a massive heart attack. Frantic efforts were made to revive him but to no avail.

Sid James was dead.

He was a great performer and a good friend. I have many happy memories of dining with him and his beautiful wife Valerie in their lovely house in Iver. Val and I have still kept in touch and we still see each other occasionally.

An interesting by-product of 'BLESS THIS HOUSE' was the emergence of the writer Carla Lane. As part of our remit to find new writers for Thames, Harry and I used to receive scripts from budding sitcom writers. One day a script landed on my desk. It was from two Liverpool writers, Carla Lane and Myra Taylor. It was all about a conversation in the womb between two unborn babies. Although it would have been virtually impossible to make a 25 minutes sitcom out of what was really only a ten minute sketch, I was so impressed by the originality of the idea and the quality of the writing that I rang them and asked them to come down and see me and said that Thames would pay their expenses. At that moment, they were writing a BBC sitcom series, THE LIVER BIRDS which was a spin-off from a COMEDY PLAYHOUSE, and went on to be a big success. Anyway, a few days later Carla and Myra arrived at my office - Harry was taking a few days off - and I was confronted by this couple of bubbly, wise cracking Scouse girls firing on all cylinders. I discovered that they used to sit in the lounge of Liverpool's famous Adelphi hotel making a pot of coffee last a few hours while they came up with ideas and scripts. They were like a breath of fresh air, full of enthusiasm and confidence. I took them to lunch in the executive restaurant and explained why I thought their 'womb' sketch wasn't quite right for a sitcom series. However, I asked them if they would like to write a sample script for 'BLESS THIS HOUSE'. I gave them a copy of the format and off they went back to Liverpool. Three days later a script arrived from them. I read it, liked it and suggested a few changes, which they agreed with. I sent it along to Philip, who also liked it and agreed to commission it. We recorded it a few weeks later and it went very well, so well that Carla and Myra were commissioned to write several more scripts. They eventually split up as a writing team and Carla went on to create and write many more successful sitcoms, sadly mainly for the BBC. But I'm getting ahead of myself.

The scripts for 'BLESS THIS HOUSE' were going well and Harry and I were enjoying writing them. We had just finished writing the last script in the series and judging from the reaction of the cast, it looked as if we were on a winner. My Dad was due to travel down from Manchester to spend a few days with Judi and me and I was looking forward to seeing him and taking him to one of the recordings. Then I got a phone call from his daily help to tell me that Dad had fallen down in the street and had been taken to hospital. I immediately rang the hospital who told me that Dad was okay apart from a few bruises. They were keeping him in overnight and he would be discharged the next day. I phoned Harry with the news and told him I was driving up to Manchester early the next morning to pick up Dad and bring him back to my house. I left the house at the crack of dawn and was at the hospital about 09:30 to find Dad waiting in reception fully dressed. Apart from a graze on his forehead and looking a bit pale, he seemed all right. The ward Sister told me that he was fine but that he appeared to be a little unsteady on his legs. The last time he had come to stay with us, I'd noticed that he was walking much slower than normal but had put this down to his old age - he was in his late 70's. He was obviously glad to see me, and we drove to his house to pick up some of his clothes, before setting off on the drive back to Weybridge. During the journey Dad told me that it wasn't the first time he'd had a fall but, like me, had attributed it to his age. We stopped for a bite to eat on the way and arrived home late that afternoon. Dad was tired after the journey and went to bed early.

The following morning, I took Dad to see my doctor who gave him a thorough examination and arranged for him to have some blood tests and an X-ray. Judi and I agreed that Dad should stay with us for a couple of weeks.

I had, on several occasions in the past, suggested to Dad that he sell his house in Blackley and buy a small flat near us in Weybridge but he wouldn't hear of it. Much as he liked coming to stay with us, his roots were firmly embedded in Manchester. However, later that week certain events occurred which changed Dad's thinking. The first was a call from my doctor. The results of the blood tests and X-ray had revealed that Dad was showing the first signs of Parkinsons disease which was why he was having problems with his walking and his balance. The Doctor explained that it was an incurable and progressive disorder which would inevitably get worse but could be kept under control by the drug Levodopa. He assured me that the disease was in its early stages and that there was no immediate cause for alarm, but he felt that I should be made aware of its future effects. That night, after Dad had gone to bed Judi and I discussed the situation. We decided not to tell Dad so as not to cause him any worry, but to raise again the possibility of him moving to live nearer to us.

To my surprise, Dad didn't voice his usual objections. I felt that his recent accident had made him think more about the advantages of living close to us. He quickly made it clear that he was against living with us - he was fiercely independent and valued his privacy. I immediately rang Michael Mayhew, the estate agent through whom I had bought my house and asked him to keep his eyes open for a flat which would be suitable for my father. From then on, events moved at lightning speed. The agent told me that an hour ago he had been offered a ground floor, two bedroom flat for sale in a large Victorian house. It had fitted carpets, central heating, a fully fitted kitchen and best of all, it was only ten minutes walk from my house.

I arranged for Dad and I to meet the agent at the flat that morning. It was perfect. It had a large lounge with French windows which led out to a communal garden, a kitchen which contained a small dining area, a double bedroom, a single bedroom and a bathroom and toilet. The asking price was reasonable and I told the agent that we'd think about it and get back to him.

Dad and I returned home and described the flat to Judi who said that she would arrange to see the flat herself later that afternoon. I phoned the agent and agreed to meet him at the flat after lunch. When we met, the agent informed us that he had another client who had heard about the flat and was interested in buying it. At first, I presumed that this was the usual estate agents ploy in order to influence me to make a decision, but the agent assured me that it was genuine and invited me to telephone his client to verify the situation. Judi, Dad and I went round to the flat. Judi approved of it, Dad was more than enthusiastic especially about the central heating which was something he'd never had in his life in Manchester. Within half an hour, I found myself writing out a cheque for the deposit. I told you that events moved at lightning speed, but there's more. What happened next was even more incredible. When we returned home I rang Dad's daily help in Manchester, Mrs Humphries to give her the news and tell her that I would be putting Dad's house up for sale. There was a small silence then she asked what price I was thinking of. I told her I'd ring her back then I phoned Michael Mayhew to ask his advice. He suggested I ask for £5,500 and be prepared to accept £5,000. I rang Mrs. Humphries back and spoke to her husband who, to my surprise, accepted my first offer. We concluded the deal on the phone and exchanged contracts within a week. I arranged for a removal company to bring Dad's furniture down to Weybridge and a few weeks later he was happily ensconced in his new flat. He never went back to his old home again.

Meanwhile, Harry and I carried on writing more episodes of 'BLESS THIS HOUSE' which went from strength to strength, but we were anxious to devise a new sitcom for Jimmy Jewel, who had performed so well in 'NEAREST AND DEAREST' and who had become a very good friend of ours since we wrote the 'COMEDY PLAYHOUSE' in which he starred for the BBC and the series of 'NEAREST AND DEAREST' for Granada television. Jimmy, once half of the highly successful comedy double act, Jewel and Warriss, was one of the few comedians who had made the transition from comedy to drama. He and his partner, Ben Warriss, who was also his cousin, were the most successful British comedy double act in the forties and fifties. They had their own radio series, 'UP THE POLE' which was heard by millions of listeners and made them national names. They became the highest paid double act in the country earning up to £2,000 a week in summer season shows and pantomimes.

However, the advent of television and the demise of the variety theatres in the fifties took its toll on variety performers and Jimmy and Ben were reduced to appearing in working men's clubs until one day when Ben announced to Jimmy that he had invested in a restaurant and was quitting the act. Jimmy was devastated. Through the good days, he had been careful with money investing in property and could afford to retire, but show business was in his blood and he began to accept small parts as an actor in TV plays which led to him being cast in our 'COMEDY PLAYHOUSE' and subsequently in 'NEAREST AND DEAREST'.

He was a lovely, generous man with only one fault - he was the world's greatest hypochondriac. One soon learned never to greet him with a conventional 'How are you Jimmy?' Or he would reply by describing the state of his heart, (he was convinced that every little twinge was the onset of a major heart attack) his lungs, (he smoked 50 cigarettes a day and was sure that he had lung cancer) and his bowels (he was either constipated or had diarrhoea). Rumour had it that there was a clause in his will stipulating that when he died, he wanted to be buried next to a doctor!

We rang Philip Jones and told him that we intended to come up with a sitcom idea for Jimmy Jewel, which we would write under our long term contract with Thames Television. Philip immediately voiced his approval and we told him that we would start work on it the following day. But fate, as usual had other plans. Leslie Grade and his brother Bernard Delfont had noticed the success of the sitcom series 'NEAREST AND DEAREST' and decided that it would be an ideal vehicle for a summer season stage play. As Harry and I owned the copyright they asked us to write the play which would open for a season at the Blackpool Grand. They had already cast Hylda Baker to play her TV role as Nellie Pledge. We asked them who would play Jimmy's part as, in view of the animosity between him and Hylda, we couldn't for one moment envisage Jimmy agreeing to do a long summer season, twice nightly, with her. To our surprise Leslie Grade told us that Jimmy had agreed, in principle to do the play. Harry and I couldn't believe it but we overlooked one important fact - everyone has their price and Jimmy was no exception. Leslie revealed that he had made Jimmy an offer he couldn't refuse. In addition to a weekly fee, Jimmy was to receive a percentage of the box office takings. Money talks louder than principles!

The rest of the play was cast with Joe Gladwin and Madge Hindle playing their TV characters. Diedre Costello played the love interest as Jimmy's girl friend and Barry Howard played Cyril, Walter's brother due to the fact that Eddie Malin, the original TV Walter was unavailable. Harry and I began work on the play and devised a plot in which an old admirer of Nellie's played by Roger Avon, turns up and begins to woo her. We discover that he is a con man whose only interest in Nellie is to get his hands on her money and the pickle factory. We finished the script, met with the director, Denis Spencer and started rehearsing in a room above a synagogue in Soho. It wasn't long before Jimmy and Hylda were at each other's throats again, both of them trying to add funny lines and visuals to their individual parts. We got through a week's rehearsal somehow with neither of them word perfect, particularly Hylda. Prior to opening in Blackpool, we were due to have a week's trial run at the

Bristol Hippodrome and I travelled down to Bristol on Sunday, the day before the Monday opening night. Harry Driver had decided not to come with me to Bristol, but to wait until the show opened at Blackpool the following week. So I drove to Bristol, checked in at a hotel near the theatre and decided to walk to the theatre and look at the set which was a replica of the Pledge's living room exactly as portrayed in the TV series. I arrived at the theatre and was just about to make my way to the stage door, when I saw Hylda. She was measuring something on a poster advertising the show.

'What are you doing Hylda?', I asked, causing her to drop the tape measure and almost fall off the chair.

She shrugged. 'I'm measuring the billing to make sure the 'J' for Jimmy isn't larger than the 'H' for Hylda!'

'You're joking Hylda,' I said.

'No I'm not,' she replied. 'Billing is very important and I'm the star of this show. I've got top billing and my name should be bigger than his.'

I pointed out that, as far as I could see, both names were the same size. Hylda sniffed, 'Aye, well - as long as mine's at the top. It's me they'll come to see you know - not him,' she added with a knowing wink. I nodded, smiled and walked into the theatre with an uneasy feeling that the ensuing 26 weeks at Blackpool would not be without it's problems. The curtain was up as I walked down the aisle. The set was excellent and I felt a tremor of excitement and anticipation as I looked forward to the following night's opening. It was going to be a full house - all the tickets had been sold - there was no need for the age-old custom of 'papering' the house which occurred when there were lots of unsold tickets and empty seats. In such cases the theatre management would distribute complimentary tickets to various organisations for their members to fill the empty seats. But tomorrow, every seat would be taken and paid for, with the exception of about 20 reserved for the Lord Mayor, his Lady Wife and a host of Civic Dignitaries.

At that moment the director, Dennis, arrived accompanied by Jimmy Jewel who had driven him to Bristol from London. We made our way up to the Circle Bar, to join the rest of the cast, where coffee and sandwiches had been prepared and where Hylda was already seated drinking her second port and brandy. Dennis was looking decidedly seedy, which I discovered was due to a combination of Jimmy's erratic driving and a two hour dissertation on the various malfunctions of his internal organs!

Eventually, we returned to the stage where Dennis held a read through, with scripts, then a full rehearsal without scripts. It soon became obvious that Hylda could neither remember her lines nor her moves and the rehearsal was a shambles. Surprisingly, Jimmy was practically word perfect. He was always a quick study and had adopted a system of recording any script he had to learn on a tape recorder, but omitting his own lines, then playing it back to himself. It obviously worked. Dennis dismissed everybody and told them to go back to their various hotels, learn their lines and we would meet up again in the theatre the following morning at ten o'clock.

Jimmy and I were staying at the same hotel and we arranged to meet for dinner. Dinner with Jimmy was always an ordeal. One reason was that he didn't drink, whilst I was an apprentice alcoholic! There is nothing worse than having dinner with someone who drinks tonic water while you are imbibing large whiskies, and tries to convince you that alcohol rots your liver. The result was that I drank twice as much as I would normally have done, and Jimmy had to help me to bed!

The following morning, we all met at the theatre. The first read through was no better than the previous day. Hylda still didn't know her lines. Dennis was distraught. In less than seven hours the curtain was due to rise on a full house and the leading lady couldn't remember her lines. What were we to do?

Jimmy came up with a solution. He told us all to go to lunch and come back in an hour.

When we returned, we assembled on stage where Jimmy and Dennis were waiting. Dennis started to speak. 'During the past hour, Jimmy and I have been through the script and marking various points in the dialogue with which Hylda is having difficulty.' Hylda cut in, 'It's not my fault. The script's badly written. It's difficult to learn.' Jimmy glared angrily at her and was about to reply, when Dennis hastily intervened. 'Be that as it may, Jimmy told me that when he and his partner Ben Warriss were faced with doing a TV sketch series and had to learn two or three new sketches each week, they used to write little notes containing certain cue lines and distribute them around the studio set to help them remember. Well, we've done that with the play.' He went on to explain to Hylda that she would find several notes scattered about the stage to help her. We rehearsed again and this time, with the help of the notes, it was much better. We did one last dress rehearsal before it was time to break and prepare for the opening. The audience began to arrive. Dennis called me into the Production Office to discuss the traditional curtain speech which every star makes after a show. Dennis was worried because, contractually, Hylda and Jimmy had equal billing and he was uncertain as to who would make the curtain speech. So he arrived at a compromise. He suggested that Jimmy should start by saying a few lines then he should introduce Hylda who would do a normal curtain speech before handing back to her co-star. I agreed with Dennis and he asked me to go with him to explain it to Hylda. We went to see her in her dressing room and Dennis started to tell her about the curtain speech. He got as far as saying 'Jimmy should start ...' when Hylda cut him short with 'Just a minute. I'm the star of this f***ing show. I do the f***king curtain speech!' We both stared at her, nodded, bowed and shuffled out backwards. We then went next door to Jimmy's dressing room to talk to him. We had hardly got inside the door when Jimmy, who had heard our conversation with Hylda through the paper thin walls of the dressing rooms, said 'If she does the curtain speech, I'm driving back home to London first thing in the morning!.' Dennis and I did what any sensible persons would do - we went to the Circle Bar and ordered large whiskies! By now the Lord Mayor and his entourage had arrived. At that moment, the stage manager dashed into the bar, a look of horror on his face. 'They've gone Dennis,' he said, 'they've all gone.' Dennis stared at him blankly, 'Who's gone?' he asked. 'The notes for Hylda. The cues. They've all been taken down. Some super efficient scene hand must have removed them.'

Dennis and I looked at each other. At that moment the orchestra struck up the overture. Dennis held his head in his hands. 'What are we going to do Vince?' I said, 'I don't know about you Dennis but I'm going to have another large whisky!'

Dennis and I watched the show from the back of the circle. There has never been an opening night, before or since to equal it. For the first ten minutes or so, all went well. Then Hylda stumbled over a line, searched in vain for a cue then froze, Jimmy walked to the footlights and announced, 'She's forgotten her lines. I told her to put more water in her whisky.' There was a roar of laughter from the audience who thought it was all part of the script. Hylda, like the trouper she was, retorted, 'shut your face', and hit him with her handbag. Another roar of laughter from the audience. And so it went on. Each time Hylda forgot a line Jimmy would make a sarcastic comment to which Hylda would reply with an appropriate insult. The audience loved it thinking that it was all part of the script. At the interval, Dennis and I went down to Hylda's and Jimmy's dressing rooms to tell them how well it was doing and to keep up with the verbal insults. They both ignored our advice and it became obvious that they were now so deeply involved in a personal battle as to which of them could 'top' the other in terms of getting laughs, that the plot of the play became a secondary consideration. Fortunately the supporting cast held the plot together and the play finished to tumultuous applause and a standing ovation.

Dennis and I waited. The cast took their bows and the applause died down. The theatre grew silent as the audience awaited the curtain speech. An eternity seemed to go by. Then Hylda nudged Jimmy. 'Go on then,' she said. Jimmy stepped forward and said. 'Thank you Ladies and Gentlemen. You've been a wonderful audience. If you enjoyed the show go home and tell all your friends. If you didn't enjoy the show, keep your mouth shut! But now it's my great pleasure to introduce the star of our show - Miss Hylda Baker.'

Hylda made a very good speech. She thanked the audience, she thanked the Lord Mayor - she even managed to thank

Jimmy Jewel. She was presented with two large bouquets of flowers. The audience applauded and the curtain came down only to go up again immediately. They took five curtain calls before it finally stayed down and the audience started to leave. Dennis and I were in the wings waiting to go and congratulate Hylda and Jimmy, Dennis turned to me and said that the show exceeded his expectation and that the over efficient stage hand had done everyone a favour by removing all the notes. I nodded and smiled. Not for one moment did I believe it was a stage hand - I was convinced that it was an act of revenge perpetrated by a certain person standing not too far away. Dennis and I made our way across the stage to congratulate Hylda, Jimmy and the rest of the cast. The management had provided two bottles of champagne and a glass was handed to everyone, even Jimmy accepted one. Dennis called for a toast to the success of the forthcoming Blackpool season and said to Hylda 'It's going to be a big hit Hylda,' to which she replied 'Aye, well that's because I re-wrote most of the script!' Jimmy stared at her, a look of fury on his face. 'You lying sod!' he said, 'you couldn't even write your bloody name!' With that, he threw the rest of his champagne in her face and walked off the stage followed by a stream of insults from Hylda. Contrary to what you may have expected, Jimmy didn't leave the show. He turned up at the theatre the next morning to rehearse but you could have cut the atmosphere between him and Hylda with a knife. They barely looked at each other let alone speak to each other. I wondered how that evening's performance would go. But to my amazement it went like a bomb! Each time that Hylda and Jimmy insulted each other, the audience roared, still under the impression that it was part of the show. And so it continued throughout the rest of the week. I had phoned Harry to tell him what had happened and he couldn't wait to travel up to Blackpool to see for himself.

Opening night at the Blackpool Grand was unbelievable. It was 'standing room only'. Harry and I watched the show with Leslie Grade from a box that had been specially reserved for us. The more Hylda and Jimmy insulted each other, the more the audience laughed. There was one moment during which Hylda was delivering a particularly comic speech when

Jimmy stood behind her and started to pull funny faces at the audience. Hylda turned, saw him and proceeded to hit him with her umbrella. The audience went into hysterics. That night, the curtain calls seemed to go on forever. After the show, Harry and I, along with Hylda and Jimmy were invited to join Leslie Grade for dinner at his hotel. When we were all seated, Leslie, an astute businessman and showman, who knew of the enmity between Hylda and Jimmy and what had occurred at Bristol, addressed us all.

'What we have here,' he said, 'is a smash hit - more by accident than design.' He looked at Hylda and Jimmy. 'I am aware that, on a personal level there is no love lost between you. But you are both professionals and for the next 26 weeks, you must put your personal feelings to one side and learn to work together for the good of the show. Vince and Harry have written a good script which works in spite of your mutual animosity and the audiences love the way you insult each other. So let's keep the insults and the laughs flowing until the end of the season.'

Hylda and Jimmy were both intelligent enough to see the sense in Leslie's observations and the show carried on to become one of the Grand Theatre's biggest summer season's hits. Hylda and Jimmy still remained at loggerheads. They rarely, if ever, spoke to each other for the rest of the 26 weeks. When the season ended, Leslie Grade began negotiating for a further season, the following summer. But Jimmy flatly refused to ever work with Hylda again and he didn't. He wasn't the only actor to have problems with her. In 1973 she was appearing in a summer season show at the Windmill Theatre, Great Yarmouth. Her co-star was Jack Haigh, a funny and respected comedian. Shortly after the play opened, Jack took a whole page in The Stage newspaper. In the middle of the page he put an announcement which stated his name, where he was appearing and with whom. Underneath in large capitals was one word - HELP!. Hylda did another television series in 1974. It was commissioned by Leslie Grade's son Michael who was then the Programme Controller at London Weekend Television and written by Tom Brennand and Roy Bottomley who had written several of the TV episodes of 'NEAREST AND DEAREST'. The series was set in a pub and ran to 17 episodes but was only moderately successful. Shortly after, Hylda became ill and was having trouble with her memory. Her condition worsened and she was eventually admitted to Brinsworth House the Entertainment Artists' Benevolent Home in Twickenham where she spent the rest of her life until her death in 1986. A remarkable woman. Yes, she was difficult but she was one of the funniest comediennes I have ever worked with and I was very fond of her.

Chapter Eleven:
A WEDDING, A BIRTH AND A DEATH

Judi and I were on our way to Ernie and Doreen Wise's house in Dorney Reach, Maidenhead on the banks of the Thames. Some months ago, Philip and Florence Jones had invited a few friends to dinner at their home. There was Judi and I, Ernie and Doreen Wise, Billy and Sandra Dainty and Pearl Carr and Teddy Johnson. Billy was a buck-toothed, singing, dancing comedian who I first met in 1967 when Harry and I wrote a TV sitcom pilot 'THAT'S SHOW BUSINESS' which was made for ABC Television, but failed to impress neither Philip Jones or the viewers. However, Billy and I became firm friends and from time to time I wrote bits of material and gags for him to use in his TV guest appearances. Pearl Carr and Teddy Johnson were old friends of Philip and Florence's having worked together for Radio Luxembourg. Philip as a producer and Teddy as a disc jockey. Florence was Philip's secretary before they got married. We had a terrific evening with lots of jokes and show business reminiscences. A couple of weeks later, Billy and Sandra returned the compliment and we all went to Billy's house where we were joined by Harry and Kay Worth. A couple of weeks later, Judi and I hosted a dinner party with the same set of guests, then Pearl and Teddy did the same. It soon became a regular thing and we thoroughly enjoyed them. On this particular occasion after being wined and dined during which we swapped lots of show business anecdotes, we all made our farewells to Ernie and Doreen and headed back to our respective homes. Judi was driving and I switched on the car radio to listen to the news. There was an item about the recent influx of West Indian immigrants and the problems this was causing. Members of the public were being interviewed. One man said that his worry was, that the house next door to his was up for sale and that if a West Indian family bought it, it would affect the price of his own house when and if he came to sell. I agreed with the man's views which prompted Judi to accuse me of being a racist. We argued all the way home but by the time we arrived home, we had stopped arguing, in fact we weren't even speaking.

The following morning, I got up early and drove to Harry's house. He was still in bed. His wife was up and made me a coffee which I took into Harry's bedroom. He was sitting up in bed listening to the radio. He looked surprised to see me at such an early hour.

'Has she kicked you out then?' he asked. 'Listen,' I replied. 'I've had a fabulous idea for a sitcom.' 'I'm listening,' he said. I nodded, 'There's this white couple, husband and wife, who live in - say Twickenham - in a semi detached house. The house next door becomes vacant, and a West Indian couple buy it. What do you think?'

Harry shrugged 'What do you mean - what do I think?'

'Can't you see it would make a great series? We could exploit all the attitudes and prejudices between whites and blacks. The white guy could be working class and very left wing. The black guy could be intellectually superior and right wing. It'll practically write itself.'

Harry frowned, 'Well I hope so, 'cos I'm not going to write it with you.'

I looked at him in astonishment. 'Why not?' I asked.

'We'd be on a hiding to nothing,' he replied. It's too controversial. The critics would tear us to pieces.'

'Oh come on Harry,' I said, 'who cares what a few critics think?'

'I'll tell you who cares,' said Harry. 'Philip Jones for a start. Then the Independent Television Authority followed by the advertisers, then the viewers.'

I couldn't believe what I was hearing. Harry and I rarely, if ever, disagreed and I didn't understand why he couldn't see the possibilities in the idea and what a great sitcom it would make. For several minutes, I pointed out all the plusses in the situation, but he was adamant. Finally, he said, 'All right Vince, I'll tell you what I'll do. Give Philip a ring and run the idea past him. If he likes it and agrees to make a pilot, I'll write it with you. Okay?'

I rang Philip who was in a meeting so I decided to drive to the studios, take him to lunch and put the idea to him, face to face. I drove to Teddington, still bemused at Harry's reaction. After parking my car, I went up to the Terrace Bar, leaving a message with Philip's secretary for him to meet me in the bar. I was on my second large Bell's when Philip arrived. He was anxious to know why I wanted to see him, and I was equally anxious to tell him. We went into the Executive Restaurant, ordered lunch and a bottle of Gevrey Chambertin and I spent the next 45 minutes trying to convince him that my idea of a sitcom about a black family living next door to a white family could be Thames Television's next big success. To my surprise and disappointment, Philip's reaction was the same as Harry's had been. 'It's too controversial luvvie . . . We'd never get it past the I.T.A. ... we'd be crucified by the press.' I reminded Philip that Johnny Speight's 'TILL DEATH US DO PART' starring Warren Mitchell and considered by some critics as being racist was a big success on the BBC, but Philip's opinion didn't change and I gave up. Being exclusive to Thames, I couldn't offer it to another broadcaster so I decided to admit defeat.

Harry and I continued to think of an idea for Jimmy Jewel and eventually came up with a good one. Jimmy would play Tommy Butler, an elderly widower living in an old terraced house which was due to be pulled down. He was going to be re-housed in a new block of high rise flats miles away from where his daughter Vera and son-in-law Brian lived. He refused to move and barricaded himself in his terraced house. Eventually, Vera agreed that her father could live with her and Brian in their modern semi-detached house. At the same time, 12 year old Charlie Harris was living nearby with his divorced mother Betty in a rented flat. Tommy and Charlie met and, despite their differences in age, struck up a friendship. Tommy became a kind of surrogate father to the young boy, while Charlie took the place of Tommy's young son who tragically died when he was only five years old.

Harry and I both firmly believed that in devising a potentially successful sitcom, it must contain certain ingredients. Firstly, the situation and the characters must be believable. Secondly, it must have areas of comedy, drama and even pathos. We felt that this new sitcom filled all those requirements. There was plenty of scope for comedy and drama in the situation of an elderly parent living with in-laws, there were areas of comedy and pathos in the relationship between the aged, often cantankerous Tommy and the cheeky young boy. Philip Jones liked the pilot script, and commissioned our old friend Stuart Allen to produce and direct it. We all liked the end result and we decided to go ahead with a series, which we called 'SPRING AND AUTUMN'. However, Philip couldn't find a slot in the schedule for at least six months.

Harry and I were all set to start writing the scripts, but Philip advised us to wait. He had something much more important in mind which would re-unite us with one of our first successes. Philip had long been an admirer of Harry Worth and after one of our show business dinners, had offered him the opportunity of doing a series for Thames. To his delight, Harry who had always worked for the BBC, agreed. Harry Driver and I were then asked to think of a suitable idea. We agreed that, as Harry Worth had done over a hundred episodes of situation comedies we should look for something different and decided that we would devise a thirty minute sketch show and came up with the title 'THIRTY MINUTES WORTH' which we thought was quite clever. Each thirty minutes would contain 3 or 4 sketches plus a couple of quickies which would feature Harry bumbling and dithering his way through various comic situations with different supporting casts. So far, so good. The next problem was to find somebody to write it. Harry and I had never been at our writing best with a sketch show format so we looked around and were fortunate in finding not one, but three experienced sketch writers who had written successfully for BBC radio and TV. They were Mike Craig, Lawrie Kinsley and Ron McDonnell, a trio of Northern writers with a decided flair for broad comedy. Ideal for Harry Worth. They were contracted and wrote three successful series.

Harry Driver and I decided that we needed a holiday and we took a couple of weeks off to drive to the South of France, Harry, his wife and their son Stephen being driven in their Rolls Corniche by Jack Ripley, with Judi and I following in our Rolls Bentley.

Rather then taking the car ferry from Dover to Calais, we decided to use British Air Ferries which flew from Lydd to Le Touquet. Each squat, little plane could take about 4 cars and passengers on the twenty minute trip across the Channel. After landing Jack and I set off in convoy to join the Route National 7, the main three lane highway to Nice, nicknamed the 'Murderess' because of the high number of fatal casualties which occurred each year. Fortunately we did the journey safely and after an overnight stop in Macon, we arrived at the Cote d'Azur in brilliant sunshine.

Harry and his family were staying in an apartment at the Cannes Palace and Judi and I were staying at a villa further along the coast in Eze-sur-Mer. During our stay, we spent most of our days just relaxing in the sunshine on the beach, fortified by glasses of Orangina for Harry and Biere Pressions for me. If someone had have said to me when Harry was first struck down with Polio and we were struggling to make a mark as comedy writers, that we would one day be sunning ourselves by the sea in the South of France, I would have said they were mad. But here we were, doing just that. How fortunate we were, doing a job we both loved, working in an industry we both enjoyed and meeting so many talented and wonderful people. One good thing came out of the holiday. We all decided to drive to Monaco one day and behave like tourists. We went to the Oceanographic Museum with its world famous aquarium then made our way toward the 16th Century Palais du Prince. On the way, we passed the 19th Century Cathedral where Prince Rainier of Monaco married the famous Hollywood film star, Grace Kelly. Co-incidentally, as we passed a wedding was taking place and we stopped to watch the bride and groom leaving the Cathedral. Judi, always the romantic and easily moved to tears, dried her eyes. I looked at her and whispered, 'Maybe it's time we got married', which produced another flood of tears.

We returned from our holiday, refreshed and raring to go. Mike Craig and his co-writers had written the first three scripts for 'THIRTY MINUTES WORTH' and they were extremely funny. Philip still hadn't got any recording dates for 'SPRING AND AUTUMN' so Judi and I went ahead with our wedding plans. I rang Billy Dainty and invited him to be my best man which he accepted. As I was a lapsed Catholic and divorced, a church wedding was not an option so we decided to have a Registry Office wedding. I posted the banns in Epsom then began the formidable task of compiling the list of people we wished to invite. For the actual ceremony at the Registry Office we had about 20 guests which included my father, my cousin Ivy and her boy friend, Judi's parents, her brother and his wife, Harry and Edith Driver, the Ernie Wise's, the Harry Worth's, the Philip Jones's and the Sid James's. The ceremony went off without incident apart from the moment the best man had to produce the wedding ring, and Billy did a comedy routine, pretending that he'd either mislaid it or that one of the celebrity guests had picked his pocket. Fortunately the Registrar had a sense of humour. After Judi and I had signed the wedding certificate and had it witnessed we left for the wedding reception at the Seven Hills Hotel in Cobham, where over fifty guests were waiting to congratulate us. We had invited many of the celebrities with whom Harry and I had worked. Ronnie Baxter and the cast of 'NEVER MIND THE QUALITY' ... Irene Handl, Wilfred and Mabel Pickles, Stuart Allen and the cast of 'FOR THE LOVE OF ADA', Alan Tarrant, Peggy Mount, Michael Grade (He couldn't come but sent his chauffeur with a case of Champagne). It was a wonderful day. Billy made a terrifically funny speech which I wish I'd recorded, before escorting Judi and I out to our taxi which was to take us to London Heathrow for our flight to our honeymoon in Rome.

We stayed at the Hotel Quirinale and did all the usual things - we threw coins in the Trevi Fountain and made a wish, we climbed the Spanish Steps, visited Vatican City and the Sistine Chapel, walked down the Appian Way and called in at the Church of Domine Quo Vadis where there is a copy of the footprint traditionally believed to have been left by Jesus when he turned Peter back to Rome.

We returned home to find that, due to Thames's very busy output there was still no news of any recording dates for 'SPRING AND AUTUMN'. Studio space was limited - Thames only had three studios which had to be shared by the Drama Department, Light Entertainment and Children's programmes so we had to take our place in the queue. Thames was the most successful of the various ITV companies. Last year they had produced a staggering number of 86 programmes which included such favourites as 'AND MOTHER MAKES THREE'. 'ARMCHAIR THEATRE', 'BENNY HILL', 'BLESS THIS HOUSE', 'CALLAN', 'FATHER DEAR FATHER', 'FOR THE LOVE OF ADA'. 'FRANKIE HOWERD', 'DAVE ALLEN', 'MAGPIE', 'MAX BYGRAVES', 'MIKE AND BERNIE', 'NEVER MIND THE QUALITY ...', 'OPPORTUNITY KNOCKS', 'THE SOOTY SHOW', and 'THIS IS YOUR LIFE' to name but a few. No wonder the studios were stretched almost to breaking point.

Howard Thomas, the Managing Director of Thames Television decided that all the production staff should spend a weekend in a Brighton Hotel during which ideas would be exchanged, and people from the various departments, many of whom rarely met each other, could mix and mingle. Philip asked me to go along and talk about the Light Entertainment Department's plans for the future. Little did I know that the events of the next hour would have a lasting and remarkable affect on my career. We assembled in a large conference room, Howard Thomas made a short welcoming speech and called on Philip Jones to address the gathering. Philip spoke about the current state of Light Entertainment then asked me to elaborate. I stood up and went through our plans for the future - another series of 'FATHER DEAR FATHER' written by Brian Cooke and Johnnie Mortimer, more 'HARRY WORTH SHOWS', and a new series for Jimmy Jewel. I glanced across at Howard Thomas and then took a gamble.

'But what I would really like to do is a series about a West

Indian family moving to live next door to a white family.' Beside me, Philip groaned and shook his head. Then Howard Thomas said, 'That's a very interesting idea. We should do a pilot.' The Head of Drama, Jeremy Isaacs echoed Howard's remarks and said that he had also been considering a similar idea for a drama series. In fact, when I last met Sir Jeremy, as he is now known, his recollection was that he mentioned the drama idea first, but I'm sure my memory is the correct version. However, I was elated and couldn't wait to get back and tell Harry. Philip was still worried about the idea but couldn't very well go against the wishes of his own Managing Director, and agreed that we should go ahead and do a pilot programme.

True to his word, Harry agreed to write the pilot script with me and, with Stuart Allen as Producer/Director we went into production. Stuart, with a little prompting from me, cast Jack Smethurst to play Eddie Booth, the bigoted, left wing white neighbour with Gwendolyn Watts playing his wife. The West Indian neighbours were played by Rudolph Walker and lovely Nina Baden-Semper. The pilot was approved by Howard Thomas and Philip gave us the green light to do a series of seven shows. Due to a contractual difficulty, Gwendolyn Watts was unable to do the series proper so we had to remake the pilot, with Kate Williams taking on the role of Eddie's wife. We deliberately made Eddie Booth a working class Labour supporter, and his neighbour, Bill Reynolds a slightly more intellectual Conservative to capitalise on the comedy we could use in their different attitudes, politically, socially and personally. We are now talking about attitudes which existed in the early 1970's when it was common for British workers to address each other by using nicknames. Thus, a Welshman was a Taffy, a Scotsman a Jock, an Irishman a Paddy, an Italian an Eyetie, a Chinaman a Chink, a German a Kraut and a black man a Sambo. These names were used not as insults but as a matter of course and were said and received with good humour. The re-made pilot went well and was transmitted a few days later. We all waited anxiously for the reviews. The television critic of one of the daily tabloids tore the programme to pieces. 'Disgraceful - downright racist - Powell and Driver should hang their heads in shame - Thames Television deserve to lose their licence' and so on.

Meanwhile, in the same newspaper a few pages further on, some enterprising journalist had sat and watched the programme with a West Indian family who thought it was terrific and laughed all the way through. The series was a huge success. The critics hated it but the viewers loved it especially the black communities. They looked upon it as their show. It was the first situation comedy in which leading roles were played by black actors. At its peak it reached audiences of over 17 million viewers. The series ran for 56 episodes in the UK over eight series. A feature film based on the series was made by Hammer Films and became the highest grossing British movie in 1973, a stage play based on the series played to packed houses at the Winter Gardens Theatre Blackpool for 28 weeks in the summer of 1973, then 26 weeks the following summer at the Windmill Theatre Great Yarmouth, a ten week British tour in 1974, then an 8 week tour of Australia. America and Australia made their own TV versions. The British TV series was a big hit in the West Indies where it was watched by the whole population night after night and the series was sold all over the world. If that isn't success I don't know what is. It just goes to show how out of touch the TV critics were with the viewing public.

It's true, we did get letters from some viewers complaining about the white actor calling his black neighbour 'Sambo' and 'Nig Nog' but we never received one letter from a viewer complaining about the black actor calling his neighbour 'Honky' (Pig) and 'Snowflake'. Perhaps we got the balance right in spite of what the critics thought.

Harry and I finished writing the first series of 'LOVE THY NEIGHBOUR' and due to it's immediate success, Philip asked us to start writing a second series, again produced and directed by Stuart Allen. It was such an enjoyable series to write and won the readers of the Sun newspaper award for the best situation comedy.

At the start of the second series, I found out that I was going to become a father, for the first time. Both Judi and I were delighted and when I broke the news to my Dad that he would soon be a Grandfather, he wept tears of joy. His condition had slightly worsened and he was walking much slower. I decided to advertise for a housekeeper for him and was lucky enough to find a charming Welsh lady, Vera. She was divorced and had a 9 year old daughter Karen, so she accepted the position, which was ideal for both her and my Dad. We arranged for Judi to have the baby at Mount Alvernia, a Catholic maternity hospital in Guildford which was owned and maintained by the Franciscan Missionaries of the Divine Motherhood, a dedicated order of Nuns. A date was fixed around the day our baby was expected. All we had to do was wait.

While we waited, Harry and I completed writing the second series of 'LOVE THY NEIGHBOUR' during which a catchphrase was born. We had written a scene in the social club of the engineering firm at which both Eddie and Bill worked. Eddie was ordering drinks for his mates Arthur, a Cockney played by Tommy Godfrey and Jacko, a cloth capped Northerner played by Keith Marsh and Bill. The dialogue went something like this:

EDDIE: Right barman, that's a pint for me. How about you Sambo?
BILL: I'll have a pint.
EDDIE: Arthur.
ARTHUR: I'll have a pint.
EDDIE: Jacko.
JACKO: I'll 'ave 'alf.

For some reason, the studio audience laughed - don't ask me why. So in the next episode we repeated the sequence and they laughed again. And it became a catchphrase. Long after the series ended, whenever Keith was spotted in the street, people would greet him with 'I'll 'ave 'alf.' I still don't know why audiences found it so funny.

At the end of the second series, we got a call from Leslie Grade, inviting us to write a stage play based on 'LOVE THY NEIGHBOUR' which he wanted to present the following year at the Winter Gardens Theatre in Blackpool. We began work on it immediately and finished writing it in January 1973, which was fortunate as a week later, in the middle of the night, Judi went into labour. I bundled her into the car and drove to Mount Alvernia. For over an hour I paced up and down a waiting room until one of the Nuns came in and told me that Judi was about to be wheeled into the delivery room, and would I like to be present at the birth. I nodded and followed her down a corridor. As we went through the door to the delivery room, I glanced up and saw a sign reading 'Bethlehem' which I thought was rather apt. Judi was lying in bed with her legs in the breech position - not a pretty sight. Our gynaecologist was in attendance urging Judi to push hard with each contraction. Neither Judi or I knew whether we were about to have a son or a daughter, as both of us had declined to be told after the scan. Finally, after heaving and grunting accompanied by a few choice swear words, our baby appeared. The first thing I noticed was a penis, then the umbilical cord was cut and he was smacked on the bottom which resulted in him greeting his arrival with an ear piercing cry. I stayed with Judi for a couple of hours, by which time she was tired so I drove back home and called on Dad to tell him he had a grandson. We drank to his health with a few large Bell's, then I returned home and spent the next few hours on the 'phone to my many friends to give them the news.

The next day, I drove to Mount Alvernia to see Judi and our son. Sister Maria reminded me that, as a Catholic I should have our son baptised as soon as possible. However, Judi wasn't a Catholic but agreed that our son could be baptised into the Catholic faith. Although I had never been inside a Catholic church for a long time, the many years of being taught the Catholic faith still had its effect. Once a Catholic, always a Catholic they used to say. After a lot of deliberation we finally chose the name Dominic. A baptism was arranged at our local Catholic Church, St. Charles Borromeo and we asked Billy Dainty, Florence Jones and Judi's brother Errol to be Godparents. My old Parish Priest, Father Ignatious insisted on travelling down from Manchester to officiate and Dominic was baptised on the 24th of March 1973.

Meanwhile, Harry and I put the finishing touches to the stage play of 'LOVE THY NEIGHBOUR' which was to be directed by Stuart Allen. The initial signs were encouraging.

Although it was only March, and the show was not due to open until early June, the advance bookings were beyond all our expectations and we all looked forward to a bumper summer season.

We were looking forward to writing the next series of 'LOVE THY NEIGHBOUR' when we got a call from Hammer Films asking us to write a movie based on 'LOVE THY NEIGHBOUR.' There was only one snag. Could we write it in a week as they had a gap in their studios? Never the ones to turn down an offer of work, we agreed and worked night and day to complete the script. The successful director of Thames TV's 'BENNY HILL' series, John Robins was brought in, and the film was shot mostly on location at Elstree film studios. As I have mentioned earlier it was a big box office success with the movie audiences but not surprisingly with the film critics who again accused us of racism. However, Harry and I never let the adverse criticisms we received worry us as they were more than compensated by the script fee and our share of the profits!

Shortly after the film opened Philip announced that he now had some dates available for us to record 'SPRING AND AUTUMN' so we started to write the scripts. Due to the fact that the pilot had been recorded almost a year ago, and by now, a couple of the original cast and the Producer/Director were no longer available, we had to re-cast and remake the show. Our old friend Ronnie Baxter was called on to produce and direct the series, which was a gentle comedy and was well received by both the critics and the viewers and a second series was planned for the following year.

The play of 'LOVE THY NEIGHBOUR' opened in Blackpool to excellent revues and 'Standing Room Only' notices. Life could not have been better. We had a further TV series of 'LOVE THY NEIGHBOUR' to complete, plus a second series of 'SPRING AND AUTUMN'. But, as had happened before, fate dealt us a cruel blow which totally changed the rest of my life.

I was awakened one Sunday in the early hours of the morning by the telephone ringing. It was Jack in an obviously distressed state. 'Vince' he gasped, 'its Harry. He's dead!'

Chapter Twelve:
A NEW BEGINNING

Harry had died peacefully in his sleep. His lungs had given out just as the doctors had predicted when he first contracted Polio in 1957. A life expectancy of fifteen years they'd said. Well, he'd proved them all wrong. He'd lived for 16 years. As you can imagine, it was a huge shock to us all. Harry was cremated at Randall's Crematorium in Leatherhead after which we had two wakes, the first at Harry's bungalow in Weybridge which went on for a couple of hours, then as people began to drift away, I invited some of the show business element over to my house to carry on drinking. The cast of 'LOVE THY NEIGHBOUR' and 'SPRING AND AUTUMN' came as did Philip Jones. Naturally, as you can guess the main topic of conversation was about the future. What was going to happen to the projects which Harry and I had in the pipeline? I was in no mood to think about the future - to be honest I was in no fit state to think about anything, being more than a little drunk. Philip suggested that he and I meet the following morning at the studios and we all began to disperse.

I hardly slept that night. I was still in a state of shock at Harry's death. We had been friends and collaborators for almost 25 years. Various images from our long association flashed in and out of my mind - our first meeting, the double act we formed, Harry trapped in his iron lung, our first writing success, and subsequent rise to fame, Harry proudly sitting in his Rolls Corniche, our office overlooking the Thames, a smiling Harry sitting with me on top of the Arc de Triomphe and many more. My mind was in a turmoil. I tossed and turned for hours until I finally fell asleep through sheer exhaustion. The next day, I drove to the studios where I met with Philip.

'You look terrible,' said Philip.

'I feel terrible,' I replied.

Philip produced a sheet of foolscap paper and pushed it toward me. 'I've done a lot of thinking since last night Vince. I realise that probably the last thing you feel like doing right now is writing a comedy script, so I've made a list of possible writers with whom you may feel you could collaborate to help you finish the current series of 'LOVE THY NEIGHBOUR' and the forthcoming second series of 'SPRING AND AUTUMN.'

I pushed the sheet of paper back across the desk. 'I appreciate that Philip, but I won't need this. I too, have done a bit of thinking and I've decided that the best tribute I could pay to Harry would be for me to continue to write the scripts on my own. Finding a new writing partner would not be easy. Harry and I had such a good writing relationship that it would be very difficult to find another comedy writer with the same sense of humour to take Harry's place.'

Philip was very understanding and we agreed that I should go ahead and write the next episode of 'LOVE THY NEIGHBOUR' and see how it turned out. We shook hands and I went back home to start writing. I couldn't face trying to write sitting alone in our empty office surrounded by memories. So I sat in my study and tried to think of a plot for the next episode. It wasn't easy. The problem was, without Harry, I no longer had a sounding board from which to bounce ideas off. In the past, whenever one of us had a funny idea or a funny line, we used to try it out on each other to get a reaction. Now, I had nobody to try it out on and nobody to give me a reaction. I had to rely on my own judgement as to whether a line was funny or not. I realised that many writers' who habitually wrote alone had been doing this for ages, but it didn't make it any easier for me. However, I persevered, came up with a workable plot with which I was happy and wrote the script. When I had finished, I drove to the studios, handed a copy of the script to Philip's secretary and told her I would be in our - (sorry - force of habit) - my office. I helped myself to a large Bells and waited nervously for

Philip. He arrived holding the script. For a moment he didn't speak, and then he broke into a huge grin and shook my hand.

'Congratulations Vince,' he said, 'it's a very funny script. It's every bit as good as the ones you and Harry wrote together.' I breathed a sigh of relief. From that moment on I became more confident about writing alone. I completed writing the final 3 scripts in the series which, as before, were well received by the viewers although still hated by the critics. At the end of the series the Producer/Director Ronnie Baxter was head-hunted by Yorkshire Television and joined their Light Entertainment department where he went on to direct several successful situation comedy series.

This was a big disappointment to me as Ronnie was one of the best Producer/Directors I had ever worked with. Not only did we have to find another Director for 'LOVE THY NEIGHBOUR' but also for 'SPRING AND AUTUMN'. I knew that 'SPRING AND AUTUMN' was a series close to Ronnie's heart. It was a gentle series, along the same lines of 'FOR THE LOVE OF ADA' which Ronnie also produced and directed. Ronnie was a very sensitive director who used a language of his own. He once said to me about an idea I'd suggested, 'Let's run it up the flagpole and see if anyone salutes it.' To an actor, commenting on his performance he said, 'Find something to hang your hat on!' To an actress, trying to advise her on how to deliver a certain speech, he said, 'When you say those lines, can you go through the gears?' I knew what he meant but not many other people did. He lived in Shepperton and I have many fond memories of sitting in his dining room eating fish and chips with him and his lovely wife Rita and trying to improve my latest script.

However, Thames's loss was Yorkshire's gain and Philip invited me in one day to meet a young director who he thought would be ideal to direct the next series of 'LOVE THY NEIGHBOUR'. His name was Anthony Parker and he was formerly an actor having appeared in several films including 'EXODUS', 'THE WORLD OF SUZIE WONG' and 'QUATERMASS.' He also starred in the long running TV series of 'DIXON OF DOCK GREEN' before deciding that his future in television would be better for him behind, rather than in front of, the cameras.

He joined Associated Television as a Floor Manager, responsible for ensuring that everything in the studio was ready and in position on each recording day, including props, sound and cameras. Eventually, he attended a Thames training course on producing and directing and after directing several children's programmes was chosen by Philip to produce and direct the next series of 'LOVE THY NEIGHBOUR'. Philip arranged for the three of us to meet for lunch in the Executive Restaurant. I was a little nervous and I expect that Tony felt the same. The relationship between a writer and his director is a sensitive one. It's vital that both parties are on the same wavelength, particularly so in the often difficult area of comedy. Fortunately, we found that we both had one thing in common - a love of red wine!

Lunch went well and was the start of a long and happy friendship between Tony and I which still exists to this day. I started to write the next series with Tony producing and directing which, as usual, went well and remained Thames's highest sitcom in the audience ratings. On the strength of that a further series was planned, but before that could take place, I had to write the second series of 'SPRING AND AUTUMN'. Tony was unavailable as he was involved in directing a comedy pilot starring John Alderton so Philip gave the job to Mike Vardy who had recently joined Thames after directing several sitcoms for London Weekend Television. The series went equally as well as the first one and I presumed that a further series would be planned. However, Philip had never been over fond of gentle comedy and preferred the more robust, laugh-a-minute genre. Consequently, he took the decision not to proceed with 'SPRING AND AUTUMN'. This meant that I had a few weeks gap before I plunged into writing the next series of 'LOVE THY NEIGHBOUR'. Over lunch with Tony Parker one day I mentioned that I'd always wanted to write a gritty comedy about a working class Liverpool family. Tony was interested and suggested that I think of a plot and write an outline of the idea. So I set to work. I invented the Clarkson family - a husband Billy and wife Mary. She was a devout

Catholic and an even more devout supporter of Everton - he was a Protestant and a fanatical supporter of Liverpool. They have three children, 21 years old Tony, a student at Southampton University, 18 year old Bernadette and 16 year old Raymond still at school. The children are all Catholics and have two grandparents, Billy's widowed mother, Maggie and Mary's widower father, Joe.

Convinced that I had given myself plenty of opportunities for humour, conflict and moments of drama I wrote the outline for an opening episode in which Billy returns home from two years at sea in the Merchant Navy. At least that's his excuse. In reality he had been a guest of Her Majesty in Walton Prison. Mary, out of loyalty to her husband has kept this fact from her family, only to discover that they knew about it all along, having read a report in the local Liverpool newspaper. A homecoming party is planned at which all the family attend and which soon turns into arguments about politics, religion and football ending with Billy looking forward to resuming his conjugal rights. However, Mary is in no mood to share neither her bed nor her body after two years of celibacy and the episode ends with Billy sleeping on a bunk bed in Raymond's room.

Tony liked the plot, took it to Philip and convinced him that it would be full of the broad, earthy humour which Philip preferred. He did such a good selling job that Philip decided to dispense with the usual system of doing a pilot episode first, but to go straight into a series of seven half hours. Tony immediately started a casting session and invited me along to attend. To play Billy and Mary, we cast Liverpool born Ken Jones and his real life wife, Sheila Faye, and as their son Tony we cast David Casey, the son of BBC writer/producer James Casey, who, in turn was the son of the famous northern comedian, Jimmy James. To play their daughter, Bernadette we cast the Liverpool born and now extremely famous, Alison Steadman in her first ever situation comedy. For the role of their youngest son Raymond we chose Keith Chegwin, another Liverpudlian, later to achieve fame as a successful children's television presenter and an appearance on 'GET ME OUT OF HERE I'M A CELEBRITY'. Finally, we cast actress and comedienne Pearl Hackney, married to comedy actor Eric Barker to play Billy's mother, Maggie and to play Mary's father we cast Joe Gladwin, a talented character actor, later to star in 'LAST OF THE SUMMER WINE'. What a talented cast. We felt we couldn't go wrong. I started to write the scripts. After I'd written three, Philip called me into his office. He revealed that he was a little concerned at some of the earthiness in the scripts and wondered whether a few of the lines were a little too crude. I argued that I thought that they would be acceptable and reminded Philip that it was he who preferred the more broader comedy. He was eventually swayed by my arguments and I carried on writing.

Tony and I went up to Liverpool for a few days to do some preliminary filming, during which we devised an opening sequence using a montage of shots of Liverpool landmarks - a ferry crossing the River Mersey, the Liver Birds, the Catholic Cathedral, a Salvation Army Band and a mucky kid kicking a tin can in a back entry. We were lucky enough to have the help of a Liverpool actor, Bill Dean whom we had cast to play a publican in the series. When he heard we were going out filming, he offered to pick us up early in the morning at the Adelphi Hotel, where we were staying, and drive us to the various locations. True to his word, he picked us up at 6am and of we went, Tony, myself and a film crew. A couple of hours later, I mentioned to Bill, that I wouldn't mind stopping for a drink, meaning a cup of coffee. To most Liverpudlians, the word drink only has one meaning - alcohol. Consequently Bill drove us to his local pub, The Lord Nelson, or as he affectionately called it, The One Eyed Sailor. It was still only about eight thirty in the morning. Bill got out of the car and hammered on the pub doors. Eventually, an upstairs window was pushed open and the bleary eyed face of the pub landlord peered out at Bill.

'Oh it's you Bill,' he said, 'what do you want?'

'What to you think we want?' said Bill. 'We want a bloody drink.'

The landlord scowled. 'Do you know what time it is?'

Bill shrugged. 'Aye well, we're doing a bit of filming. I've got these fellers here from the television. You know what they're like. Can you open up?'

The landlord sighed. 'Hang on.'

His face withdrew and he shut the window. I tried to explain to Bill that all we wanted was coffee but he wouldn't listen. I'd said we wanted a drink and that's what we were going to get!

We waited. The pub doors opened and the landlord beckoned us inside. I asked for coffee but the landlord insisted on serving us all large brandies. Not wishing to offend, we drank them only for him to refill our glasses. He told us that he had only recently come out of hospital after having his legs filleted. We subsequently discovered that he had been operated on to have his varicose veins removed! By now, we were each on our third large brandy and all thoughts of coffee had been forgotten. None of us were in a fit state to carry on with the filming, so we did the only thing we could do - had a fourth brandy and took a taxi back to the Adelphi Hotel! We finished the filming the following day and returned to Teddington to start rehearsals for the first episode.

We all enjoyed recording the series and the studio audience laughed in all the right places. Philip was still worried about the scripts being too avant-garde but the reaction of the studio audience appeared to reassure him. We finished recording the last episode the week before the first episode was to be transmitted. Tony and I couldn't wait to read the critics reaction. We were convinced we were on the brink of a huge success. How wrong we were. So anxious were we to discover what the critics had to say, we drove into London at midnight, so that we could buy the early editions of the newspapers as they came hot off the press. To our surprise and dismay, they didn't like it. They said it was crude and vulgar. I drove home that night in a state of shock. How could I have got it so wrong? I have asked myself that question many times since and the only conclusion I have ever come to is that perhaps it was too avant-garde. One drama critic friend of mine suggested that, if I had written it as a drama and recorded it without a studio audience, it would have been perceived as a slice of Liverpool life. Maybe he was right - who knows?

The following day, Philip sent for Tony. He'd spent hours

viewing the rest of the series, and making notes. He told Tony that he wanted him to edit out all the cruder references from each episode, even if it meant that some episodes would only run for under twenty minutes. Tony, out of loyalty to me, protested. He felt that Philip was over reacting, and persuaded him to phone Jeremy Isaacs, Thames Controller of Programmes, to ask his opinion over such a drastic action. Jeremy spoke to Tony and asked him which of the following six episodes yet to be transmitted contained the most questionable vulgar references. Tony chose an episode which had some strong sexual jokes. Jeremy then spoke to Philip and said that this episode would be dropped but that the rest of the series would be transmitted without any editing. And that's what happened. Somehow, the news was leaked to the press and a statement was made to the effect that Thames would not make any more episodes. The next day, a banner headline appeared in The Sun newspaper reading 'GIVE US BACK OUR WACKERS'. The paper carried out a survey of its Liverpool readers and discovered that they were divided in their opinions. Fifty percent loved it and fifty percent loathed it. I don't think Philip ever forgave me but I still think it was a good series and, given time, would have been a big success. It was 'BREAD' a BBC series written by Carla Lane, ten years before its time. I am proud of having written it.

Philip's decision not to do any more of 'THE WACKERS' left Thames with a hole in their schedule which I decided I would try and fill. I devised a Jewish comedy about a 35 year old Jewish man, Reuben Greenberg, running the dry cleaning business started by his late father. Reuben was still a bachelor living with his mother Fay and literally, tied to her apron strings. He would love to leave home and get his own place, but every time the subject comes up, Fay throws a wobbly and feigns a heart attack. I wrote it with Bernard Spear, the Jewish actor who had been in 'NEVER MIND THE QUALITY. . . ' in mind. Tony cast Lila Kaye, a talented Jewish actress to play the part of Reuben's mother. I wrote a script for a pilot episode and called the series 'MY YIDDISHER MOMMA' and wanted to use Anne Shelton's recording of the song as the signature tune. That was my first mistake. Certain members of the Teddington staff objected saying the title was anti-semetic. How they could say that this popular song which was a tribute to a Jewish mother was anti-semetic I will never know. I would lay odds that every Jewish household owned a copy.

However, Philip, still very much mindful of the controversy over 'THE WACKERS', yielded to the objections and the title was changed to 'MY SON REUBEN'. We recorded six episodes, all of which were well received even by Philip who said that a decision to go ahead with a second series would be taken in a few weeks time.

In the event, Philip decided not to go ahead with a second series. I suspect that he was still suffering from the 'fall out' from 'THE WACKERS' and was concerned lest 'MY SON REUBEN' might be seen by some television critics as being anti-semetic. And so another good idea bit the dust. However, I barely had time to lick my wounds when an event occurred which was to change the course of my life again. I had a call from my accountant inviting me to lunch in London. I arrived at his office and we went to his favourite Italian restaurant. Over lunch, he informed me that, as I had now taken on all Harry's contractual commitments in addition to mine, I would be earning twice as much and therefore be liable for a very heavy income tax bill. There was only one solution which I already explained on the first page of this autobiography. If I went to live in France for an entire tax year, I would not incur any tax liabilities either in France or in the UK for the whole of that year. It was quite legal and was known as tax avoidance, as opposed to tax evasion. He advised me to think about it seriously before coming to a decision. I went home and talked it over with my wife, my agent and Philip Jones. My own personal opinion was to go and live in the south of France for a tax year, but that would mean re-negotiating my contract with Thames. Although I could still write scripts for them while living abroad, they may not agree to this and I certainly couldn't act as their comedy adviser from such a distance. Judi's opinion was that she would support any decision I made, but only I could make that decision. My agent advised caution pointing out the advantages and disadvantages of the situation which I was already aware of. There was also my father to consider. Although his condition was fairly stable, he was not getting any younger and there was no telling whether his illness would become worse. If I chose to go abroad for a tax year, I would not be allowed back in the UK under any circumstances during that year without becoming liable to pay the tax due for that year. After several meetings with everybody involved, including Philip, a mutually agreeable decision was arrived at.

My family and I would rent a suitable villa and go and live in the South of France for a tax year.

I would give up my contract with Thames to act as their comedy adviser, but continue to write a minimum of 13 situation comedy scripts a year and would remain under exclusive contract to Thames.

I would write a further series of 13 scripts for 'LOVE THY NEIGHBOUR' plus 2 pilot scripts for other sitcom series.

Tony Parker would visit me once a month to edit and approve of the scripts. Thames would pay his air fare and I would accommodate him in my villa.

Philip agreed that my main priority should be to continue writing scripts for the successful 'LOVE THY NEIGHBOUR' series which was still getting huge audiences as well as being sold to countries abroad.

I contacted Michael the estate agent through whom I had bought my father's flat and he agreed to let our Weybridge house for the year we were away.

I made a flying visit to Nice where I met with an estate agent, found a suitable villa in St. Jean Cap Ferrat and signed all the necessary documents to rent it for a year, before returning home to start planning my exodus which would be in a couple of months. Before I left I decided to write another pilot script for a future sitcom series which I could then write when I got to France. It was an idea which I had been toying with for some time about four sailors who had been shipmates in the Royal Navy and who, when they got demobbed, made a vow to meet again in 25 years time in London. They were an Englishman, an Irishman, a Scotsman and a Welshman, and I called the series 'RULE BRITANNIA.'

Tony cast four good character actors for the pilot - Tony Melody for the Englishman, Joe Lynch for the Irishman. Russell Hunter for the Scotsman and Richard Davies for the Welshman. The pilot episode mainly revolved around whether they would all remember their vow to meet and would they turn up. We meet each of them in turn, and they all do turn up. It was very jokey with lots of laughs and augured well for a future series, and I looked forward to writing the series during my time as a tax exile

The time was almost near for me to leave for France. I threw a farewell party on the boat at Thames attended by Philip and most of the people with whom I'd worked, to say my farewells. The following day, Judi helped me pack my gold Rolls Bentley and I set off en-route for Dover, stopping to pick up Tony who had volunteered to accompany me on this new and exciting adventure.

Chapter Thirteen:
C'EST LA VIE

After our journey across France in the Rolls, I quickly settled in at Villa Solanam. Tony helped me turn a garden shed into an office in which I could sit and write and after a few days, during which we enjoyed the sunshine, it was time for us to return to England, Tony to go into pre-production for the next series of 'LOVE THY NEIGHBOUR', and me to pick up Judi's Mini, and bring it to the Villa. Judi and our son Dominic would be flying to Nice a few days later to join me.

The drive went without incident. I stood on the deck of the cross Channel ferry looked at the White Cliffs of Dover slowly disappearing into the distance and wondered what lay ahead for me in the year ahead. At Calais, I sailed through Customs with no problems and made my way to the Gare Maritime where I loaded the Mini on to the Auto Couchette and found my sleeping compartment. A ham sandwich and a half bottle of Rose later and I was ready for bed.

Justa and Manuel were pleased to see me when I arrived at the villa the following day and told me that they were looking forward so much to the arrival of Judi and Dominic who were due to land at Nice Airport the next day. I too, was really looking forward to their coming. Early next morning, I gave the Rolls a polish and set off for Nice. I parked the car outside the arrivals door opposite a sign that said 'No Parking'. One distinctive advantage in owning a Rolls Bentley on the Cote d'Azur in those days was that you could park it anywhere you wished. The plane was on time and as they had only hand luggage, they were virtually the first to come through customs. We made our way to the car and headed for Cap Ferrat. Justa and Manuel were waiting at the villa with champagne at the ready and we all sat by the pool in the sunshine and drank to our new life.

I soon settled in to a working routine and started to write

the scripts of the new series of 'LOVE THY NEIGHBOUR'. I would get up early, say around 6:30am and have breakfast - usually coffee and croissants and be at my desk by 7:30am. I would then write non-stop until - 11:30 - a good solid four hours without any interruptions. No phone calls, no scripts from other writers to read, no meetings with Philip to attend - it was so productive. I used to get as much done in those four hours as I used to do in a whole day in my office at Thames.

At 11:30, I would put the cover on my trusty typewriter - word processors and P.C's were still in the future - and stroll down to the port of St. Jean to collect the English newspapers, which I would read sitting in the sunshine at a table outside the Bar Civette with a cold beer. Then it was a gentle stroll back to the villa and a refreshing dip in the pool before sitting down to a delicious lunch prepared by Justa. Most afternoon were spent sightseeing with trips to Nice, Cannes and Monaco and evenings eating out at one of the many excellent restaurants in Cap Ferrat. What a hard life it was!! A far cry from the gasworks of my childhood.

However, life wasn't always one long round of pleasure filled days. Scripts still had to be written and deadlines kept. As soon as I finished each 'LOVE THY NEIGHBOUR' script I posted a copy to Tony who read it, then arranged to fly over and discuss it with me.

I looked forward to his visits as, apart from doing any re-writes which Tony felt were needed, we had many enjoyable days mostly connected with food and drink. I recall one memorable day when we decided we would drive to Bordeghera just over the Italian border at Ventimiglia for a working lunch. We drove along the Moyenne Corniche in the gold Rolls Bentley with the windows down and a cassette of Frank Sinatra singing 'Strangers in the Night' at full volume. We slowed down at the border, but the border guards, no doubt impressed by the car, waved us through without the usual formalities. We reached Bordeghera and parked outside a small family restaurant. The owner welcomed us as if we were old friends and we ordered a bottle of Valpolicella. To our surprise, it was a large two litre bottle. We shrugged, poured ourselves a glass each and started to drink. We ordered the speciality of the house, which was, as I recall, Veal Escalope with Spaghetti. As we ate, we filled our glasses from time to time and we had got through over half a bottle of the wine when we noticed the owner peering at us from out of the kitchen and muttering. By this time, the restaurant was filling up and I noticed that most diners had a 2 litre bottle of Valpolicella on the table. I then noticed that all the bottles contained different amounts of wine, and that one or two diners had left the restaurant without finishing their wine. I remarked on this to Tony and we were just discussing it when we noticed a waiter collecting the bottles, marking the level of the wine left in each bottle and writing the table number on the label. The penny dropped. Obviously, it was the restaurant's custom to serve each table with a 2 litre bottle of wine. The diners drank a glass or two and after marking the level the bottle was kept for the customer for his or her next visit. It wasn't obligatory to drink the whole 2 litres! Tony and I looked at each other and shrugged. Oh well, we'd come so far - might as well go the whole hog. So we finished the bottle. The owner came to our table followed by the chef and a couple of waiters. The owner looked at us admiringly. 'Never before', he said in halting English, 'have anyone drink all the bottle.' Then he, the chef and the waiters all applauded us. With a flourish, he produced a bottle of Italian brandy and poured Tony and I a generous measure each. 'On the house,' he cried!

We left the restaurant in an alcoholic haze of euphoria, climbed into the Rolls and headed back to the border where the guards, recognising us, cheered and waved us through to shouts of 'Viva Inglaterra.' We replied with cries of 'Viva Italia' and made our way along the Moyenne Corniche with it's hairpin bends. It was a miracle we arrived safely back at the villa.

Tony's visits were always full of incidents such as the occasion when we were dining in the Bar du Port in St Jean. Halfway through the meal, Tony felt the need to answer the call of nature and went through a curtain leading to the toilet. I carried on with my meal but when Tony hadn't returned after ten minutes, I became a little worried, especially when a male customer had gone behind the curtain and returned with his legs crossed and muttering angrily to the barman. Just then the curtain was drawn aside and Tony's worried face peered out and beckoned me over. I left the table and went to join him. He revealed that he had been washing his face when one of his contact lenses had fallen out of his eye and down the plughole of the sink. Could I ask the barman to help? Perhaps he could call a plumber. I went to speak to the barman with everybody giving me strange looks. Not having the greatest command of the French language I said. 'Pardonez moi M'sieu. Mon ami avez perdu une yeux dans la toilette. Avez vous un plombier?' which brought a babble of conversation from his customers. Literally translated, I had said, 'Excuse me, my friend has lost an eye in your toilet. Have you a plumber?'

The barman picked up a torch and a length of wire and together we went to the toilet. I called for Tony to let us in and he unlocked the door. The barman shone his torch down the sink and was about to poke the wire down the plughole, when Tony pulled his arm away shouting that contact lenses were very expensive and could he find a plumber to dismantle the sink. Just then I gave an almighty shout and pointed to the sink. There balanced upright on the tap and caught in the light from the torch was Tony's contact lens. With a cry of relief, Tony plucked it from the tap, washed it and replaced it. From then on, he was referred to as 'the Englishman who lost his eye in the toilet!'.

One further story about the Bar du Port is worth recalling. The agent through whom I rented my villa spent most of his working day in the bar. His name was Claude and he used to open his office each morning purely to collect his mail. He would then leave a notice on his office door, stating he could be found in the Bar du Port. He had his own table from where he conducted business and drank several glasses of white wine. He once asked me if there was an English equivalent to the French expression of 'Ooh La La'. Feeling in a frivolous mood I said that the English equivalent was 'Bloody Hell'. From then on, every time Claude and I met, I would greet him with 'Ooh La La' to which he would reply 'Bloody Hell'. I often used to wonder years later, if he was still using that expression.

The good life continued. I pressed ahead with writing the 'LOVE THY NEIGHBOUR' scripts and Tony made his monthly trips to give me his comments and suggestions. I also finished writing the scripts for 'RULE BRITANNIA' so I was kept busy. It wasn't all play! During my daily routine of going down to the port for my papers and a couple of beers, I often used to see some of my celebrated neighbours and had an occasional beer with David Niven and Oliver Reed. On one occasion, while I was sitting having a drink, Judi arrived in her Mini, closely followed by Rex Harrison in his Rolls Corniche. He parked next to Judi and proceeded to chat her up. He offered to buy her a drink, which she accepted and led him to the table at which I was sitting. Rex pointed out that somebody was already sitting at that table to which Judi replied, 'Yes, it's my husband!' Rex, ever the charmer, didn't bat an eyelid. He shook my hand, joined us for a drink and we discussed the various merits of our respective cars before he drove off.

During our time in France, we had several visits from friends and relatives, including Judi's parents, my father, my agent, Jimmy Jewel, Jack Smethurst, Philip Jones, Sid James and his wife and of course Tony's monthly trips. On one of Tony's visits he had some surprising news for me. The week before his visit, Jeremy Isaacs, Thames' Controller had held a meeting of the Light Entertainment department to discuss ways and means in which they could improve it's output. During the meeting one of the producers happened to ask Jeremy why the series of 'SPRING AND AUTUMN' had been discontinued. Jeremy called on Philip to reply, and when Philip said that he thought it had run it's course there was a murmur of disapproval. After a lively debate, it transpired that the majority of opinion was that the series should be revived. Consequently Philip instructed Tony to tell me to start writing another series. It had been my intention to write a detective novel during my year abroad, and indeed I did start to write it but with this new commitment to Thames I had to put it to one side after writing about six chapters. Those chapters are still gathering dust in my study waiting for me to continue with them again. One day please God!

One afternoon I received a phone call from England which led to a meeting with a Corsican restauranteur who became one of my closest friends. The call was from a beautiful French actress, Dany Robin who was married to Mike Sullivan who, you may recall, was Sid James's agent. Finding that I was now living on the French Riviera, she rang to tell me I must go to a restaurant in nearby Villefranche-sur-Mer, Chez Bidou, owned and run by a friend of hers. He was a Corsican and his real name was Marcel Bonifaci. When he was a baby, his mother used to call him Bidou which was a Parisian slang term for 'beautiful baby'. Consequently, when he opened his restaurant he called it 'Chez Bidou' and the name stuck. Very few people ever referred to him as Marcel. The following day, I decided I would go and have lunch at Bidou's. I drove to his restaurant which was on the seafront in Villefranche at the far end of the Promenade des Mariniers, parked outside, went in and found a table. The restaurant had an open cooking area; behind which stood a short, plump, cheerful man wearing a white chef's uniform including a tall chef's hat who turned out to be Bidou. He welcomed me in fractured English and offered me a complimentary drink on the house. I decided not to mention I had been recommended by Dany Robin and ordered the house speciality - grilled lobster and a bottle of Chablis. Bidou was fascinating to watch. He sang snatches of songs as he cooked and at one point, sat at a piano and played a few bars of the National anthems of France, Germany and Italy, then when he discovered I was English played 'God Save the Queen.' He had a perpetual grin on his cheerful face, but after I paid the bill and told him about Dany Robin, he scowled.

'Why you not tell me you are friends wiz Dany Robin?' he said, 'If I know zat you would not 'ave to pay for ze wine.'

'That's why I didn't tell you,' I replied.

He scurried behind the bar, and returned carrying a bottle of Armagnac. He poured two incredibly large measures and raised hi glass. 'To ze friends of Dany Robin.'

That was the start of a long and lasting friendship. I got into the habit of calling at his apartment which was next to his restaurant, every Wednesday the one day in the week which he didn't open. We both used to go to different restaurants for long lunches and as everybody knew Bidou, we rarely had to pay. After lunch we usually played the French game of Petanque or, as it was more familiarly called, Boule, with some of his friends such as Albert Duchateau the owner of the five star Hotel Verseilles, Joe Calderoni the Mayor of Villefranche and Remy the owner of the restaurant La Mere Germaine. Bidou had a unique sense of humour and told me some wonderful stories such as the one about his local parish priest who complained to him that he rarely came to Mass, to which Bidou replied, 'True Father, but then you rarely come to eat in my restaurant.'

I discovered that he was going through a divorce. His wife had left him and run away with a Belgian businessman, taking their son Armand with her. She was sueing him for maintenance and he was refusing to pay her, as a result of which he had to go to court. He elected to represent himself, and told the judge that he would not pay his ex-wife a penny. The judge explained that it was the law that an ex-wife received payment for herself and their son. Bidou told the judge that he would pay for their son but not for her. The judge again explained that it was a legal obligation. Bidou stared at the judge.

'Judge', he said, 'tell me. If your wife run off to live wiz anozer man, would you give her money?'

The judge frowned as he considered the question. 'No,' he said.

'Voila!' said Bidou.

He won his case.

On another occasion, I went to his restaurant for lunch to be told by Bidou that the previous day, there had been a shooting at the restaurant. Naturally I asked him about it. This is what he told me in his own words.

'It was terrible. Ze man come in and orders ze best meal on ze menu. Ze prawns, ze lobster, ze cheese, ze everyzing. 'e 'has ze bottle of Beaujolais Village, cognac and ze coffee. When ze waiter give 'im ze bill, 'e says. I cannot pay. I 'ave no money.' Ze waiter comes to bring me. I go to ze man and ask him for ze money. Zen ze man jumps up and runs out of ze restaurant. I run after him. Zen 'e stops, pulls out a gun and shoots 'imself. Poom!

'That's terrible,' I said.

Bidou spluttered, 'Of course it's terrible. If 'e is going to shoot 'imself, why doesn't e shoot 'imself in my restaurant? Zen I 'ave all ze publicity. I can say 'Look - zere is ze blood on ze floor - zis is where 'e was sitting - ziz is ze plate 'e was using.' What a character!

One day, Bidou drove me to Peillon, a perched village in the hills high above Nice. It was a small, pretty village with about 30 houses, a church and a small hotel/restaurant called the Auberge de la Madonne run by the Millo family, father, mother, son Christian and daughter Marie Jose. It was the first of many pleasurable visits for me and we became good friends. The restaurant employed a Belgian student, Carrine, as a gardener. She and Christian fell in love, married and raised a family. When Christian's father died, Christian and Carrine took over the running of the Auberge. Bidou and I used to go for lunch then have a game of Boule in the courtyard next to the restaurant. I very rarely won because he was a terrible cheat. When he thought I wasn't looking he would either slyly kick his boule nearer the small wooden jack, or kick my boule further away. Happy days and happy memories.

During my year as a tax exile I attended a wedding and a funeral. The wedding was that of Yves Duchateau, the son of Albert and Odette, the owners of the Hotel Verseilles in Villefranche. What an occasion it was. The wedding was celebrated with a Nuptial Mass in the 17th Century church of St. Michel. After the ceremony we all went into the adjoining square where several trestle tables had been set up containing several barrels of wine. The square was packed and it seemed as if the whole of Villefranche had been invited to celebrate the occasion with a glass of wine to toast the happy couple. On a table in the centre was a huge wedding cake. The groom's father lifted up the top of the cake and a dozen white doves flew out to loud cheers and applause. The cake was then cut and distributed among the villagers before the bride, groom and invited guests, which included my wife Judi, son Dominic and I, returned to the hotel for a private wedding lunch which lasted until the evening.

The funeral was that of Bidou's elderly Corsican father, Ange. According to tradition, it was customary for the corpse to be laid out on a bed, fully dressed the night before the funeral with a member of the family keeping vigil over him. I volunteered to sit with Bidou through the night. Between us, we drank a whole bottle of Ricard, Ange's favourite tipple from dusk to dawn. We were both very hungover the following morning when we attended the funeral in the local cemetery.

A few weeks later, Bidou had occasion to go to Corsica to settle some of his late father's affairs and he asked me if I would like to go with him. I jumped at the chance and we flew to Ajaccio where we picked up a rental car for the drive to Bonifacio. After driving along the coast road for a few miles, Bidou suddenly turned into a car park of a shabby looking bar/restaurant.

'My cousin', said Bidou.

We went into the bar in which were half a dozen rough looking bearded men wearing ammunition belts and carrying shotguns. I felt as if I'd wandered into a film set of a spaghetti western. Bidou explained that they were a hunting party setting out to shoot quail, a local delicacy which would later be on the menu in the restaurant. Bidou introduced me to his cousin who insisted we sat outside on the terrace overlooking the sea. She produced a bottle of white wine and told us to help ourselves.

Bidou and I sat in the sunshine, sipping our wine and quietly enjoying the view. It was a beautiful day, not a cloud in the sky. Bidou sighed and said, 'You know Vincent, my cousin, she tells me that she is thinking of selling this place. We should buy it.

'Pardon?' I said.

'Yes. You and me. We should call it The Corsican Bandits. We should put up a big sign. 'If you have money, you can come in. If you have no money, go away.' And if we don't like how they look we don't let them in.'

I listened fascinated as he warmed to his theme. 'We only serve Champagne - no wine, no whisky - just Champagne. And we only have two choices of food. Either steak or fish. And when they ask for l'addition we put everything on the bill. A bottle of Champagne, steak and chips, salt, mustard and pepper, coffee, knife and fork, plate, chair, napkin - everything.'

I smiled at the thought, then said, 'You know Bidou, your idea is so bizarre that if we did it, people would be queuing up to eat here, if only to boast that they actually managed to get in.'

We couldn't put the theory to the test as we never bought the restaurant. We finished the wine and carried on to Bonifacio where Bidou met with his late father's lawyers and signed the necessary legal document, then we drove back to Ajaccio to catch the plane back to Nice.

Back at the villa, I carried on writing the series of 'LOVE THY NEIGHBOUR' and made a start on the new series of 'SPRING AND AUTUMN.' Back in England, Tony went into production with 'RULE BRITANNIA' but ran into difficulties particularly with one of the actors, Joe Lynch. Joe kept re-writing his lines and trying to re-write everybody else's lines. This caused a great deal of friction among the cast with poor Tony trying to keep the peace. It wasn't a happy experience and had an adverse affect upon everyone's performances which showed, so much so that, when the series went to air, the viewing figures were much lower than we had hoped for. The end result was that Philip took the decision not to go ahead with a second series. This was a blow to my ego as I was convinced that it had all the makings of a big success. However, I had more than enough work ahead so I put my disappointment to one side and carried on writing the projects in hand. The days passed pleasantly by and all too soon my year as a tax exile was drawing to a close. Part of me was sad at the thought of leaving the South of France, while another part of me was looking forward to going home and becoming involved in the day to day business of television again.

I had enjoyed an unforgettable year and met some wonderful people with whom I have remained friends ever since, some of whom you will be meeting again during the course of this book.

All too soon, the day was finally here. A taxi arrived at the villa to take Judi and Dominic to Nice airport for their flight to London. After a tearful farewell from Justa and Manuel, off they went, leaving me to finish packing the Mini before driving to Frejus to catch the Auto Couchette to Calais. I got back home the following afternoon and after a good night's sleep got a taxi to Heathrow to catch the noon flight to Nice.

I was booked on the Auto Couchette for the following evening so I spent my last night with my friend Bidou at his restaurant. I had quite a bit to drink, and as I drove back to Villa Solanam I decided to call on Rex Harrison. He was, at the time married to Elizabeth, who was formerly married to film star Richard Harris. They were living in a villa called Beauchamp near the lighthouse on Cap Ferrat. I pulled up outside their gate and began to sing all the songs from My Fair Lady at the top of my voice. Nothing happened - no light came on and nobody stirred so I drove back to Solanam and bed. I found out later that both Rex and Elizabeth were both holidaying in England. C'est la vie.

The following day, I finished packing the Rolls Bentley and said my goodbyes to the Cote d'Azur. Another tearful farewell from Justa and Manuel.

Chapter Fourteen:
BACK HOME

It was good to be home again, but there was bad news about my Dad who was approaching his 80th birthday. His condition had worsened inasmuch as his walking had deteriorated and although he was able to walk about his flat, he found it difficult to walk to the local shops or to our house. Luckily my doctor had managed to get Dad a wheelchair from the local National Health hospital which was a big help.

Philip and Tony welcomed me back with open arms and in no time I found myself in the rehearsal room for a read through of the first episode of the new series of 'SPRING AND AUTUMN.' All the old cast were there to welcome me back. Jimmy Jewel still coughing and complaining of pains down the left hand side, Charlie Hawkins, now a year older and a few inches taller but with the same cheeky grin. The lovely talented June Barry, Larry Martyn one of the most under-rated actors I have ever worked with, and the equally talented Jo Warne. The first episode of the new series was as a result of my journey back from France. I was driving toward Boulogne when I spotted a sign to Etaples and a notice pointing to a military cemetery. Out of curiosity I followed the sign and came across the cemetery which was maintained by the Allied War Graves Commission. I climbed the steps to the huge cross and gazed down at the moving sight of hundreds of identical white headstones each marking the grave of a fallen British soldier from two world wars. I walked down among the graves and read some of the inscriptions, one of which brought tears to my eyes. After the soldier's name, age and rank was this inscription - 'He gave all he had to his country - his life'.

Before I left I visited the office where there was a Book of Remembrance which visitors could sign and leave a comment. One such entry again moved me to tears. It only said six words - 'We came son. Mam and Dad.' I was so moved by my experience that I couldn't stop thinking about it on the journey back to Calais. After I loaded my car on to the cross channel ferry, I sat in the bar and before we landed at Dover, I had worked out a plot in which Jimmy Jewel's character decides to go and visit his late father's grave in the cemetery at Etaples. Tony loved the idea and arranged for a film crew to go over to France. We filmed it in three days and I consider it to be one of the best things I have written. The whole series was an instant success and Philip immediately commissioned a further series. I was happy to be back doing what I wanted. It was almost as if I'd never been away. Unfortunately my Dad's health was not getting any better, and he kept falling down in his flat. My doctor arranged for him to be admitted to hospital for observation. I went to visit him and he seemed confused not knowing where he was. I went back home, worried and concerned. About 2:30am my phone rang. It was the hospital telling me that Dad was drifting in and out of consciousness and that I should go to the hospital. I quickly dressed and drove there where I was given the news that they didn't expect him to last much longer. I sat by his bed holding his hand, thinking back to all the times we'd had together. Funny one always thinks one's father is indestructible. I phoned the local Catholic Church and asked them to send a priest. The priest arrived and administered the Last Rites. Shortly after, almost as if he had been waiting, my Dad gave a sigh and passed away. I cried over his body. My link with the past had gone. Never again would I be able to ask my Dad about events and people from my youth.

He was buried in the local Catholic cemetery and using the French custom, I had the stonemason affix a glazed plaque to his headstone taken from a photograph of my son Dominic then aged eighteen months sitting on my Dad's knee. It's been over thirty years now since my Dad died but I still miss him every day.

I carried on writing the second series of 'SPRING AND AUTUMN' and life went on as usual. Philip decided that after 56 episodes of 'LOVE THY NEIGHBOUR' the series had run it's course particularly in view of the adverse criticisms we were receiving from the Race Relations Board, so no plans were made to do any more. I started to feel guilty about accepting a fee for being exclusive to Thames Television, and went to speak to Philip about it. By now Thames was the major commercial broadcaster with a track record in Light Entertainment second to none and able to commission many sitcom writers and I put it to Philip that they cancel my exclusivity contract. After some discussion, Philip agreed and so I became a freelance writer again. I worried if I had done the right thing. After my long association with Thames would any of the other broadcasters want my services? I needn't have worried. The next day I got a call from Michael Grade the Controller of Programmes for London Weekend Television. He said that he'd heard I was now freelance and was I free for lunch. Naturally I said I was and he invited me to join him for lunch at the Café Royal on Regent Street the next day.

We met in that wonderful baroque Grill Room so often favoured in the past by Oscar Wilde. Over lunch, Michael told me that now I was freelance he would like to offer me the opportunity of writing for London Weekend. Did I fancy writing a sitcom for Larry Grayson? No I didn't. However, I told Michael that I had what I thought was a great idea for a sitcom.

I explained that when my family and I returned from France, we brought with us a young French au pair, Yvonne, to look after our young son, Dominic. Every morning when the post came, she would say to me 'M'sieu Powell are there any French letters for me.' It never failed to make me laugh and I never revealed to her why it was so funny. Yvonne used to go to the local College of Further Education to improve her English and occasionally she would bring one or two of her foreign classmates back to our house. Their efforts at English were often hilarious and I began to wonder if there wasn't an idea for a sitcom about a class of foreigners learning English. I visited the College, told the teacher of my idea and asked if I could sit in on one of her classes to which she agreed. It just so happened that they were discussing double vowels such as the double 'ee' and the teacher cited the word sheet as an example, whereupon an Asian student raised his hand. 'Oh dearie me,' he said, 'that is very naughty word - sheet!'

I burst out laughing and at that moment 'MIND YOUR LANGUAGE' was born. I told all this to Michael who liked it and recommended that I try and get hold of a copy of American writer Leo Rosten's book, The Education of H*Y*M*A*N K*A*P*L*A*N. It was published in the U.S. and it's theme was foreigners learning English. I told Michael that I didn't think it was a good idea to read Leo Rosten's book in case it influenced my sitcom idea.

I left the Café Royal with a promise from Michael that he would commission me to write a pilot episode of 'MIND YOUR LANGUAGE' for London Weekend. At that time, my old friend Stuart Allen was at LWT producing and directing 'THE FOSTERS,' a sitcom comedy series which was a spin off from an American TV series, and Michael gave him the job of directing the pilot of 'MIND YOUR LANGUAGE.' I have to say that Stuart did a marvellous job in casting the series. It couldn't have been easy. He had to find a young male English teacher, a middle-aged female Principal, and ten foreign students - five male, a Pakistani Muslim, a Punjabi Sikh, an Italian, a Greek, a Spaniard and a Japanese, and five females, a German, a French girl, an Indian Lady and a Chinese girl. Not only did he cast every role brilliantly, a large part of the eventual success of the series was due to Stuart's inspired casting. We recorded the pilot and, to use a show business expression, it 'went like a bomb'. Fifty percent of the audience were foreigners either as a result of the cast inviting friends and relatives or LWT inviting students from the Adult Education Centre. I hadn't heard laughs like that for a long time. John Birt, who was then Head of Entertainment at LWT, immediately commissioned me to write a series of seven episodes as soon as possible. I'd just finished writing episode 4 when John rang me and said that, on the strength of the audience reaction to the first shows, he had decided to extend it to a series of 13.

It was one of the happiest sitcom series I ever wrote. I never laughed so much during rehearsals as I did on 'MIND YOUR LANGUAGE.' Stuart had cast Barry Evans, who had found fame in the popular and successful 'DOCTOR IN

THE HOUSE' series, as the English teacher and Zara Nutley as the formidable College Principal. When the series was transmitted the viewers loved it but, wouldn't you know, the TV critics said it was racist and that all the actors were stereotypes. In spite of that, the series ran for 29 episodes until LWT, under pressure from the Race Relations Board decided to drop it. The series was sold all over the world. It became the highest ratings show in India, and in Singapore it was shown on TV every night. According to LWT's own records it made more money from overseas sales than any other sitcom series at that time. The format was sold to America who made their own version which ran for 26 episodes, then Tri Films, an Independent British company made a series of 13 episodes which again were sold all over the world. So much for the critics.

On the work front, things were okay. But on the home front, things were not so good. Ever since we came back from France, relations between Judi and I had deteriorated. History was repeating itself. I was spending too much time writing, going to rehearsals and recordings and not enough time with her and Dominic. We eventually agreed to separate and I left the marital home and bought an apartment near Teddington studios on the river. It was a miserable time for me as I loved my son Dominic, whom I now only saw at weekends. I became one of that vast legion of weekend fathers who frequented the many London steakhouses with their offsprings, before going to the matinee performance at a nearby cinema. It wasn't easy trying to write comedy scripts while going through the throes of a divorce, but somehow I forced myself to do it. It was a very depressing period of my life. To cap it all, my Rolls was too large for the car parking space which went with the apartment, so I sold it and bought a much smaller car. It was around this time that I first came in touch with Gerald Thomas who, with his partner Peter Rogers had created one of Britain's most successful and long running series of 'CARRY ON' films. Peter produced the movies and Gerald directed them. I was invited to their office at Pinewood studios where they were having a problem with their latest film, 'CARRY ON EMMANUELLE'. They weren't happy with the script, which they felt was much too raunchy and explicit and wanted me to do a quick re-write on it. I booked myself into the Strand Palace hotel for a week and spent every day in my bedroom typing away. I finished the re-write and sent it to Peter and Gerald. They were delighted with what I had done, paid me generously and promised me that I would be offered a contract to write their next 'CARRY ON' film.

Before that, however, I had a phone call from Bill Robertson, John Inman's agent. John had just recently finished the last episode of the BBC's hugely successful sitcom series 'ARE YOU BEING SERVED' set in a department store in which he played a camp sales assistant in the Gents department. The agent told me that John was anxious to star in his own show and had I any ideas. After a lot of thought I came up with the idea that John would inherit his late father's rock factory. I took it to Philip Jones who liked the idea and commissioned a series of six with a title of 'ODD MAN OUT'. He called in Tony Parker to direct it, and asked Gerald Thomas to produce the series. It was not one of the best series I had written although it might qualify as one of the worst. I went way over the top with John's character. He was far too camp and there were too many gay jokes. I think the reason it failed was that although his character in 'ARE YOU BEING SERVED' was blatantly gay, he was only one of a team and, as such, his role was limited, whereas in 'ODD MAN OUT' he was the star and rarely off the screen. It was just too much for the viewers to take and it sank with hardly a trace.

However, true to their word, Peter Rogers and Gerald Thomas invited me to lunch at Pinewood to reveal that they were planning another 'CARRY ON,' film - 'CARRY ON DALLAS,' a send up of the long running U.S. soap, 'DALLAS,' and wanted me to write it. It was a perfect vehicle for the 'CARRY ON' team even without the legendary Sid James. I wrote the script, changed the name of the lead character from J.R. Ewing played by Larry Hagman, to R.U. Ramming played by Kenneth Williams. I also changed the nature of the business from oil to fertiliser. Everyone approved of the script - Gerald told me that he thought it would be one of the best 'CARRY ON' films they had made.

Lorimar Productions the American company which made 'DALLAS' got to hear of the proposed film and threatened to sue Peter and Gerald if they proceeded with it. Consequently the film never got made.

Since returning from France I had resumed the monthly get-togethers with Philip, the Ernie Wise's, Billy Dainty's and so on. One such evening at Billy Dainty's house we decided to play the familiar parlour game 'CHARADES.' We had so much fun doing it that I suggested to Philip that it might make a good gameshow for television but he wasn't enthusiastic about the idea so I didn't pursue it.

It was around this time that I got the news that my old mentor, Ronnie Taylor was in hospital with a chest complaint. It was at first thought to be nothing serious - just a rather nasty flu bug. I rang his wife to arrange to go and visit him but she told me that he was over the worst and that he was expected to be discharged in a few days so I decided to wait until he was back home. I rang the hospital the next day and was surprised to be told that he was in intensive care. His temperature had shot up overnight and he was having difficulty breathing.

He died later that day. It turned out that he had been suffering from Legionnaires Disease, a comparatively new illness caused by an air borne virus which bred in certain air conditioning units. What an awful shock!

I went to his funeral in Berkhamsted and afterwards joined his wife, daughters and a few close friends in a local pub for the traditional wake. During the proceedings I was speaking to one of Ronnie's daughters, Diane and happened to mention to her the debt I owed to her father for saving my writing career all those years ago and his encouragement and help in the years that followed. She told me that the BBC North Region in Manchester were planning to hold a memorial service for Ronnie and asked me if I was prepared to say a few words on his behalf at the service. Never having done anything like that before I was, at first, hesitant but felt that I owed it to Ronnie's memory to agree. For days, I agonised over what I should say then one day, I found a sitcom script which Ronnie and I had written together and decided to base my eulogy around that. The memorial service was arranged to take place at St. Pauls, the Actors Church in Covent Garden, and I duly arrived at the appointed time. There was a huge crowd which included many television executives and producers as well a several TV celebrities such as Cilla Black, Jimmy Tarbuck, Val Doonican and many stars Ronnie had helped on their road to stardom. I was handed an Order of Service card and was surprised to discover that there was to be a total of four readers including me. They were, Harry Worth, Richard Wilson, David Jason and me, in that order. We all took our seats on the front row and the service got under way with an opening prayer by the Vicar followed by a hymn. Then Harry Worth rose and recited a prayer about the resurrection of the body all fairly deep and gloomy. Then there was another hymn and a short prayer by the Vicar, after which Richard Wilson rose to speak. After a brief acknowledgement of Ronnie's talents he gave a reading from the prophet Kahil Gibran about life after death. I started to get a little worried - my reading was going to be much more light hearted. I became much more worried when David Jason rose and, after listing some of Ronnie's successful TV shows, ended with a reading from the Old Testament. By now I was in a state of panic. I'm sure that Harry Worth, Richard Wilson and David Jason, were each in their own way, in deference to the religious aspect of the memorial service, paying serious tributes to Ronnie's memory. In those days it wasn't customary to deliver comic eulogies.

As the congregation sang 'Guide me, O thou great Redeemer', I quickly went through my prepared jokey speech in my mind and for one brief moment considered doing a quick reading of 'The Lord is my Shepherd' then sitting down. But I thought of Ronnie and decided to go ahead with what I had. I stood up, looked at the packed church and started. I told about my meeting with Ronnie when Harry Driver and I did 'What Makes a Star', how he saved me from packing in my career before it had even started, then recalled some of the jokes and anecdotes we had shared while writing together. Then I finished with a reading from the sitcom script we had collaborated on. At first there was silence from the congregation then a few chuckles and great roars of laughter at the end. I sat down to loud applause, the Vicar ended the service and we all made our way outside where Cilla, Jimmy and Val all congratulated me and said 'Thank goodness someone spoke about Ronnie the way we remembered him.' Some years later, my eulogy was to have a surprising effect on my career as you will discover later.

Meanwhile, I had the new series of 'SPRING AND AUTUMN' to write. By now, Jimmy, his wife Belle and I had become close friends and he often invited me to join them for dinner in their penthouse flat on Kensington High Street. Belle was Australian and a dancer. She was from a famous Australian show business family called the Bluetts who actually had the honour of having a street named after them in Sydney. Her sister Kitty later found fame playing the wife of Ted Ray in the long running radio series 'RAY'S A LAUGH'. They had two children, a son Kerry who had recently emigrated to Australia with his actress wife Elyse and their two young children Dean and Dale, and an adopted daughter Piper who sadly had had a falling out with her parents and left home. On one occasion Jimmy took me as his guest to a dinner hosted by The Variety Club of Great Britain at London's Grosvenor Hotel in honour of Gene Kelly, and I actually met the great man and shook his hand. There I go - name dropping!

After one of our monthly show business dinners at which we all played 'CHARADES' again, I brought up the idea again to Philip of doing it as a television gameshow. To my surprise, he said 'Well why don't you think of a way to do it then?' The next day I got my thinking cap on and came up with what I thought was a good format. There would be two teams, one male and one female presided over by a celebrity team captain, with two other members drawn from the world of Show Business, The Arts, Music and Politics. I typed out the format and handed it in to Philip. I waited for him to get back to me - and waited - and waited. Not a word. I mentioned Philip's silence to Tony Parker and he told me that Philip had a problem with the format for 'CHARADES'. Apparently, coincidentally he had been sent a similar format by a drama Programme Assistant called Juliet Grimm and was in two minds as to what to do. On the one hand, I had put the idea to him first, but on the other hand he was afraid of being accused of nepotism if he accepted my idea and rejected hers. I immediately went to confront Philip who was embarrassed and apologetic.

'Don't worry Philip,' I said, 'you don't have to choose between Juliet and I. We'll pool our ideas and do it between us.'

Philip breathed a sign of relief.

'Where will I find this Juliet?' I asked.

'She's in the Drama department working as a P.A. on a drama series,' he replied.

'Haven't you ever met her?' he asked.

'No Philip - I don't have a lot to do with drama department. They're all too stuck up and full of their own importance for me.'

'Well watch yourself with Juliet. She's absolutely stunning.'

I nodded and went in search of this 'absolute stunner.' I found her in the canteen. Philip was right - she was absolutely stunning. A slender willowy blonde with legs that seemed to go on forever. I was immediately captivated which was more than she was with me. I explained Philip's dilemma and my suggestion that she and I pool our ideas and collaborate - a suggestion that she didn't take too kindly to. However, when I pointed out that if she didn't agree, there was a distinct possibility that neither of our ideas may be taken up, she reluctantly changed her mind. We took the best parts of our two formats, put them together, changed the title to 'GIVE US A CLUE' and added a member of the public to each team. We then began to look around for celebrities to play the Chairman and the two Team Captains. We were fortunate in finding Michael Aspel for the role of Chairman and Lionel Blair and Una Stubbs for the Team Captains. They were all devotees of 'CHARADES' and jumped at the chance to take part. When we eventually went into production we discovered that because of it's popularity among show business people, we had no problem with finding celebrities to appear on the show - in fact many of them kept ringing us to ask if they could take part.

The series was a huge success from the beginning. Juliet

and I both received a format fee for devising the show but after the series had been on air for over a year complications set in. Thames Television's Programme Controller suddenly objected to paying Juliet and I a format fee. He argued that 'CHARADES' was a well known parlour game which was in the public domain and as such, we were not entitled to a fee. We argued that we had changed the title and devised a way to do the game on television. Thames were adamant and at a subsequent meeting made us a 'once and for all' offer to buy us out for £10,000 with the proviso that if we didn't agree, they would do their own version under the original title of 'CHARADES'. More meetings followed and we reluctantly agreed to let Thames have the exclusive British option for £10,000 but that we would retain the world rights. This was eventually agreed and we signed away the British rights. The whole business left a nasty taste in our mouths, but some months later, we managed to negotiate a format deal with TV3 New Zealand for them to produce nearly 200 episodes of 'GIVE US A CLUE' which helped to compensate somewhat for the treatment we had received from Thames Television.

Around this time, Judi and I got divorced. My solicitor had dealt with all the matters regarding the marital home and the maintenance for her and Dominic and I eventually received a letter informing me that my divorce would be heard in Kingston Crown Court on a certain day and that unless I had any objections I needn't attend. On the day in question, I happened to be in Kingston and out of curiosity decided to go. At the appointed hour, a barrister read out a list of names of those couples whose divorces were being granted, and which included mine and Judi's. That was it - quick, painless and impersonal. Five years of marriage wiped out in just a few seconds. I came out of the court thoroughly depressed, drove to my riverside apartment and got extremely drunk.

Chapter Fifteen:
DOWN UNDER

I settled down into a bachelor life again. I still had a second series of 'SPRING AND AUTUMN' to finish so I sat in my office scribbling away. Then, out of the blue, an unexpected offer came my way. The entire television series of 'LOVE THY NEIGHBOUR' had been sold to Australia where it had been a big success. A well known theatrical impressario, Paul Dainty and his partner Garry Van Egmond had heard that there was a stage version of the show and were keen to do a 30 week Australian tour of the play. Jack Smethurst, Rudi Walker and Nina Baden-Semper were all approached and agreed to do it. Unfortunately, Kate Williams had a young daughter and was reluctant to do the tour. I managed to re-structure the script to cover her absence and it was with great excitement I arrived at London Heathrow for my flight to Australia. Paul Dainty had arranged for my old friend Stuart Allen, who had directed the play in England, to direct the Australian tour. The play was due to open at the Memorial Theatre in Ballarat just outside Melbourne for a week before going on to Sydney's Theatre Royal for four weeks. Stuart and the cast had already been rehearsing in Melbourne for two weeks and I was looking forward to joining them. Paul Dainty had booked me on Concorde which in those days flew to Singapore as the runway at Sydney airport was too short to accommodate Concorde. Concorde was superb - so smooth and quiet. We were served champagne and a roast beef lunch, and broke the sound barrier. I arranged to stay at the world famous Raffles Hotel for the night and found myself in the Somerset Maugham suite. I sat at the desk at which he must have sat hoping to draw some inspiration from that fact but nothing came. The next day I flew to Melbourne for the last two days rehearsal before we left by coach for Ballarat and the Travel Lodge at which we were

staying. Ballarat reminded me of an old Wild West town with it's wooden sidewalks and rows of shops with wooden awnings. The Memorial Theatre was a lovely old building and we rehearsed onstage for a couple of hours before going across to a nearby pub for drinks and a bite to eat. We had hardly sat down before the landlord, a huge mountain of a man approached us.

'Get the Sheila's outta here,' he bellowed. This was our first introduction to one of the Aussie drinking rules - that in those days women were not allowed in certain rooms, and this was one of them. We went back to the Travel Lodge and had a drink and a sandwich in the bar. We rehearsed again in the afternoon then the audience started to arrive. The theatre was packed. It was standing room only. The opening music was played and the curtain went up to loud cheers and applause. The audience loved it. They cheered and clapped at practically every line. We had never had such tremendous audience reaction when we did the play back in England. At the end of the show, the audience wouldn't stop applauding and the cast took curtain call after curtain call. Jack made a funny curtain speech and the audience called for Rudolph and Nina, so they both said a few words.

The audience reaction to each performance for the rest of the week was the same - wild applause and cheers. After a couple of days, Stuart and I flew to Sydney to prepare for the opening night at the Theatre Royal. This was the big one. Stuart and I were met by television crews from the major TV channels, radio reporters and the press all wanting interviews. We had no idea that 'LOVE THY NEIGHBOUR' was so popular down under. We discovered that the entire 30 week tour was heading toward a sell out. We eventually got to the theatre and had meetings with the set designer, lighting director, sound engineer, make-up and wardrobe who were all excited about being involved with such a high profile production. It was now Wednesday and the cast were due to fly from Melbourne to Sydney on Sunday so Stuart and I spent a couple of days exploring Sydney - a fascinating and vibrant city. We took a Captain Cook boat tour of the harbour, visited the Opera House and The Rocks which was where the First Fleet landed in 1788 with it's human cargo of

British convicts, and the colony of New South Wales was established and over which now towers the impressive Harbour Bridge, known to Sydneysiders as The Coathanger. We ate at The Old Spaghetti Factory, sadly no longer there, and at a revolving restaurant a thousand feet above the ground in the AMP Tower. The 360 degree views, often stretching for over 50 miles, were stunning. Eventually, Sunday came around and Paul Dainty picked up Stuart and me in his white Rolls and drove us to the airport to meet the cast. Again there were crowds of TV crews, radio reports and journalists - their arrival was on every television channel later that day. When the cast eventually managed to make their way through customs and into arrivals where Paul Dainty, Stuart and I were waiting they got another surprise. There were several hundred people, all fans of the series, cheering and waving. It was an incredible scene and I suddenly thought of Harry Driver. What a pity he hadn't lived to see this moment - how he would have loved it. It took us over half an hour to make it through the crowds - everybody wanted an autograph - but we finally got outside to where a fleet of cars waited to take us to our hotel. It was a day I'll never forget.

We were all booked in at one of Sydney's prestigious hotels the Sebel Town House which was favoured by visiting celebrities. Paul hosted a dinner for us all. We ate and drank and went to bed in a happy mood, looking forward to the Sydney opening. For the next two days, we rehearsed in the theatre in readiness for the grand opening night. As in Ballarat, the theatre was packed and it was standing room only. The curtain rose to a burst of enthusiastic applause from an appreciative audience and at the end, the cast took several curtain calls. I decided to capitalize on what happened in Ballarat and wrote three funny curtain speeches, one for each of the three stars, and it worked like a charm. Back at the hotel, the management had arranged for supper to be served to us in a private dining room and we all toasted our success in vintage champagne.

Stuart and I didn't stay in Sydney for the four weeks. Once the play was up and running, there was no reason for our presence so after a couple of days, we caught a flight back to

London where I continued to write the rest of the series of 'SPRING AND AUTUMN'. From time to time I got a phone call from Paul Dainty or Jack Smethurst giving me a report on how well the play was doing on tour and I wished I were with them all. I missed Sydney and promised myself that, one day, I'd return. That day was to come sooner than I expected. I was sitting in the bar at Teddington - where else? - when producer William (Bill) G. Stewart walked in, - remember him? He was the one who said 'FOR THE LOVE OF ADA' hadn't a laugh in it! We'd long since become friends and he had produced and directed the successful series of 'BLESS THIS HOUSE.' He bought me a drink and asked me to join him for lunch.

Bill had recently returned from Sydney, where he had produced and directed the Australian version of the British sitcom 'FATHER DEAR FATHER' for Lyle McCabe Productions. The series had been shown on Channel 7 and had been well received. Bill had spoken to Lyle McCabe and suggested doing an Aussie version of 'LOVE THY NEIGHBOUR' and wondered would I be interested in writing it. Would I? I jumped at the chance. I told Bill that we wouldn't be able to do it until the play had finished touring, but he said that Lyle was okay with that. It would give me time to write six episodes in advance. Bill said I would be required to fly out to Sydney for the recordings and that was just fine with me. He had been in touch with Jack's agent and Jack was available and eager to do the series. There was only one snag. Due to the fact the Lyle McCabe was reluctant to pay three air fares and hotel bills for Jack, Rudi and Nina, was it possible for me to devise a format for the series in which only Jack featured. There was another problem. Australia, due to their strict immigration laws, had no black actors. I looked upon it as a challenge and came up with the idea of Eddie Booth, the character played by Jack, deciding to emigrate to Australia and going on ahead of his wife in order to find a place to live. He had got a job in a Sydney suburb. I could hardly believe my luck when, during my research, I discovered a suburb some 30 miles west of the city centre called Blacktown. It couldn't have been more perfect. The first episode started with Eddie arriving at digs in Blacktown to find that his next door neighbour was a pot-bellied beer swilling Aussie who hated the English or, as he called them, 'whinging Pommie bastards!' The format worked perfectly. I wrote the six episodes which Bill and Lyle liked, and an Australian writer, Ken Sterling was drafted in to fine tune the scripts and make sure that the dialogue was authentic. All I had to do now was wait until the 'LOVE THY NEIGHBOUR' tour had finished and it would be off Down Under again.

However I wasn't idle for long. Stuart Allen had been directing and producing a series for ATV, 'A SHARP INTAKE BREATH' written by the late Ronnie Taylor and starring David Jason. It was assumed that the series would end with Ronnie's death, but ATV wanted to continue it and Stuart thought I would be ideal to take it on. I met with David and we quickly developed a rapport. He was an excellent actor, as later events have demonstrated only too well, and one of the most inventive performers I have ever worked with. He added so many visual touches to my scripts and contributed so much to the two series which I wrote for him. A lovely and talented man.

By now, the last series of 'SPRING AND AUTUMN' had been transmitted, and despite its continuing popularity, Philip made the decision not to do any more. It was never one of his favourite sitcoms being too gentle for his taste. Jimmy took me out to dinner and together we tried to think of a new idea for him. By this time, Jimmy had by now developed into a fine dramatic actor and had appeared in several drama productions and was currently involved in a drama series based on his own family and their life as a family troupe in the early days of Music Hall but his first love was still comedy, and I promised I would keep thinking of a suitable idea for him.

Finally, the 'LOVE THY NEIGHBOUR' tour ended at the end of November and the cast all returned home. Jack and I met as soon a we could and I gave him copies of the six scripts of the Australian series, to read over Christmas. He loved them and a few days later, we checked in on a Qantas flight to Sydney. We were travelling economy class but were soon upgraded to business class where the chief steward made it his personal business to keep our wine glasses permanently full.

When we landed at Sydney airport, we were greeted by a cheerful uniformed man who got us through customs without having to queue. His name was Tony Maddock an ex-Mancunian who was the airport manager for Thai Airlines. Tony had been part of the Royal Navy submarine fleet and had been stationed in Sydney. When he got demobbed, he married Linda a Blackpool girl and they emigrated to Australia under the then £10 assisted passage scheme. They quickly settled down and raised a family as Tony rose to become Airport Manager. He had read reports of our impending arrival and made it his business to meet our flight. We quickly became good friends and, indeed I recently spent a three week holiday in Sydney and stayed with him and his wife.

We had arrived in Sydney on New Years Eve and checked in our hotel. Being New Years Eve the hotel had a Gala Dinner arranged. Jack and I were found a table and we sat in a roomful of romantic couples. We got a few funny looks from people who obviously thought we were a couple of consenting adults. When the chimes of midnight range out, everyone held hands and kissed. Jack and I joined in the fun, embraced and kissed thus confirming what most people had been thinking.

Another person we met and had also become a good friend was Tricia Colgan who was a hotel P.R. lady and helped us to get the best hotels whenever we needed them. Tricia and I became very close friends and had many happy dinners together. We have kept in touch and on my aforementioned recent trip, I spent a lovely weekend with her and her husband Richard.

A few days later, Jack and I left the hotel to share a modern two bedroom apartment booked for us by Channel 7. It was in a complex in Lane Cove with a swimming pool. The TV station had arranged for us to have the use of a rental car from Avis, and their Head Salesman called on us to take us to their showroom. His name was Bruce Rollo, and he was totally stagestruck. He was also a dead ringer for Jack Lemmon and did a remarkably accurate impersonation of

251

him. Bruce took it upon himself to be our personal guide for the weeks we were recording the TV series. He took us to several league clubs which were really gambling and drinking clubs attached to a local rugby team. He became a really good friend, a friendship which has lasted several years.

We completed recording the series which was well received although it didn't break any records. My opinion was that the Australian version didn't live up to the successful British version and that the viewers were disappointed in it. The one good thing that came out of it was that I managed to get Jimmy Jewel's son, Kerry a job as a warm-up man, that is, someone who greets the studio audience and introduces the cast and show with a few well chosen gags. I saw quite a bit of Kerry and his lovely wife Elyse during the series - I was able to report to Jimmy that they seemed to have settled down in Australia and took lots of photographs of them and their two small sons to take back and show to Jimmy and Belle.

One day, Lyle took us out on his boat. He had a 30 foot cruiser and arranged a picnic lunch on board. We sailed round the harbour, then headed toward Middle Harbour. We dropped anchor prior to having our picnic lunch. It was a glorious day and Jack and I decided we'd have a swim. We changed into swimming trucks and went over the side. We saw Lyle giving us strange looks but thought nothing of it. Eventually he called that the food was ready. Lyle welcomed us back on board and said we were both very lucky. He went on to say that the spot in which we were swimming was where many sharks came to spawn and that we were fortunate not have been eaten!

What with sharks, funnel web spiders, poisonous snakes and crocodiles, I came to the conclusion that Australia could be a dangerous place to live. Nevertheless I had enjoyed my trips Down Under and wouldn't have missed them for the world.

Jack and I flew back home and I sat at my desk in my Riverside apartment looking at the river and wondering what to do next. I had, by now, given up my office at Teddington Studios although I had Philip's permission to use the facilities of the restaurant and bar. I phoned Stuart Allen

252

to discuss an idea I had been thinking about for Jimmy Jewell and about an old man retiring, only to find that retirement wasn't as pleasant as he had imaged it to be. He and his wife started to get on each others nerves. Stuart liked the idea and suggested the talented Thora Hird to play Jimmy's wife. It was an easy script to write and I finished it in a week. I sent it to Stuart, who liked it and sent it to Michael Grade at London Weekend Television who also liked the idea. I then decided to take a holiday and fly to my favourite place in the world - the South of France. I phoned my friendly travel agent and booked a ticket for Nice for the following morning. I'd just put the phone down when it rang. It was the lovely Juliet to tell me that the P.A's were on strike at the studios and why didn't we have lunch. I immediately said I had a much better idea and why didn't she come with me to France, to which she agreed. We had a wonderful week - remember, I was a bachelor at the time. We discovered that Sacha Distel was appearing at a dinner and cabaret in the Sporting Club of Monte Carlo and booked to go and see him. I wondered if he would remember me from the Mike and Bernie Winters special he had appeared in. As it was a very up market venue, I wore a silk shirt with gabardine trousers and cashmere cardigan that had cost me an arm and a leg from Harrod's. I called for Juliet to hurry, and she emerged from the bathroom wearing a brocade waistcoat and hotpants. I stared at her.

'Darling,' I said, 'this is the Sporting Club of Monte Carlo not the Working Man's Club of Wandsworth. They won't let you in dressed like that.'

'Too bad.' she replied, 'this is what I'm wearing.'

I signed. 'Okay, but don't blame me if you can't get in.'

We drove to Monte Carlo, parked the car and took our place in the line of people waiting to enter. Most of the women were wearing evening gowns. I looked at Juliet's hotpants and shook my head. Eventually we reached the head of the queue where a uniformed Maitre d' was examining tickets. He looked at us and raised a hand.

'I'm sorry but I cannot let you come in.'

'I stared at Juliet. 'What did I tell you?'

The Maitre d' shook his head. 'No no M'sieu. It is not

Madame - it is you. You are not wearing a jacket!'

Juliet burst out laughing, and I tried to explain to the Maitre d' the cost of my cashmere cardigan, but to no avail. We were not allowed in. I was furious and Juliet couldn't stop laughing. We left and went to Gianni's an Italian restaurant nearby. I was still fuming as we were shown to a table until I saw, sitting at the next table, Richard Burton - there I go, name dropping again! It would be nice to say that I had a meaningful conversation with him but I didn't. We merely exchanged pleasantries then he paid his bill and left. Juliet and I had a meal then walked along the Avenue Princesse Grace to where we had parked our car. On the way we came across a cabaret club - Gregory's After Dark - and decided to go in for a drink. It turned out to be a large basement room with no tables and chairs but a series of seats around each wall with huge soft pillows for one to sink back in. The only drink they served was champagne - Bidou would have approved.

The cabaret was Gregory himself singing a selection of popular ballads. He wasn't a Sacha Distel, but had a pleasant voice. At one stage, he came across to where we were sitting and addressed Juliet.

'What is your name?

Juliet told him, and he proceeded to sing to her the Tony Bennett hit, 'The Shadow of your Smile.' It was a fun evening and helped to compensate for our earlier disappointment.

When we eventually flew back to London, I found three messages on my answer phone all from Gerry Thomas and all asking me to ring him urgently which I did immediately. He wanted to see me and invited me to his club in Soho the following day for lunch. When I joined him the next day, he said that he and Peter Rogers had been approached by an Australian producer called Marc Josem who was prepared to invest in a 'CARRY ON' film set in Australia and they wanted me write the screenplay particularly with the knowledge I had recently acquired about OZ. Naturally, I accepted and was asked to come up with a synopsis as quickly as possible which they would send to Marc Josem in Melbourne prior to my flying out to meet Marc. I could hardly wait to get back to my flat and start writing. The title was obvious - 'CARRY

ON DOWN UNDER' and I devised a storyline in which Kenneth Williams and his sister, played by Joan Sims had been left an opal mine by an aged Aussie relative. They had to fly to Sydney to claim their inheritance. At the same time, a half brother, played by Kenneth Connor and his girl friend, played by Barbara Windsor, found out and decided to fly out ahead and claim the inheritance for themselves. To complicate matters, the location of the opal mine could only be found by solving several coded messages. The synopsis was faxed to Marc, who like it and I was then told to pick up a return air ticket to Melbourne at Heathrow for a meeting with him. I was met at Melbourne by Marc's secretary who drove me to the Chateau Commodore to sleep off my jet lag. The following day Marc himself picked me up and took me to his Production Offices where I met with the set designer, casting director and location manager with whom I spent two days discussing the technicalities involved in the making of the film. Marc told me that he wanted me in Australia during the shooting of the film and that I would be given a courtesy title of Associate Producer. We discussed the fee I would be paid for writing the screenplay which would be paid to me by the Production Company in the following stages - one third on signing the contract, another third on delivery and the final third on the first day of shooting. I agreed and left to fly back home the next day, hardly believing my good fortune. I would be spending at least four weeks in Australia, all expenses paid and a script fee of £12,000 to boot. I started to write the screenplay at once without waiting for the contract to arrive which the Writers' Guild and every writer's agent advise against. Fortunately, the contract arrived a few days later, so I quickly signed and returned it, together with an invoice for the first stage payment and carried on happily writing the script. My career was on a roll.

But there was even more good news in store. ABC Television in Sydney had struck a co-production deal with Thames Television whereby Thames would provide a sitcom script set in Australia, and a British director, and for their part, ABC would provide the studio plus all the production costs. I was summoned to a meeting with Philip who asked me if I was prepared to write a script. The deal was that I would write the script and it would be sent to ABC TV in Sydney for their approval then, providing they liked it they would fly me and the British director over to produce a pilot programme which, if it was successful would lead to a series. The Gods were certainly smiling on me. There was only one small problem - Philip had decided to hedge his bets and had also asked the writing team of Johnnie Mortimer and Brian Cooke who had written 'FATHER DEAR FATHER' and 'MAN ABOUT THE HOUSE' to write a sitcom for Australia. It therefore became a contest. Which sitcom would be chosen to be made into a series? I was a bit miffed about this, but accepted the challenge and got down to some serious thinking about an idea which would appeal to the Aussie viewers. During my time Down Under, I had noticed that whenever I caught a taxi, the driver would invariably be an Italian who, despite the fact that he had been living in Australia for several years, still spoke broken English (or should that have been 'broken Australian?). No matter. So I devised a situation whereby a taxi driver, Enzo Pacelli had emigrated to Sydney some 16 years ago with his wife, Maria and their two year old son, they had two further children who were born in Sydney. Consequently the children all grew up with Australian values and attitudes while Enzo and Maria still maintained the values and beliefs of Italy and their Catholic faith. The finished script which I had called 'HOME SWEET HOME' was sent to ABC TV as was the script by Mortimer and Cooke, which was based on an ex-Aussie Army sergeant trying to come to terms with life as a civilian after 20 years in the Army. We all waited to find out which script had won. Meanwhile, Michael Grade had decided to make a pilot of 'YOUNG AT HEART' the idea I had devised for Thora Hird and Jimmy Jewel. Nothing, it seemed, could go wrong for me.

I was summoned to a meeting with Philip, at which Mortimer and Cooke were present. To our joint surprise, ABC TV had decided to make a pilot of each of our ideas before choosing which of them they would select to become a series. My pilot would be directed by Michael Mills who had directed the successful 'SOME MOTHER'S DO HAVE THEM' and 'CLOCHEMERLE' for the BBC before joining

Thames Television. The other pilot would be directed by Mark Stuart who had produced 'PLEASE SIR' and 'THE FENN STREET GANG' before joining Thames and producing most of the Tommy Cooper shows. They flew us all to Sydney and put us up in the same apartment complex that Jack Smethurst and I had stayed in. Michael Mills started to cast my script. To play Enzo, he picked John Bluthal, who you may recall, played Manny Cohen, the Jewish tailor in 'NEVER MIND THE QUALITY FEEL THE WIDTH'. John was an Australian/Polish/Jewish actor whom Michael had directed in an episode of a Spike Milligan series and who was well known in Australia for series of commercials. Michael and I worked closely with the casting director to choose the rest of the cast. I had written a small part for a pub barman in the pilot and managed to persuade Michael to cast Kerry Jewel, Jimmy's son, in the part. In the audience the night that we recorded the pilot was Thames Australian representative, Mike Callaghan, and after the recording he told me that when he first read my script, he thought it was excellent. It was such a simple idea, he said, superbly tailored to appeal to Australian viewers. He couldn't believe that nobody had ever thought of it before. I had no idea how the Mortimer/Cooke pilot was doing, as we were in separate studios and at different times.

One good thing about my time Down Under was that ABC's Light Entertainment Production Manager was a beautiful Aussie redhead called Geraldine Moore to whom I was immediately attracted. We went out for dinner several times and enjoyed each others company. In due time a decision was reached as to which of the two pilots would be made into a series. Much to my relief, the verdict went to 'HOME SWEET HOME'. This was not to say that the Mortimer/Cooke pilot was a failure - it was just felt that 'HOME SWEET HOME' would have a better chance of success with the Australian viewers. Be that as it may, arrangements were set in motion. Michael Mills and I would return to London where I would start writing six scripts after which we would both be flown back to Sydney to go into production. Also, during my time in Sydney, various Australian writers would be invited to submit scripts for future series on which I would edit. So lots to look forward to. But a couple of pieces of bad news. The first stage fee for the 'CARRY ON DOWN UNDER' movie still hadn't arrived. I spoke to Gerry Thomas who told me not to worry. Marc Josem was filming somewhere in Europe and as only he could authorise the payment it would have to wait until he returned. So I put writing any more of the screenplay on hold to concentrate on 'HOME SWEET HOME'.

The other piece of bad news was that Michael Grade didn't like the pilot of 'YOUNG AT HEART' and that London Weekend would not be doing a series. Michael thought the pilot was too soft centred and gentle - he was expecting a lot more laughs. What a disappointment. I rang Jimmy and told him and he too was disappointed but not unduly worried as he was in the middle of rehearsals for a play at the National Theatre. I pressed on with the scripts for 'HOME SWEET HOME' which were coming along well. I phoned Geraldine in Sydney a few times to tell her I was looking forward to seeing her again when I came over to do the series.

Then I got a phone call from Stuart Allen with some unexpected news. He was very excited and told me that he had been speaking to John Scoffield, the current Head of Comedy at ATV and had mentioned the 'YOUNG AT HEART' pilot which Michael Grade had turned down. Jon expressed an interest in seeing it, and Stuart gave him a copy. Jon thought it was very good but had two observations to make. His first was that he thought it was too jokey, which was the exact opposite of Michael Grade's comments. His second was that he didn't like the casting of Jimmy and Thora. Television is full of executives with conflicting opinions. When Ray Galton and Alan Simpson wrote the first Steptoe script as a one-off Comedy Playhouse, I heard that it was first suggested that Harold and Wilfred Steptoe could be played by Alfred Marks and Graham Stark. Would it have been as successful? I doubt it. Anyway, there we were. If I could re-write the pilot, take out the jokes and put in some more gentle comments, referred to in the business as 'Schmaltz' and Stuart could recast, Jon Scoffield would commission a series. My part was relatively easy and I re-wrote the pilot script which Jon liked. Recasting proved to be much more difficult. Day after day, Stuart and I went through Spotlight looking for the right characters but with no luck. One day, after a particularly liquid lunch, I was in Stuart's office idly turning the pages of Spotlight when I came across a picture of John (now Sir John) Mills. It was a still from the film 'THE FAMILY WAY' in which John had played the lead. I showed it to Stuart.

'He wouldn't be bad in the part,' I said.

Stuart gave me a withering look. 'Are you drunk?' he said. 'He's one of our famous actor/knights. He's not going to want to appear in a situation comedy.'

I wasn't drunk. But I had drunk enough to make me stubbornly pursue the thought.

'You don't know, he might,' I said, 'I'll ring his agent.' His agent's telephone number was on the picture in Spotlight. I rang him and explained the situation. He gave a bored sigh and asked if I had a script. I told him I had and he asked me to send him a copy. I put down the phone and looked at Stuart.

'You see,' I said, 'you never know.'

'I know', said Stuart, 'for a start, the agent may never send the script to John. And if he does, John may never read it. And if he does read it, he's never going to agree to do it.' The following day several things happened in quick succession. First the agent rang to say that he had sent the script to Sir John. Then I got a phone call from Sir John's wife, Lady Mills who as Mary Hayley Bell was no mean writer herself. She told me that she and John had read the script, which they both liked and could Stuart and I come and see them to discuss it the following day. We immediately went to tell Jon, who arranged for a private hire car to take us to Denham Village which was where Sir John and Lady Mills lived.

The following morning Stuart and I arrived at Hill's House their lovely old timbered cottage in Denham. We were greeted at the door by Lady Mills who took us into the lounge where Sir John was sitting in an easy chair wearing an elegant smoking jacket. The room was full of pictures of Sir John with practically everybody - Sir John with the Queen, Sir John with the Duke of Edinburgh, Sir John with the Queen Mother, Sir John with Sir Noel Coward, Sir John with

Sir Richard Attenborough, Sir John with Judy Garland, Sir John with David Niven, Sir John with Julie Andrews, Sir John with Alfred Hitchcock, Sir John with Margaret Thatcher - there were so many it was difficult to take it in. Sir John rose and offered me his hand.

'Nice script Vince,' he said.

'Thank you Sir John,' I replied.

He pulled a face. 'Call me Johnnie. And you can call my wife Mary.'

What a charming and lovely couple they were. They complimented me on my script and Johnnie confessed that he loved doing comedy and that he was looking forward to taking part in his first ever situation comedy. He then did something which endeared me to him forever. He picked up a decanter and poured us all a generous measure of whisky and we sat toasting each other. At ten thirty in the morning!

Meetings were then arranged between Jon Scoffield and Johnnie's agent to find a suitable date to record the pilot. Due to Johnnie's prior commitments and the availability of a studio and crew at ATV, it appeared that the only available date would be several weeks away at which time I would be in Australia. In actual fact, when I got back to my flat, there was a message from Philip to tell me that ABC TV in Sydney wanted me to fly out the following week and finish writing the scripts out there with Michael Mills travelling out two weeks later.

I rang my friends Tony Maddock and Bruce Rollo to give them the news. When I landed in Sydney, they were both there to meet me and once again, Tony whisked me through Customs and Bruce drove me into Sydney and provided me with a top of the range rental car courtesy of ABC TV. I drove to the usual apartment complex, unpacked and went straight to bed to sleep off the jet lag. The next morning I met with John O'Grady ABC'S senior Light Entertainment executive. It was his job to go through my scripts and make sure there were no inaccuracies in the way of Australian idioms and language structure. He was a talented writer in his own right, and had been responsible for running ABC's Light Entertainment department virtually single handed for many years and had a great track record for devising it's many successful variety and sketch shows. He was a big help to Michael and I during the series.

I finished writing the scripts for the series, and had dinner a few times with the lovely Geraldine, with whom I was becoming more and more enamoured while I waited for Michael to join me. He eventually arrived accompanied by his beautiful actress wife Valerie Leon who had found fame for a series of commercials for Karate aftershave in which she appeared dressed in black leather and wielding a whip. She later found further fame as a Bond girl in several of the Bond movies. Michael was allowed a week to get acclimatised and settle in before having to start pre-production, during which time, Gerry Thomas arrived to look for suitable locations in which to film 'CARRY ON DOWN UNDER'. Still no word from Marc Josem but Gerry was as enthusiastic as ever about the project. He did a deal with Qantas airlines whereby, they would provide four free air tickets for the four principal actors in exchange for me writing in the screenplay that they would be travelling by Qantas and making sure that there would be lots of footage of Qantas planes. This happens a lot in movies and helps to lighten the budgets. I remember when we were shooting the film of 'LOVE THY NEIGHBOUR', I couldn't understand why there were several shots which had nothing to do with the storyline - a long close-up of a tin of Crown paints, a scene of crates of Watney's beer being delivered and lots of shots of extras opening packets of cigarettes, all Senior Service. I complained to the producer who explained that the companies involved were paying half the production costs for the publicity they were getting.

Gerry did several other similar deals with various hotel pubs and restaurants. One night I invited Gerry to join Geraldine and I for dinner at a fish restaurant on Balmoral Beach called Mischa's, a favourite eating place of mine. During the meal, Gerald excused himself to go to the toilet. When he came back he was grinning broadly, the reason of which became clear when I went to pay the bill. Mischa revealed that instead of going to the toilet, Gerry had talked to him and hammered out a deal whereby, in exchange for Gerry filming some scenes in his restaurant, Mischa would provide free meals including the one we had just eaten! What a smooth talker Gerry was. Over the next couple of days I accompanied Gerry in his search for suitable locations. We still hadn't heard from Marc Josem and Gerry decided to fly to Marc's offices in Melbourne to see what was going on. He phoned me from Melbourne with the shocking news that Marc had pulled out of the project. There was no investment money, no script fee, nothing. The project was dead in the water. I still have 90 pages of the script in my study at home, gathering dust. What a blow! Irving Berlin got it right when he wrote 'There's No business Like Show Business!'

Meanwhile, we went into production with 'HOME SWEET HOME'. Michael was a perfectionist as a director. Everything had to be just right - the one thing he couldn't stand was inefficiency. He had been a Naval Officer during the war, and treated each TV project on which he worked as though he was still in the Navy and his production crew as if they were naval ratings bullying them unmercifully. Luckily, Michael and I had one thing in common - the eventual success of the series. And it was a success. It won for ABC TV their highest audience ratings they had ever achieved since they commenced broadcasting. It was an exciting and happy time, made more exciting for me by the fact that I was falling in love with Geraldine. One night, I took her for dinner to an Italian restaurant at the famous Bondi Beach and as we sat and talked about the show, it suddenly occurred to me that I would shortly be leaving Sydney to return home. I mentioned this to Geraldine and boldly suggested that she might like to come with me for a holiday.

She nodded and said, 'That would be nice.'

Half an hour and half of bottle of Chianti later, I became even bolder and asked her to leave Australia to come and live with me in England.

She smiled at me, 'That would be nice.'

Fifteen minutes and two large brandies later, I threw caution to the wind and proposed marriage.

Geraldine smiled again, 'Ah yeah, that would be nice.!'

Chapter Sixteen:
THIRD TIME LUCKY

After my somewhat unorthodox proposal, things moved at a hectic pace. Geraldine phoned her parents who were on holiday up the coast and spoke to her mother. The conversation went something like this.

'Hello Mum. I've got some news for you. You remember that English writer I went out with a couple of times last year? Well he's out here again and he's asked me to marry him.'

Geraldine went on. 'He's 52 (Geraldine was 34) he's been married and divorced twice and has a 7 year old son.'

There was a long silence as her mother digested this information. Finally, she spoke.

'What's the weather like darling?'

How's that for changing the subject?

However, when they returned from holiday, we all met and they approved of me. It was decided that I would stay on in Australia and that we would get married in Sydney before flying home, then to the South of France for a honeymoon. About three weeks before the wedding was due to take place I got a phone call from Stuart Allen. The pilot of 'YOUNG AT HEART' had been scheduled for the coming weekend. I decided that I should be there and rang my friend Tony Maddock at Sydney airport who managed to book two seats on a Thai Airlines flight - one for me and one for Geraldine. It was a hectic weekend. We landed at Heathrow in the early hours of the morning, and got a taxi to my Teddington flat for a quick shower and freshen up. I rang Gerry Thomas and arranged to have dinner with him the following night, then we left for the studios and the recording. Stuart had cast the experienced Megs Jenkins to play Johnnie's wife. They were old friends having appeared together in the film, 'THE HISTORY OF MR POLLY.' Geraldine and I sat in a viewing room to watch the show. I was nervously biting my nails. The studio was full. The floor manager introduced Johnnie and they gave him a rousing reception. He was such a popular actor. You could almost feel the warmth of affection for him from the audience. The recording commenced and went like a dream. We all met afterwards in the hospitality room to celebrate. John Scoffield congratulated Johnnie and Megs and told them that he would definitely go ahead with a series.

I drove Geraldine and I back to my flat, happy but jet-lagged and we both fell into bed and were asleep before our heads touched the pillows. The following day we had lunch with Juliet and a couple of the other P.A's from Thames with whom I had worked. Poor Geraldine having to suffer meeting all those girls who she didn't know. I have often thought later that it was a little cruel of me to put her through a situation which could have been embarrassing for her. But she coped magnificently. Juliet and the P.A's all loved her, and Juliet became such a close friend that she later became Godmother to our daughter. That evening we had dinner with Gerry Thomas and his wife. Gerry told us that there was still no sign of any money for the 'CARRY ON DOWN UNDER' project. He and Peter Rogers had thought of suing Marc Josem, but had decided that it wasn't worth the time, effort and lawyers fees. We had told Gerry about our impending marriage and at the end of the meal Gerry produced a bunch of keys which he handed to me.

'This is our wedding present to you both', he said. 'The keys to our apartment in Antibes. Use it on your honeymoon. There is also the key to our garage, and keys for our little Citroen which you can also use.'

What a generous gesture, but so typical of the man.

The following day, we flew back to Sydney where we were immediately plunged into a flurry of wedding arrangements. It was decided by Geraldine that we would be married in a park with the Harbour Bridge and Opera House in the background. The wedding reception would be held in the garden of her parent's house, a short walk away. I rang Jimmy Jewel and asked him to be my best man. He jumped at the opportunity as it would give him the chance to see his son and family who had also been invited to the wedding. The great day arrived. The sun was shining. Geraldine looked beautiful and we were pronounced man and wife. It was a very romantic occasion. Among the guests was the cast and crew of 'HOME SWEET HOME'. Unfortunately, Michael and his family had returned home and couldn't be there. We got dozens of telegrams from England - Philip, Johnnie Mills, Tony Parker, Ronnie Baxter and many more which Jimmy read out before making the traditional 'best man' speech. We spent the wedding night in a Sydney hotel, and then flew off the following morning to spend a couple of days at my flat before flying off to Nice for our honeymoon. Gerry's flat in Antibes was lovely and I enjoyed showing Geraldine around my favourite part of the world. We ate at Bidou's and the Mere Germaine, we drank in Betty's bar and the Bar du Port. We sat outside the Café de Paris in Monte Carlo sipping our Kir Royales, we drove up to Peillon for lunch at the Auberge and we shopped in Galeries Lafayette in Nice. We had a wonderful week. I've been very fortunate to have had three wives all of whom have loved the South of France. I don't know what I'd have done if one of them had hated it.

Anyway, honeymoon over, we decided we should look for a house. The flat was okay but we were planning on having children and it would have been too small. This task fell to Geraldine and day after day, armed with an AZ of Surrey and a list of Estate Agents, she drove up and down the leafy lanes of Surrey looking for a suitable property. I took her to see Manchester United but the rules and skills of football were, and still are, a mystery to her. I started to write the series of 'YOUNG AT HEART' as ATV wanted to go into production at once. The scripts were a joy to write and Johnnie and Megs were a joy to work with. Johnnie was a natural actor and a quick study. On the first day of each rehearsal he was word perfect. We recorded the first six and plans were made for a second series. Meanwhile ATV went into a second series of 'A SHARP INTAKE OF BREATH' which kept me busy.

Geraldine found us a house in a delightful village called Cobham which was about 25 miles south west of London.

The house was detached with 4 bedrooms and she thought it would be ideal for us. She took me to see it and I agreed. It was empty, as the previous owners had moved to another part of the country. I met with the estate agents, put down a deposit and we moved in a few days later. It was a lovely house and we were both very happy.

Shortly after we moved in, Geraldine's Mum and Dad flew over to stay with us, and we took them to Paris for a few days. They flew back, and we spent our first Christmas in our new house. We received the best Christmas present we could have ever wished for. Geraldine was pregnant. I was so contented with life. After two failed marriages, I had finally got it right.

In the Spring of that year, I got a phone call which led to me meeting the Prince of Wales. It was from Robert Nesbitt the renowned theatre producer. Robert had been responsible for producing many of the Royal Variety shows and Royal Command Performances and had been asked to produce a Royal Gala Variety show at the Grand Theatre, Blackpool in the presence of His Royal Highness, the Prince of Wales. The show had a glittering cast of stars including such luminaries as Russell Harty, David Kossoff, Barbara Windsor, Anita Harris, Jimmy Jewel, Anne Zeigler and Webster Booth, Danny La Rue an Petula Clark. Most of the acts would be doing their own familiar self contained performances but Robert needed someone to write the linking material. Jimmy Jewel, an old friend of Roberts had suggested me and I got the job. Robert sent me the running order and I wrote most of the script before going up to rehearse in Blackpool. The Grand Theatre was one of the few remaining theatres designed by Frank Matcham and is architecturally and aesthetically stunning. The show, as you would expect, was a huge success and afterwards we were all presented to Prince Charles and shook his hand. I had arranged for Geraldine and I to stay overnight so that I could give Geraldine a quick tour of my favourite British holiday resort. We visited the Tower, the Golden Mile, the Pleasure Beach and the Central Pier. We took a ride on one of the famous trams and I proudly pointed out that the beach and promenade were seven miles long. Her only comment was that there weren't any trees along those seven miles! And you know, she was right. In all the years that I had been to Blackpool, I had never noticed.

I was still writing episodes of 'SHARP INTAKE OF BREATH', 'GIVE US A CLUE' was still going strong so there was no shortage of work. We spent a holiday on the Riviera - surprise, surprise! Lots of people ask me why I am so enamoured by the South of France. Why do I choose to go to the same spot year after year instead of places like Spain, Italy, Majorca or Tenerife? Well, I'll tell you. Apart from the huge culture shock that I experienced the first time I saw the South of France (See Chapter Two), I had made some good friends there who I wanted to keep on seeing, I liked the laid back, casual attitude of the inhabitants and their acceptance of me and many kindnesses shown toward me.

I'll let you into a secret. I once went to a séance conducted by Kate Williams, one of the stars of 'LOVE THY NEIGHBOUR' who was a spiritualist and a medium. During the séance I was told by her spirit guide that in a former life, I had been a French seaman. Make of that what you will, but I have always been drawn to the Cote d'Azur and each time I have been there, I get a strange feeling of coming home.

I'll give you a couple of instances which have always stuck in my mind. When my eldest son, Dominic was a baby and in a carry cot, my wife and I went to a luxurious restaurant called the Chateau de Madrid overlooking the bay of Villefranche. It is very expensive, so much so that I could only afford to go once, on every holiday. We entered the restaurant and were greeted by the owner, who immediately insisted on taking Dominic asleep in his carry cot and putting it in a nearby private room. When I protested, he told me that Dominic would be quite safe and that my wife and I should be free to enjoy our meal without worrying about our baby. We reluctantly agreed and went in to order. After our first course, I felt I should go and check on Dominic and went toward the private room. As I approached I saw a Labrador sitting outside the door. When I got near it started to growl. The owner appeared and saw it was me.

'Ah M'sieu it is you. I have told my dog to guard your baby.'

He patted the dog and I opened the door. Dominic was still fast asleep so I returned to the restaurant where my wife and

I had a delicious, if expensive gourmet meal. One year later - I'll repeat that - one year later, we were on holiday again and went to eat at the Chateau de Madrid. Dominic, now a year older was in a push chair and as my wife transferred him from the car to the push chair I went on ahead. I was greeted by the owner.

'Ah M'sieu' he said, 'how nice to see you again.'

Oh yes, I thought, cynically. A typical restaurateur's ploy to give customers the feeling that they are remembered. Then in the next breath he said. 'And how is Dominic?'

That remark totally blew my mind. Out of all the hundreds - no thousands of customers who had visited his restaurant in the year since we had been, how could he possibly have remembered our son's name? I still don't know. Sadly the Chateau de Madrid is no longer there - sorry I'll rephrase that - it is still there but it no longer a restaurant, it's a private residence. Rumour has it that it was bought by a wealthy Italian who arrived one day with two suitcases, stuffed with cash and bought it on the spot.

The other instance was the occasion when I was in Monte Carlo, with an elderly actor and old friend Harry Littlewood. It was Harry's first visit to Monte Carlo and I took him into the world famous Hotel de Paris opposite the Casino. We sat and ordered two glasses of wine. The waiter who served us heard us talking and asked if we were English. I told him that it was Harry's first ever visit to Monte Carlo and he went away. Harry and I finished our drinks and I called for the bill. The waiter appeared carrying several articles which he gave to Harry.

'Souvenirs' he said.

There were coasters, printed with the name of the hotel, serviettes also bearing the name of the hotel, a beautifully bound and illustrated brochure of the hotel, plus a few picture postcards with views of Monte Carlo, which one would usually have had to pay for. On top of that, he told us that our drinks were on the house.

'Just so you never forget your first visit to Monte Carlo' he said to Harry.

And Harry never forgot it. He kept those souvenirs on display in his flat and was still speaking about it years later.

Would this ever have happened in a hotel in England? I doubt it. However that's enough of that. Time to move on.

The other major event that occurred later that year, was the birth of our daughter, Genevieve. We had chosen that name as Saint Genevieve was the Patron Saint of Paris, and we were sure that's where she was conceived.

On the writing front, things could not have been better. A new series of 'GIVE US A CLUE' went into production and although Juliet and I were no longer receiving a 'devised by' fee, we still got a writing fee. 'HOME SWEET HOME' was still going strong in Australia and another series was being planned. However, not everything I wrote had the Midas touch. I was asked to write two films, one by a French Production Company and one by a Dutch film producer neither of which ever got started so I didn't get paid a fee. To offset this I spent a week in Paris and a week in Amsterdam discussing the projects, with all expenses paid so I wasn't too disappointed.

The following summer we spent in the South of France with Geraldine's parents and Tony Parker and his wife Anne where we had Genevieve baptised in a small, private Catholic chapel at Peillon in the grounds of the Auberge de la Madonne. It was arranged for us by Carrine Millo - remember her, the Belgian gardener who married the son of the owner. It was like a scene from one of M Hulot's films. Tony, an Anglican was a Godfather, as was a Jewish friend of ours Alan. The French priest spoke not one word of English and conducted the ceremony in French with Tony and Alan reading their responses from cards in French with English accents. Then there was me - Genevieve's father - a lapsed Catholic and her mother, an Australian Anglican.

Later that year there was good news from New Zealand. Their major TV channel - NZTV had bought the series of 'SPRING AND AUTUMN' from Thames. Tom Parkinson, the Head of Entertainment liked the premise and thought it could be adapted for New Zealand viewers. His idea was that Jimmy Jewel's character, a widower, travels to New Zealand to live with his only daughter who years before had gone to work in Auckland, fallen in love, married and had a son. Her husband had died quite young from a heart attack and the daughter asked her father to come and live with her and her son. The series would open with Jimmy arriving in New Zealand looking forward to meeting his only grandson. What he doesn't know, however, is that her daughter had married a Maori and that her son is a Maori boy. The idea appealed to me so off I flew to Auckland with Geraldine and our daughter Genevieve to start writing the series. We were put up in a wonderful hotel, the White Heron, which had a series of two-bed-roomed bungalows in their gardens, one of which was allocated to us. To our surprise, we discovered that staying in the adjoining bungalow was New Zealand's biggest star, Kiri Te Kanawa - name dropping again!

Anyway, I wrote the first script, we found some great locations for filming and were all set to start as soon as Jimmy arrived when we got a phone call from Jimmy. He wasn't coming! His wife had been taken ill and he felt he couldn't leave her. What a disappointment. However, NZTV decided that they would go ahead with the series and re-cast Jimmy's part. Tom and I had several meetings with the casting director and considered lots of English actors who might be suitable for the part without success. Either they were busy or they didn't want to travel and work on the other side of the world. Then another of those coincidences which seem to regularly occur, happened. NZTV bought a series of 'SYKES AND A ...' from the BBC and Tom and I were invited to a preview. We sat there laughing at the show, when a familiar figure appeared dressed as a policeman and wheeling a bike. It was Deryck Guyler. Tom and I looked at each other and nodded. The next day I phoned Deryck and told him of our situation. He agreed to do the series on one condition. Would NZTV pay for his wife, Paddy to come out with him? They agreed, and a week later I met them at Auckland airport. They were also put up in a bungalow at the White Heron and we went into production. We re-named the series 'AN AGE APART' and recorded six episodes which everyone seemed pleased about. The viewer reaction in New Zealand was good, but there was one big problem. The cost of producing the series was quite high, involving as it did, international air fares and accommodation, which meant that, in order for NZTV to make a worthwhile profit, the series had to be sold to Australia. Unfortunately, Australia wasn't keen on buying it so the first series of 'AN AGE APART' was also the last.

We all returned home where I met up with my old friend Mike Craig who, as you may recall, I had commissioned to write the sketch series for Harry Worth. He was now a radio producer for BBC Manchester and asked me to write a radio sitcom. He was keen to use Jack Smethurst so I devised a northern domestic comedy for Jack and Madge Hindle, who had previously played in 'NEAREST AND DEAREST' on both TV and the stage. It was recorded in Manchester on Sundays which was good for me as it gave me the opportunity to go and see my favourite team Manchester United play on Saturday afternoons. It was a good series with lots of laughs and it was nice to work again with old friends. The series was repeated several times so I got my script fee over and over again.

Later that year I was enjoying a drink in the bar at Teddington studios when I was approached by Peter Frazer-Jones with whom I had worked before on the Mike & Bernie Winter's special. He was now involved in a series called 'NEVER THE TWAIN' starring Donald Sinden and Windsor Davies two accomplished and distinguished actors. Donald had appeared in many films and stage plays and had recently completed a successful TV sitcom series 'TWO'S COMPANY' with American actress, Elaine Stritch while Windsor was well known for his portrayal of the bullying Sergeant Major in the popular TV sitcom 'IT 'AINT HALF HOT MUM'. 'NEVER THE TWAIN' had been created by Johnnie Mortimer and was in it's third series. Donald and Windsor were two antique dealers who not only lived next door to each other, but had adjoining shops. Johnnie had run into trouble in coming up with future plots and Peter had called in other writers to help out. He asked me if I was prepared to write an episode. At first I was offended, telling Peter that I wrote my own original series and did not contribute to other writer's series. How pretentious that must have sounded. I rang my wife and told her. To my surprise, she told me off for my attitude and practically accused me of being big headed. She said it was stupid of me to turn down a script fee. I eventually saw the sense in what she said, swallowed my pride, went to find

Peter and told him I'd write an episode. It was one of the most sensible and profitable decisions I ever made. It was the start of a lifelong friendship between Donald, Windsor and myself that still continues to this day. Some years ago Windsor and I drove to Le Touquet to celebrate New Beaujolais day and spent an enjoyable if somewhat alcoholic weekend. Windsor now lives in France and I have an open invitation to go and visit him and his wife Lynn whenever I wish. Donald, of course is still working mostly in the theatre and we speak on the phone from time to time. But apart from that, writing that first episode led to so much more. Peter, Donald and Windsor loved what I had written and when a further series of 6 were planned, I was invited to write three, with the other three being written by John Kane who had written that most successful long running sitcom, 'TERRY AND JUNE' for Terry Scott and June Whitfield. Later, when Thames were negotiating with Donald and Windsor for yet another series, they both insisted that I be commissioned to write the entire series. This was a tremendous compliment to me as a writer and, all in all, I wrote a total of 39 episodes. All thanks to my wife!

Donald and Windsor are both superb actors and yet when I went to the technical run of that first script I wrote, I was very disappointed. They were both overacting and mugging like mad. It wasn't until I saw the recording and heard the huge laughs from the audience that I realised that this was deliberate on their part and that, far from taking away the comedy it added to and increased it. They had taken overacting and made it into an art form. During the run of the series, my wife and I became very close to Donald and his wife Diana. We had many memorable meals together including one unforgettable evening when we were guests of his at his club The Garrick. On one occasion, I wrote a part in one of the scripts for Diana playing the part of a titled lady which was significant as shortly after, Donald received his knighthood and Diana became Lady Sinden! Talk about life imitating art!

I also wrote their two sons Jeremy and Marc into one episode in which they played a couple of policemen who arrested Donald. Some episodes in the series required sequences to be filmed outside their respective houses and I arranged for my house in Cobham and that of my next door neighbour to be used. Needless to say, I became a bit of a celebrity myself to all my neighbours, many of whom took advantage of cups of tea and coffee provided by the location caterers. I used to love filming on location. Never have I tasted better sausage sandwiches or bacon rolls.

On one occasion, my friend Tony Parker and I had the idea of making a TV series combining cooking, wine and travel. We put the idea to Donald and asked him if he would like to present it. He was interested but pointed out that he knew next to nothing about either cooking or wine.

'Don't worry', I said, 'Tony and I do. And when we've written the script, you'll be viewed as an authority on both!'

He agreed and, following a long held principal of mine of 'if you are looking for investment money, go to the top.' We approached Trust House Forte, at the time Europe's leading hotel chain. We managed to fix a meeting with their Managing Director, Martin South at which we used all our persuasive powers on him. We told him that our project was sure to be a huge success and would bound to be picked up by either the BBC or ITV. We elaborated on the selling power of having Donald Sinden attached to the project and the invaluable publicity Trust House Forte would receive from us filming the series in several of their hotels in Europe. Each episode would feature Donald talking to the Chef de Cuisine about food and wine after which the chef would show how to prepare and make a starter, main course and dessert. Then Donald would take the viewers on a sightseeing tour of the surrounding area. All we were looking for was sufficient funding to make a transmittable pilot from which to sell the series.

We must have done a good selling job as Martin cancelled any other meetings he had and took us to lunch. Mind you, having Donald Sinden a Presenter might have helped! Over lunch, Martin told us that Trust House Forte were about to open a brand new flagship hotel, The Bath Spa and it would be ideal if we filmed the pilot there. We quickly came to a deal. Trust House Forte would provide meals and accommodation for our production crew and Donald, a total of six rooms, for five days. They would also provide us with the services of their Chef de Cuisine, Richard Tonks. We, in return would provide the production team, cost of film and editing. Not a bad deal considering it was hammered out over a free lunch!

Tony and I acquired a two man film crew, a production assistant and a director, all willing to give their services free in return for being employed on any future series. We also co-opted my son Dominic as a 'Gopher' (go for this - go for that!) with special duties to look after Donald. We all assembled at the Bath Spa Hotel, which was the last word in luxury. We filmed every day for four days and got everything we needed. We were a little bit worried about the chef, but he took to acting like a duck to water. On the last day we shot the travel sequences, shooting all of Bath's historical connections - including the Pump Room & Roman Baths, Pulteney Bridge, Royal Crescent, Bath Abbey and the Guildhall. That night we had a celebratory meal and left for home the next day, happy and well pleased with ourselves.

Tony and I edited the pilot and it was really good. We sent off copies to the BBC and ITV and waited for their reaction. We were confident that we had created a potentially successful series which would run and run. Remember, this was in 1990 long before the current flood of cookery programmes burst on the TV scene. We were confident that we had created an original project and that it was only a question of time before it was sold all over the world and we would both be able to retire on our royalties! We couldn't go wrong. However, we could and we did.

The BBC replied that they had enjoyed watching our pilot - it was very professional and a credit to us all. However, part of the BBC's charter was that, unlike ITV they were forbidden to advertise and as our series would be a huge plug for Trust House Forte, they had to regretfully turn it down. A big disappointment for us. But we still had ITV. They would surely have no problems with advertising. So we sat back and waited for their reaction. It took a while and when it came it was not good news.

Like the BBC, they thanked us for submitting it and congratulated us on it's professional quality. Then they went on to say that they couldn't commission it as they had a similar idea in development. It was a brush off. At this point in time we are still waiting for this similar idea to make an appearance. Call me cynical if you like, but I didn't believe them. I think it's just another form of rejection, and that they were covering themselves in case they decided to develop it themselves. Anyway, we still have the tape of the pilot and one day we may take it off the shelf, dust it down, update it and re-present it.

The one good thing which happened during this year was the birth of our second child, Anthony James. So it was back to changing nappies and wiping bottoms again. But not for long.

Chapter Seventeen:
A LORRA LORRA LAUGHS

Later that year, I got a phone call from David Bell who was then the Controller of Entertainment at London Weekend Television inviting me to a meeting in his office, a meeting which was to affect the next twelve years of my life. David was a brilliant producer having been responsible for furthering the careers of many comedians including Stanley Baxter, Russ Abbott and Benny Hill. I wondered what he wanted to see me about. He got straight to the point.

'Vince,' he said, 'last week I had a meeting with Cilla Black and her husband Bobby. As you probably knew, a few years ago she put her show business career on hold to bring up her three children (I didn't know but what the heck). Well, she's now decided to resume her career and we're going to do a TV special with her this Christmas. Isn't that tremendous news?'

He was obviously so proud and excited at having secured her comeback for LWT that I hadn't the heart to disagree.

'Very good David, but what's that got to do with me?'

'She wants you to write the special for her.'

I shook my head. 'David,' I said, 'I write sitcoms. I don't write sketch shows or specials. It's very kind of her to ask for me, but I wouldn't be right.'

It was now David's turn to shake his head. 'They're both very insistent,' he said, 'look - why don't I fix up a lunch for us all, next week and we can discuss it then?'

Never one to turn down the offer of lunch, I agreed. The following week we all met at a restaurant on the South Bank. I hadn't seen Cilla or Bobby since the memorial service for Ronnie Taylor which they both reminded me of. Bobby jumped right in.

'Now listen Vince, I've just done a deal with LWT for Cilla to do a one hour Christmas special and we want you to write it.'

I was just about to repeat the arguments which I'd put to David Bell when Cilla interrupted.

'You can write for me like Ronnie Taylor used to do. You're from the North like Bobby and me. You've got a Northern sense of humour - alright, you're from Manchester not Liverpool but that doesn't matter. Ronnie spoke very highly of you.'

Bobby chipped in. 'Don't make up your mind right away. Think about it. And while you're thinking about it, have a glass of champagne.'

He handed me a glass of champagne. We all drank.

Cilla said, 'You'll do it won't you Vince?'

David said 'Of course he'll do it. I'm going to offer him a script fee he can't refuse.'

The upshot was, by the end of the lunch I had agreed to write the special and that was the start of my association with Cilla that lasted over a decade. And all thanks to dear old Ronnie Taylor. The special was very successful and I found it relatively easy to write. The studio set was designed to represent Cilla and Bobby's lounge, and the premise was that every so often the doorbell would ring and a guest celebrity would arrive. My job was to write a 4/5 minute routine between Cilla and each guest. The guests included Frankie Howerd, Diana Dors, Irene Handl, American singer George Benson, a children's choir who sang a selection of Christmas carols, with Cilla joining in and the inevitable chorus of dancers. I remember I even wrote a small part in for Bobby, playing himself. All in all it was an enjoyable experience.

A couple of weeks later, I got a call from Bobby.

'Hello Vince. Listen, I've just signed a contract with London Weekend for Cilla to do a series of people shows. It's called 'SURPRISE SURPRISE' and I've told them you'll be writing it.' Did you get that? 'I've told them you'll be writing it'. How's that for artist power?

Well, I did write it - in fact I ended up writing 130 episodes. The series, as it's title implies, was built around Cilla surprising unsuspecting members of the public by granting them wishes such as meeting their favourite celebrity, or re-uniting them with a long lost friend or relative. We had a team of researchers who collected all the information about the people who were to be surprised and the friends and relatives who were to be re-united and it was my job to put it into a suitable script form. It was a lovely show to work on. Some of the surprises, particularly the re-unions with relatives who they hadn't met for years or were separated from as children were quite moving and tearful. Many of them came from different corners of the world.

During the course of the series, I met lots of famous celebrities who appeared on the show including Cliff Richard, Dusty Springfield, Tom Jones, Barry Manilow, Wayne Sleep, Frank Bruno, Kenny Dalglish, John Barnes, Graeme Souness, Bryan Robson and Take That - how's that for name dropping?

Cilla and Bobby were a joy to work with. Bobby and I used to spend hours discussing football, in spite of me being a Manchester United fan and Bobby a Liverpool supporter. And Cilla really did say 'a lorra, lorra laughs, fur hur and Mairseyside.' They were true Liverpudlians and proud of it.

I'd been doing 'SURPRISE SURPRISE' for about a year when Bobby rang me one evening. He'd just concluded another deal with LWT for Cilla to host another people show, a British version of an Australian show called 'BLIND DATE' and both he and Cilla wanted me to be involved. As most of you will recall, the show revolved around pairing members of the public up on a date. One week a girl or woman, would choose from three lads or men, hidden from her view behind a screen, after asking each of them a series of questions. The following week would involve a lad or man choosing a girl or woman. The lucky couple would then be sent off on a date - a romantic weekend somewhere - with a film crew and on their return would be invited to tell Cilla and the viewers what happened. Did they get on or did they end up hating each other? Great care was taken by LWT not to suggest that anything untoward happened. The couple had separate rooms and were filmed everywhere they went. Unlike an episode in the Australian version in which the host asked the girl, 'Well, did he snore?' How subtle can you get?

It seemed like a fun programme, and I agreed to be involved. I was given the title of 'PROGRAMME ASSOCIATE' and we did 224 episodes, many of them in tandem with 'SURPRISE SURPRISE'. It was a massive hit with the viewers and launched Cilla into a second successful career after her years as a singing star with many hit records to her credit. Which reminds me of a funny anecdote about her, which I was told was true but could well be apocryphal. Cilla was appearing in pantomime at the Liverpool Empire in Jack and the Beanstalk in which she was playing Jack. It had got the part where Jack had chopped down the beanstalk and the Giant had fallen and was lying on the floor. Cilla placed one foot on his chest, drew her sword, faced the audience and asked, 'How shall I kill him? Shall I run him through or cut his head off?' A voice from the Gods shouted down 'Sing to him!'

I also wrote another special for Cilla, 'CILLA'S WORLD' a two part co-production between LWT and America. The first part was filmed in Miami. We stayed at the Bal Harbour Hotel and I wrote a series of interviews in which Cilla chatted to the Mayor, the Chief of Police, a millionaire property developer, the Bee Gees and Julio Iglesias. The second part we shot in the studio at London Weekend, in which Cilla interviewed Joan Collins and Mickey Rooney. I had the enviable task of meeting Mickey Rooney at the Savoy Hotel and having lunch with him, paid for by LWT of course, and discussing the questions Cilla would be putting to him and the replies he was likely to give. I had long been a fan of his and I spent an enjoyable couple of hours listening to the stories of his legendary career and his reminiscences of Spencer Tracy and Judy Garland.

It was a very pleasant period of my life, one on which I look back with fond memories. Cilla and I still exchange Christmas cards and I miss my football chats with Bobby who sadly died of cancer a few years ago.

After writing for Cilla on 'SURPRISE SURPRISE' and 'BLIND DATE' for 12 years, my association with her and the programmes came to a rather unhappy end. It was November and I had just finished a series of 'BLIND DATE' and was sitting in the bar at London Weekend looking forward to working on a new series of 'SURPRISE SURPRISE' in the spring. A light entertainment producer approached me and I happened to say to him that I enjoyed writing 'SURPRISE SURPRISE' more than 'BLIND DATE' as the former show had much more scope for me to use my writing talents, whereas in the latter, all I was doing was writing funny lines for Cilla and the contestants. That was that and I thought no more about it, until a few weeks later when I got a Christmas card from one of the associate producers of 'BLIND DATE'. In it he had written that he was sorry we wouldn't be working together on the next series. I had no idea what he meant so I rang him. He told me that the light entertainment producer to whom I had spoken in November, (no names, no pack drill, but if he happens to read this book, he'll know I'm talking about him) had told the Controller of Entertainment that I had said I wasn't happy working on 'BLIND DATE' and didn't want to write any more. What a blatant, misrepresentation of what I had really said. I immediately rang the Controller and told him, only to learn that he had taken the unnamed producer's word and that, in future the scripts for 'BLIND DATE' would be written by the researchers. I protested but it was too late. I had lost a valuable and financially rewarding contract.

I later found out the reason from another producer, now no longer with LWT. Apparently the unnamed producer was jealous of my relationship with Cilla and Bobby. He thought that I was being too familiar with them. After 12 years I felt I was entitled to a little familiarity. At the time all this happened, Cilla and Bobby were in Australia and uncontactable otherwise they may have been able to redress the situation. As it was, when they returned they were presented with a fait accompli. I'm not normally a vindictive person, but in this unnamed producer's case I'm willing to make an exception! But enough of that.

It was about this time that I was asked by Philip Jones to write a sitcom for Bruce Forsyth. Thames had done a couple of series about a supermarket starring Leonard Rossiter and were planning a further series when Leonard Rossiter unexpectedly died. You would think that at this point,

Thames would have abandoned the series but apparently the supermarket set cost so much to build, that they decided to recast and carry on. Mark Stuart, one of Thames most experienced light entertainment directors, was given the responsibility of directing and he cast Bruce Forsyth and asked me to write it. It was, at the time, and still is, Bruce's only attempt at situation comedy and there were fears that he wouldn't be able to refrain from playing to the audience and throwing in ad-libs as he normally did in his game show series. But he surprised us all. He stuck faithfully to the script and really threw himself into the part. We did two series, but unfortunately the viewing figures weren't brilliant and it was dropped. One good thing which came out of it, from my point of view, was that Bruce later asked me to contribute to his very successful game show series, 'PLAY YOUR CARDS RIGHT' by writing some funny routines between him and the beautiful girls who dealt the cards.

I still went over to France from time to time to spend a weekend in Calais, Boulogne or Le Touquet sometimes accompanied by my old friend Tony Parker. There was one occasion when we went to Le Touquet together. We were staying at a hotel on the beach and on the first day, after and excellent meal at Flavios with the usual accompaniment of two bottles of Beaujolais, we staggered back to our hotel. Our rooms were some distance apart so we arranged to phone each other's room the next morning to fix a time to meet for breakfast and retired to our beds. What followed next had all the makings of a situation comedy. I need to explain that I am rather deaf in my right ear as a result of an earlier perforated ear drum. I was asleep in bed and lying on my left side, when my bedside phone rang. As I was lying on my good ear, I didn't hear the phone. Meanwhile, in his room, Tony was wondering why I wasn't answering my phone. He tried ringing another couple of times, then decided I must have forgotten our previous night's arrangement and gone down to breakfast, so he got up, dressed and went in search of me. I was still sleeping blissfully in my room. Tony couldn't find me in the dining room, nor in any of the other public rooms in the hotel. He then wondered if perhaps I'd gone out for a walk on the beach so he went outside to look for me.

By now, he was getting a bit worried. He returned to his room and tried ringing my room again. I still didn't hear the phone. Tony went to my room and knocked on my door, but I was still asleep and lying on my good ear, so I didn't hear him knocking. Tony was then struck by a sudden thought. What if I had passed out - even worse - what if I had passed away? His imagination was running riot. How was he going to break the news to Geraldine? Should he ring the French equivalent of an undertaker? He did the next best thing. He went to the reception desk and tried to explain in his best, but far from brilliant French. He finally managed to get them to give him a duplicate key to my room and returned to my door. He put the key in and pushed open the door, dreading what he might see. There I was, lying flat out not moving. He crept toward the bed, and bent his head to within an inch of my face. At that moment I opened my eyes. I don't know which of us got the biggest shock!

That particular year had some sad moments for me. Two of my greatest friends passed away. Billy Dainty and Jimmy Jewel. Billy died from cancer at the young age of 59. I went to his funeral and a year later Roy Hudd organised a Memorial Service at the Actor's Church in Covent Garden which was attended by so many stars. Billy was the eternal optimist. The thing I remember most about him is his laughter. He had such a great sense of humour and an infectious laugh. On one occasion when I was writing a radio sitcom for him, we sat in an office at the BBC and I laughed so much that I got pains in my chest.

Two memories of Billy stand out in my mind. The first is when his son Laurence was about 5 or 6. We were at a barbecue at Billy's house, when Laurence ran into the garden and said the 'F' word. Billy and his wife Sandra were understandably shocked.

'What did you say?' asked Billy, so Laurence said it again.

Sandra said 'Where did you learn a word like that?'

Laurence replied 'I heard my Dad say it this morning. And I know what it means.'

'You don't,' said Sandra.

Laurence nodded, 'I do. It means the car won't start!'

We all collapsed with laughter.

The second was something Billy told me himself. He used to do a lot of charity work, and on one occasion he was due to open an old folk's nursing home. Naturally, he told a few gags and did his eccentric dance routine. During his performance, he noticed an elderly lady sitting in the front row, looking rather vague and not quite with it. After he finished he went to her and asked, 'Are you all right love.'

She nodded, 'Oh yes. I'm all right.'

Billy then said 'Do you know who I am?'

She shook her head. 'No, but if you ask Matron, she'll tell you!'

Jimmy on the other hand, was the eternal pessimist. He was 83 when he died and for years he was convinced that he had lung cancer. Mind you he did smoke 60 cigarettes a day, so it wouldn't have been surprising. However, on his death certificate it stated the cause of death as emphysema, which would have been a big disappointment to him. Jimmy had named me as one of his executors and I duly presented myself at his solicitors for the reading of his will. My mind went back a few years to a time when we were both lying on a beach in Juan Les Pins. Jimmy turned to me and said.

'Vince, when I die, I'm going to be cremated and I want you to bring my ashes over here and scatter them on this beach, where I've spent many happy hours with my wife and family.'

I nodded. 'Right. It'll cost you a first class fair fare to Nice and a week at the five star Hotel Provencal here in Juan.'

Nothing more was said.

To my surprise, when Jimmy's will was read, there was a sentence to the effect that he wished to be cremated and his ashes scattered on the beach at Juan Le Pins by Vince Powell. Not a word about a first class air fare to Nice or a week at the five star Hotel Provencal! However, the solicitors agreed that the cost of an economy air fare to Nice and three days at a two star hotel in Juan would be paid for out of the estate.

Jimmy was duly cremated and I collected his ashes which were in a bronze metal urn. There were, at least half a dozen forms, in triplicate to be filled in for the French customs including, would you believe, an export licence. I flew to Nice and took a taxi to Juan Les Pins, arriving at about six in the evening. It was a dark and windy November night and raining heavily. I checked in at my two star hotel and came to a decision. I would go out and scatter Jimmy's ashes that night. It was out of season, with not many people about to see me which would be less embarrassing than doing it in daylight, when there might be people walking on the beach. I unscrewed the lid of the urn to find the ashes in a stout plastic bag. I tried to pull the plastic bag from the urn, and in doing so, tore it. Some of Jimmy's ashes spilled on to the carpet, which I then attempted to brush up, using the only brush available - my toothbrush! To this day, there may still be a few of Jimmy's ashes clinging to that carpet. I then emptied the remainder of the ashes from the plastic bag into the urn, before going downstairs. It was still raining heavily, but I had an umbrella. I stepped outside clutching the urn and opened my umbrella, which the wind immediately blew inside out! I managed to turn it back the right way and set off toward the beach which was totally deserted. I stuck my umbrella, point downwards in the sand, unscrewed the lid from the urn and started to walk backwards along the beach, scattering Jimmy's ashes as I went. I emptied the last of his ashes out and made my way back to collect my umbrella only to discover it had vanished. The wind had blown it away. I looked around and saw it floating in the sea, a few yards out. It was an expensive umbrella which I had bought some years ago in Australia so I took off my shoes and socks, rolled up my trousers and waded in to retrieve it, cursing Jimmy as I did so. I headed back to my hotel and went to bed. It poured with rain all that night, but had stopped by morning. After breakfast I walked down to the beach and was astonished to see a trail of Jimmy's ashes plainly visible even after all that rain. I took a photograph of it and sent a copy to his son in Sydney.

On my return home I had a pleasant surprise. There was a message on my answer phone from Alan Randall. Alan was an accomplished musician - a jazz pianist and concert pianist. He also played the banjo, guitar, vibraphone and xylophone. We had never met, but he said that he had seen and liked most of my sitcoms and had a proposition to put to me. I rang him back and we arranged to meet in London. We met at Waterloo and he told me that he had always been a fan of George Formby - he actually did an impression of him as part of his stage act - and that he wanted to do a stage play based on George. Would I be interested in writing it? For those of you too young to remember, George Formby was a Lancashire comedian whose career spanned forty years during which time he made 22 hit films and hundreds of records. From 1938 to 1944 he was Britain's biggest star at the box office, a record still unequalled. He was awarded the OBE for his war effort in entertaining over three million Allied troops during the Second World War. His career was managed by his wife Beryl, a formidable lady who kept him on a tight lead. It is rumoured that after he was awarded the OBE Beryl said to him.

'Do you know what OBE stands for George?'

'Yes Beryl. Order of the British Empire.

'No George,' she replied, 'it stands for Owes Beryl Everything!'

And she meant it!

The idea appealed to me and in the end, Alan and I wrote it together. It was a wonderful show business story. It had everything. Music, songs - the lot. Beryl became an alcoholic, and died of cancer. Shortly after, George got engaged to a young school teacher whom he had known for some time. She was much younger than him and they set a date to be married. After all his problems with Beryl and her alcoholism, it appeared that at last he had a happy future ahead of him. But six weeks before the wedding he died of a heart attack.

We sent the play to several top theatrical managements but they all rejected it. Some of them said that it had limited appeal - it was too parochial - too northern. Eventually we managed to arrange a tour of small, independent theatres in Britain. We opened at the Blackpool Grand and got some terrific press reviews but still couldn't raise any interest from the West End theatres. So it lies on a shelf in my study awaiting an appropriate time to resurrect it.

Meanwhile, I had a call from Mike Craig with an offer to write another radio sitcom. He wanted to do a series about a couple in their late thirties who'd been courting for years.

She wanted to get engaged and he kept putting it off. He lived with his widower father and worked as an undertakers' assistant. She lived with her widowed mother and worked in a department store. Plenty of opportunities there for funny situations. It was Mike's idea - he would produce it and we would write the series together. I enjoyed the freedom that writing for radio gave. It wasn't as limiting as writing for television. On radio you could set a scene anywhere in the world - in an airplane, on a ship, on top of the Eiffel Tower or on safari in South Africa which, for financial reasons you couldn't do on TV. Mike and I got together to discuss who we should cast in the leading roles and came up with two star names, Gordon Kaye, famous for his role as Rene the French café owner in the TV sitcom hit, "ALLO 'ALLO', and Su Pollard, equally famous for her role as Peggy the chalet maid in 'HI-DI-HI'. We recorded the series at the City Varieties Theatre in Leeds to a 'standing room only' audience who laughed at every funny line and even at some which weren't funny. It was well received by the radio audience and the BBC were so pleased that they commissioned a further two series after which they decided that it had run it's course and it came to an end.

However, it wasn't the end of my association with Su Pollard. Mark Furness, a theatrical impressario who produced plays, summer shows and pantomimes was anxious to mount a touring revue for which he had some interest from New Zealand. While over there with another show, he had met with a theatre management to whom he pitched the idea for the revue. We arranged to meet for lunch to discuss the idea but when we met, I discovered that he had no idea. All he had was a title - 'THE GOOD SEX GUIDE'. He had sold the idea to New Zealand just on the title. We were then joined by Dougie Squires, a talented and well known choreographer who had formed his own television dance troupe, 'The Young Generation'. Mark wanted Dougie to be part of the creative team. Fortified by several glasses of wine, the three of us set out to create a format of sorts. Obviously, given the title, the content had to be of a sexual nature and we created the following format. It would be a musical revue, with songs, dances and sketches. Mark wanted to keep the cast down to a minimum so we settled on two stars, one male and one female, who could sing, dance and act. We chose Su Pollard and David Griffin, who had previously co-starred in 'HI-DI-HI' with Su. He was a good looking and clever actor and she had a terrific singing voice and great personality. Then Dougie held a series of auditions to find 3 beautiful dancing girls and 3 good looking dancing boys. To my surprise. Dougie insisted I be present at the auditions which were held in a rehearsal room in Garrick Street. When I arrived, half a dozen stunning looking girls were waiting in the corridor. Dougie was inside sitting at a table. I joined him and he summoned the first girl. Dougie asked me to make a few notes on her audition - marks out of ten - then he asked her a few questions - what experience she'd had, could she sing a piece of music and was she free on the dates pencilled in for the tour. Then he said, 'Right. 'Strip.' To my complete and utter amazement, the girl stripped down to her brief panties. I didn't know where to look - well, I did know where to look but I didn't dare! This routine was repeated with each of the six girls one of which actually took her panties off as well. By then I was breathing heavily and my eyes were watering. In all my years of sitting in at auditions for sitcoms, I had never had an experience like this before. Maybe I should have started to write musical revues a long time ago. Dougie turned to me and asked my opinion on the merits of each girl. I told him that as far as I was concerned, they were all terrific. He nodded and said he' already chosen the three best. By this time, there were half a dozen boys waiting outside to be auditioned. Dougie called them in, one at a time and I set there terrified that he would ask them all to strip off. Fortunately he only asked them to strip to the waist. Having completed the casting, it was time for me to concentrate on writing the revue.

I wrote several sketches all with a sexual theme, and re-wrote the lyrics to a selection of popular songs filling them full of sexual innuendos, Dougie devised several sexy dance routines, and eventually we had a two hour revue. I was a little worried that the overall content might be perhaps a little too overladen with sexual reference, but Dougie and Mark brushed my worries aside. They thought it was terrific.

We rehearsed for ten days in a school hall near Edgware Road, then they all set off for New Zealand.

I was hoping to be invited to travel with the troupe but Mark said he couldn't afford to take me along. So I sat at home waiting for the news of it's success. I had signed a contract with Mark which guaranteed me 5% of the box office takings and as there were to be a total of 63 performances I was looking forward to a considerable sum in royalties. The show opened at the end of August 1996 and normally, a writer would receive a statement of the box office takings and a royalty cheque each week, one week after opening. When it got to the end of the year and I still hadn't received any statements or royalties, I wrote to Mark remind him of our contract. I received the following reply dated January 11 1997.

Dear Vince,

This letter will confirm that you are due royalties from the New Zealand tour of "The Good Sex Guide".

Regrettably, the tour was not a financial success and lost not only its production costs but also a considerable sum in running costs. The result is that the company is financially stretched.

Exact figure of the tour gross are not confirmed yet but your 5% will certainly bring you in excess of £10,000.

I expect the company to receive income from its involvement in various overseas shows within the next six months and I would hope inroads could be made into your debt within that time frame.

Yours sincerely,

Mark Furness.

My first reaction was one of shock to learn that the revue had not been a financial success. I phoned my friend Tom Parkinson at NZTV for any information he might have. His opinion was that the majority of the population of New Zealand were of God fearing stock and that the content of the revue was far too raunchy for their tastes, which exactly echoed my earlier fears.

However, I consoled myself with the thought that, according to Mark's letter, I would eventually receive the £10,000 I was owed in royalties. Six months he said in his letter. But it was not to be. Five months later Mark Furness died from a fatal heart attack! The end result was that all his future projects were cancelled and I never got my £10,000. The only thing I was left with was the memory of those auditions!

Chapter Eighteen:
A JOURNEY TO
LOURDES

Around this time there was a gradual decline in TV sitcoms. Television was going through a financial crisis and TV executives were looking for ways and means to economise. Budgets for both sitcoms and dramas had escalated, audiences for the major TV channels had fallen owing to the increase in extra channels and the introduction of satellite TV. Competition was fierce. Then somebody had the bright idea that it would be less expensive if programmes were made featuring members of the public rather than actors. Thus - the Reality Show was born, and the viewers were bombarded with a plethora of Do It Yourself shows, Gardening and Cookery programmes, Make Over shows and more Quiz programmes. Added to all that was the slow rise of the twin evils of political correctness and ageism of which I shall speak more later.

I was naturally worried about this decline in sitcoms and started to think of other areas in which I could put my writing talents to good use. I received a cheque from Thames Television for royalties from video sales of 'LOVE THY NEIGHBOUR'. It wasn't a huge amount but it set me thinking. Perhaps I should make a video and try and sell copies. I went into my local branch of HMV and looked at what they had on their shelves. They had videos for sale on Golf, DIY, Keep Fit, Gardening and Foreign Travel. There was one on the Capitals of Europe. I was wondering whether I could do a video on France when I was suddenly struck with a brainwave. Lourdes! The most famous Catholic shrine in the world. The story of Bernadette, her visions of the Virgin Mary and the many miracles attributed to the shrine's healing waters was widely known. A feature film had been made of it and also a musical play. I talked it over with Tony Parker and asked him if he would be interested in directing the video. Although he wasn't a Catholic he saw the possibilities in the project. At the last count, there were over 9 million Catholics in the UK. If only one percent bought a video at a price of £10 we would make more than enough to cover the costs of making the video, including duplication. There was only one other problem to overcome, that of distribution. How could we bring the public's attention to the existence of the video? Because of the subject matter, the video would mainly appeal to Catholics therefore advertising in the national press would not guarantee that it would be read by every Catholic, even if we placed an advertisement in every national newspaper which would be far too expensive.

I then had another brainwave. I remembered that at the back of every Catholic Church was a repository - a stall which sold religious objects - prayer books, rosary beads, holy medals and pictures. If we could get every Catholic Church to display copies of the video, most members of the congregation would be sure to buy one. Tony agreed and we decided to put my theory to the test. We wrote to the Parish Priest of one hundred churches asking if he would be prepared to take ten videos on a sale or return basis and put them on display in the repository. As an added incentive we offered to donate £1 from every video sold to that particular parish's fund. We posted the letters and waited for the replies. To our surprise and disappointment, only a few bothered to reply, and most of those who did were not interested. In spite of the offer of a donation, they couldn't be bothered in collecting the monies on our behalf, paying it into our bank and returning any unsold videos. We couldn't believe it but there it was.

However, we were still convinced that we had a viable project and I decided we should write to the then head of the Catholic Church in England, His Eminence Cardinal George Basil Hume the Archbishop of Westminster telling him of the idea and enlisting his support. He replied almost immediately and suggested that we talk to Monsignor Provost Raymond Lawrence, the then President of the Conference of Pilgrimage Directors in Brockenhurst. We rang him and invited him to lunch. He was a charming man, deeply devoted to Our Lady of Lourdes and with strong views on what a video about Lourdes should contain. He told us that most existing videos about Lourdes fell between being a documentary or a travelogue and that, in his opinion, none of them contained the spiritual essence and religious aura of Lourdes. He promised to help us in any way he could and gave us the names of several important members of the official organisation in Lourdes to whom we should write.

Encouraged by his words Tony and I went ahead with planning the video but soon came up against a major obstacle. No matter how hard we tried, we could not interest anyone to invest in the project. We tried our banks, our accountants, insurance companies, investment brokers and film companies - all to no avail. Nobody wanted to know. They all agreed that it was a good idea, but weren't sure they would see a return on their investment. Inevitably, the idea went on the back burner. And there it stayed for four long years when an amazing series of events occurred which later made me wonder if some mysterious unseen hand was at work.

Having put the Lourdes project to one side, I came up with another bright idea. I would capitalise on all the knowledge and experience I had gained over the years and start a writing school to pass on this accumulated wisdom to budding writers. I contacted an old colleague of mine, George Evans an experienced comedy writer who had been writing as long as I had. Our paths had crossed several times over the years and we had collaborated on a couple of occasions. He had written for many of our top comedians and was co-author of radio's longest running sitcoms, 'THE NAVY LARK.' George liked the idea and suggested that the project should take the form of a correspondence course in creative writing and cover every aspect of writing. We decided that the course would consist of 10 lessons each one dealing with a different genre, TV comedy, radio comedy, TV drama, radio drama, stand up comedy, one-liners and so on. At the end of each lesson, we set every student some homework to complete inviting them to send us their efforts, which we would then comment on. It was a good idea, and at first worked extremely well but its success contributed to its downfall. We found that we were spending far too much of our time on reading and analysing each student's homework, that it left little time for either of us to concentrate on our own individual projects. So we reluctantly cancelled our website, and wound the course down. We are now seriously thinking of publishing the entire course in book form - we'll wait and see.

Meanwhile, I wrote another radio sitcom series for Harry Worth which turned out to be his last. He hadn't been in good health for some time and it was discovered that he had contracted a form of cancer. He underwent a course of chemotherapy and seemed to be recovering, so much so that he and I discussed the possibility of me writing his biography. Sadly, he died before we could take it any further. I then became involved in writing a pilot with Jim Bowie a genial Scot who had been the Senior Manager of Entertainment at Thames. We wrote a couple of pilots, one a sitcom, the other a drama set in and around Waterloo Station which we are still trying to get off the launching pad. We worked well together and collaborated on a talent show series after talking Teddington Studios into putting up some investment money. We also talked them into letting us use an office, rent free, for us to think and develop future projects. One day we were in the bar - fortunately, Jim shared my liking for Bell's whisky - having a drink with the Head of Catering, Barry Rey, when Barry said apropos nothing at all, that if we ever needed any investment money in the future, he would be only too happy to oblige. At that moment I had a sudden flash of inspiration.

I said, 'Funny you should mention that Barry, but there is an idea for which we're looking for some investment money.'

Jim looked at me in astonishment. He had no idea what I was talking about. I went on, 'It's called 'A JOURNEY TO LOURDES.''

Jim was even further astonished. It was the first he'd heard of it.

Barry then said, 'I don't know much about cricket.'

It was my turn to look astonished until I realised that Barry had misheard me and thought I'd said Lords, not Lourdes. I quickly put him right and told him about the idea.

Remember me saying about an unseen hand being at work? Well, you ain't heard nothing yet. In the first place, what made Barry offer to invest in a project and in the second place why should the Lourdes idea pop into my brain after a lapse of nearly four years?

Barry then asked me how much money we were looking for. Not having any idea, I plucked a figure from the air.

'£25,000,' I said.

Barry replied without blinking any eyelid. 'Right - you've got it. Draw up a draft contract between us.' And with that, he left the bar.

Jim was looking more and more confused so I told him about the video idea which I had tried to develop in the past with Tony. Jim liked the sound of it and we agreed that we should resurrect the idea especially now we had Barry's promise of £25,000. We went back to the office and I phoned Monsignor Lawrence to tell him the good news and remind him of his offer to help us. All we got was an answerphone. I left a message and asked him to ring us back. Over the next two days I kept ringing and ringing and left two further messages. He never rang back. As his parish was in the diocese of Portsmouth I decided to ring the Bishop of Portsmouth. I got through to the Bishop's secretary and told him that I was trying to get in touch with Monsignor Lawrence. For a moment there was a silence on the line, then the Bishop's secretary spoke.

'I'm so sorry to have to tell you that Monsignor Lawrence passed away last week!'

The news came as a shock to Jim and I. We were discussing what we should do when the phone rang. It was the Bishop's secretary. He told me he had listened to my messages to the Monsignor and advised me to get in touch with the new President of Pilgrimage Directors, a Father Vladimir Feltzmann. He was Czechoslovakian by birth and was the Westminster Diocesan Chaplain to Young People. He gave me his telephone number and I rang him immediately to invite him for lunch with Jim and I. To our delight, he was very enthusiastic about the Lourdes video project and suggested we accompany the Westminster Pilgrimage to Lourdes which would be led by Cardinal Hume and attended by the Duchess of Kent both of whom we could film. This was terrific news as their presence would add so much to the appeal of the video. However, our joy was short lived as Father Feltzmann told us that the Westminster Pilgrimage would be leaving for Lourdes in two weeks time. I told Father Feltzmann that there was no way we could possibly meet that deadline. Neither Jim nor I had ever visited Lourdes and we would need to do a recce in order to work out a shooting script. Not only that but we would need to hire a camera crew and arrange flights and accommodation. Father Feltzmann sighed.

'Pity,' he said, 'you'll have to wait until next years Westminster Pilgrimage.'

'Isn't there another pilgrimage we could go with?' I asked.

'Yes there are several,' he replied, 'but you won't get the Cardinal or the Duchess of Kent. It's either next fortnight or next year.'

He saw the look of despondency on my face. 'Cheer up Vince,' he said, 'look on it as a challenge. You've got two weeks. You can do it.'

I shook my head 'No way. It would take a miracle.'

He smiled, 'God will find a way.'

Well, we tried. During the next week I phoned practically every travel agent in the Yellow Pages. They all told us the same thing. Flights and accommodation were impossible. Many pilgrims booked their flights and hotels each year for the following year. Jim phoned every film crew he could think of. Not a chance. All were busy. We were resigned to putting our project away for another year when two things happened. I swear that what you are about to read is the truth, the whole truth and nothing but the truth. Jim and I were sitting at our desks in our office, consoling ourselves with large Bells when Jim's phone rang. He picked up the receiver and listened. His face lit up, he said 'We'll get back to you,' and hung up.

'That was Caren Moy, a freelance lighting camera operator. She says that she and her colleague, John Marchbank, a sound engineer, who work as a team, are unexpectedly vacant for the dates we need them in Lourdes.' Whilst I agreed that this was good news, I pointed out that, without flights and hotels, we couldn't book them. At that moment my phone rang. It was John Tangney a tour operator. He told me that he had just had a cancellation of four flights plus accommodation for the dates we had asked for. Did we still need them? I could hardly wait to tell him that we did, hung up and told Jim to ring Caren and book her and John. I had said to Father Feltzmann it would take a miracle. Was that a miracle? Who knows? I immediately phoned Father Feltzmann to tell him the good news. And what did he say? He said, 'Didn't I tell you that God would find a way!'

Anyway, we booked the flight and everything and got to Lourdes the following midday. We checked into the hotel and over lunch, Caren asked me for the shooting script so that she could study it before we started shooting the following morning. With a confidence I was far from feeling, I told her not to worry and that there would be a shooting script ready the next morning. I was lying of course. I had no idea what I wanted to shoot or how.

That afternoon, Jim and I went to register with the Lourdes authorities and were issued with 4 passes which allowed us to enter the SANCTUAIRE DE NOTRE DAME DE LOURDES with permission to film in all the holy and sacred places. We then walked all round the area - the Grotto, where the vision of the Virgin Mary appeared to Bernadette, the Stations of the Cross, the Basilica of the Rosary, the Baths in which the pilgrims were immersed in the healing waters, the route of The Torchlight Procession which took place every night, the Medical Bureau with its records and photographs of the miraculously cured pilgrims and the Notre Dame Hospital. As we walked round I was desperately trying to work out a shooting script. We only had four days to shoot our video and I still had no idea what I was going to do. I then had another flash of inspiration. I said to Jim, 'Look Jim, we're seeing all this for the first time. Let's shoot it as though we're the camera. Many people who may buy the video will never have been to Lourdes so they'll be seeing it for the first time. What do you think?'

Jim agreed and that's what we did. The next day, I led Caren and John round the Sanctuaries and I told her what to film. She couldn't understand that I had no script and that she was filming a series of seemingly unconnected shots, but I assured her that it would all eventually make sense when I'd edited the complete shoot.

We filmed for four days and shot everything I wanted - a Mass in the Grotto, a picnic in the forest, the Stations of the Cross, a blessing of the sick, the Castle, two processions and much more. When we had finished we had over eleven hours of film in the can, which I would eventually have to edit down to 90 minutes. We celebrated the 'wrap' with a slap up meal and went to bed, tired but happy.

My impressions of Lourdes are mixed. There is no doubt that there was an aura of holiness about the place. France is noted for the sound of car horns from impatient drivers, but during the entire time we were there, I never heard one car horn. In spite of the fact that many pilgrims were suffering from painful illnesses and disabilities, everyone seemed cheerful. It was an incredible experience.

The next day, we packed our bags and flew home. Jim and I went into our office and began our editing. It took us two weeks in which we worked from morning till night, taking out a few frames here and there and moving sequences about. At last we had it in a shape we were both satisfied with. We added titles, music and a commentary and made a few copies, one of which we sent to Cardinal Hume. To our surprise, he telephoned us to say that he thought it was the best Lourdes video he had ever seen. He then offered to let us film him doing a short introduction to the video which we did in the throne room of the Westminster Cathedral, and for which he wore his full cardinals robes.

Our investor, Barry, was delighted in what we'd done and we organised an official launch of the video in the Cathedral Hall. Barry provided drinks and sandwiches and we invited several Catholic dignitaries. Cardinal Hume presided over the launch at which he was presented with a cheque for £700 as a donation to the Westminster Pilgrimage Fund from advance sales of the video. In all, we sold 5,000 copies and gave £5,000 in donations to various parish funds in addition to paying Barry back his investment and making a few bob for ourselves.

During the making of the video we became quite friendly

with the Cardinal and it came as a shock when we learnt that he had terminal cancer and only had a short time to live. I met him at a function shortly after, and offered him my sympathies at the sad news. He smiled and said something I will never forget.

'You know Vince, when I was diagnosed, all the clergy here at Westminster said how sorry they were, just as you did. Last week I went to see the Bishop of Ampleforth. He didn't say he was sorry. He said 'I wish I were going with you!' Think about that for a moment. What a supreme example of faith is in that remark.

As a result of our association with the Cardinal, Jim and I met Father Michael Seed who was the Ecumenical Officer and had been instrumental in helping many leading figures to convert, including The Duchess of Kent and the former Prime Minister, Tony Blair. Through Father Michael, Jim and I became involved in the ceremonies planned for the forthcoming Millennium. We suggested that, at midnight on New Years Eve, a huge illuminated cross, suspended from a helicopter, was flown over Westminster Cathedral and planted outside in the Piazza. At first everyone was enthusiastic about the idea, but Westminster Council vetoed the helicopter and we just had the cross erected at the ceremony attended by Prince Andrew the Duke of York.

In spite of my visit to Lourdes and my involvement with the late Cardinal, I still remain a lapsed Catholic which will come as a disappointment to the Archbishop of Birmingham, Vincent Nicholls. I met him in Lourdes when he was a Bishop and part of the Westminster clergy. He said he thought the making of the Lourdes video was a good idea and that I was obviously a Catholic.

I shrugged, 'Well - not really,' I replied.

He frowned, 'What do you mean - not really?'

'Well, I don't go to Mass any more. I suppose I don't believe in it anymore.'

'Nonsense', he said, 'were you born a Catholic?'

'Yes', I replied.

'Were you baptised a Catholic?'

'Yes,'

'Well then, you're a bloody Catholic. And don't you forget

it!'

I haven't forgotten it Archbishop. How could I? Once a Catholic, always a Catholic!'

Chapter Nineteen:
TELEVISION COMEDY TODAY IS NO LAUGHING MATTER

Once upon a time people used to rush home straight from work or dash back from the pub after only one drink in order to watch television. Patients and nursing staff in hospitals used to gather round a television set. Streets were almost deserted as millions of viewers switched on to watch their favourite programme. What were these programmes which had such vast appeal and drew such large audiences? They were called 'situation comedies' - or - 'sitcoms' as they are more popularly known. During that period, now often referred to as the 'Golden Age of Comedy', there was as least one sitcom, often two, on our screens every night - sitcoms which gave viewers some of the most famous and best loved, entertaining programmes in the history of British Broadcasting.

Just to list them brings a nostalgic smile to my face. 'Hancock's Half Hour', 'Till Death Us Do Part', 'Steptoe & Son', 'Please Sir', 'Are You Being Served?', 'The Good Life', 'Nearest & Dearest', 'Bless This House', 'Sykes and ...', 'On The Buses', 'Love Thy Neighbour'. 'The Likely Lads'. 'Some Mothers Do 'Ave 'Em', and many more. They were all wonderful sitcoms and appeared regularly in the National Top Ten television ratings.

And what about Variety? Where are the programmes to take the place of 'Sunday Night at the London Palladium',

'Morecambe and Wise', 'The Comedians', 'Tommy Cooper' and 'Max Bygraves?'

The current situation with regard to the state of television comedy fills me with despair. I believe that the majority of the viewing public still wish to be entertained by witty and entertaining programmes whose sole purpose is making people laugh, rather than the plethora of cost-effective television shows so loved by TV accountants, such as gardening programmes, cookery programmes, DIY and makeover shows, people shows, quizzes and reality shows. This is not to say that the aforementioned shows have no merit and are not enjoyed by many viewers, but there are far too many of them.

So what has led us to this sorry state of affairs? Why are broadcasters no longer producing quality sitcoms and variety shows as we did in the past? One reason is that, in my opinion, many of those experienced and talented writers, producers and directors who were responsible for those successful shows during the 'Golden Age' are either no longer with us or retired - or worse - considered by present day television executives, as being 'past their sell by date' and 'old fashioned'. What utter rubbish!

Another contributory factor to the decline of television comedy is the growing army of script editors and script readers, some of whom have little, if any, experience of writing comedy. I recently submitted an idea for a sitcom to one of a major broadcaster's senior Light Entertainment producers. I received the idea back with a curt rejection letter from a script editor of whom I had never heard, and who to my knowledge had never written a sitcom. Yet here he was, passing judgement on my script and rejecting it, before it even fell on the desk of the producer to whom it was sent. This was not an isolated incident. Many writer friends of mine have had similar experiences. One such writer had his sitcom script returned with a brief one line observation 'This is not what we are looking for.' Wouldn't it have been more helpful and constructive if he had indicated what he was looking for? I suspect that the reality was that he didn't know himself.

Many of today's light entertainment television producers

regard those sitcoms of the 70's and 80's as old fashioned and dated. This is far from the case, as witness the popularity of the repeats of those programmes on UKTV GOLD and ITV3. I recently submitted a sitcom script to the BBC based on the adventures of three Chelsea Pensioners all living in the Royal Chelsea Hospital. One was an ex-Naval man, another an ex-Army man and the third an ex-Airforce man. I thought the idea had good comic possibilities with lots of opportunities for conflict and character comedy. I wrote the script and sent it off. A couple of weeks later, I received a letter inviting me in for a meeting with a producer to discuss the script. 'Good', I thought, 'he must like it or he wouldn't waste his time wanting to discuss it.' Wrong! He didn't like it and told me that the BBC weren't interested in scripts about old people. He then went on to say that their target audience was between the ages of 18 and 35. I tried to tell him that the largest viewing audience in Britain were all over 35, but he refused to acknowledge that fact. I then decided to devise a sitcom aimed at young people so I wrote a script about two sixteen year olds falling in love for the first time, with all the agony and ecstasy that a first love affair contains. I was pleased with the script. It was gentle, funny and at times, even moving. I decided submit it to one of the ITV companies. A week or so later, I received a letter from somebody with the title of Head of Comedy Development, inviting me to come and see him. I duly presented myself at his office. He was sitting at a desk, wearing granny glasses, an open necked shirt, scruffy jeans and trainers. I discovered that he had joined the broadcaster straight from University and spent a couple of months as a researcher, before being elevated to Head of Comedy Development. He asked me to sit down then asked me what I had written in the past. I was sorely tempted to tell him that if he didn't know who I was or anything about my track record, he had no right to be sitting behind that desk. However, I bit my tongue and he went on to discuss my script. He said that he found it interesting but then, eyeing my grey hair he sighed and said, 'With all due respect Vince, what do you know about sixteen year olds?' I rose from my chair slowly, leaned across the desk and replied, 'This may come as a big shock to you, but once upon a time I was sixteen. I now have a thirteen year old son and a sixteen year old daughter.' I then snatched the script from the desk and left! I recount this tale as an example of an insidious attitude that is now prevalent in television.

It is called Ageism.

It's a strange thing, but Ageism appears to be an attitude which is exclusive to television light entertainment. Nobody ever tells a novelist that he or she is too old to write another book. Somerset Maugham was 70 when he wrote 'THE RAZOR'S EDGE', Agatha Christie was still writing her novels in her 80's. Similarly, nobody tells a composer that he is too old to write another song. Irving Berlin wrote 'CALL ME MADAM' when he was 62, Ken Dodd is 80 but so far nobody has told him that he is too old to tell another joke. Richard Attenborough produced and directed 'CHAPLIN' at the age of 69 - nobody told him he was too old. Journalists are never too old to write articles for the Press, painters are never too old to paint another portrait and actors never too old to act. So why are writers of television comedy considered to be over the hill once they have passed the age of 40? It baffles me.

Let us not overlook Political Correctness, another attitude which is partly responsible for the decline in comedy. In my opinion, Political Correctness is a form of censorship. Writers are no longer allowed to make jokes about people of other ethnic origins. I'll give you an example. I had written an episode of 'NEVER THE TWAIN' in which Donald Sinden and Windsor Davies were on their way to have dinner at a Chinese restaurant. They parked their car on the fourth floor of a multi-storey car park and got in the lift. On their way down, the lift suddenly stopped between floors. It was stuck. They looked for an emergency phone but it had been vandalised. Donald tried to prise the doors open, then said, 'I think it's moved a bit. I can see a little chink,' to which Windsor replied, 'He's probably from the Chinese restaurant!' Shock! Horror! I was being politically incorrect, if not to say downright racist!

Too many of today's comedy writers are relying far too much on jokes about bodily functions, blatant sex and four letter words. British comedy has had a long history of bawdy humour as witness the success of the 'CARRY ON' films but it never sank to the level of television comedy today. Comedy writers of my generation spent time and care in creating laughter by using clever innuendos or puns. After all, the art of situation comedy is to create laughter from devising situations in which the lines become funny because of the situation in which they are said. Many of today's comedy writers take the easy way out by using shock tactics to get laughs. I saw one so-called sitcom recently, in which there was a scene where one character vomited and another urinated. I can't remember whether the audience laughed or not - I certainly didn't. Don't get me wrong - I'm not a prude - I enjoy a risqué joke as much as anybody but there's a time and place for everything and I don't think that early evening on national television, when young children may be watching, is the right time and the right place for such vulgarity. I do quite a lot of after-dinner speaking and as a comedy speaker on various cruise liners, and the one question I am repeatedly asked above all other is 'When are we going to get some good comedy programmes back on television, like we used to have?' It's a question for which I have no answer.

Lest any of you reading my memoirs may think that this chapter is written in a spirit of 'sour grapes' by a grumpy, old, retired writer let me assure that this is not the case. I have four more comedy cruises in the pipeline, and several after-dinner speaking engagements, I'm writing a comedy play for the theatre, am developing my own one-man theatre show 'AN EVENING WITH VINCE POWELL', and writing a novel. Not many 'sour grapes' there!

Epilogue:
FUTURE
INDEFINITE

Well, we're now at the end of my life story. I'd like to thank all those of you who have got to the end of this book and hope you enjoyed reading it as much as I enjoyed writing it. As to the future, who knows? Perhaps there's a light entertainment producer somewhere out there who also regrets the passing of good 'old fashioned' sitcoms and is willing to take a chance and commission some of those 'old fashioned' writers, such as Ray Galton and Alan Simpson, (Hancock and Steptoe) Jimmy Perry and David Croft, (Dad's Army), Dick Clements and Ian Le Frenais, (The Likely Lads), Carla Lane, (The Liver Birds), Eric Chappell , (Duty Free & Rising Damp), Ronnie Wolfe and Ronnie Chesney (The Rag Trade & On The Buses), John Esmonde & Bob Larby (Please Sir), Brian Cooke (Father Dear Father & Man About The House), Roy Clarke (Last Of The Summer Wine and Open All Hours) and of course myself. All these writers and others could be commissioned to write a sitcom each, which could be produced and transmitted as a series under the old generic title of 'COMEDY PLAYHOUSE' which in it's day spawned several successful sitcom series. Who knows what a new series might spawn?

Fingers crossed!

Hope springs eternal in the human breast!

www.apexpublishing.co.uk